DATE DUE

HISTORICAL DICTIONARIES OF RELIGIONS, PHILOSOPHIES, AND MOVEMENTS
Edited by Jon Woronoff

1. *Buddhism,* by Charles S. Prebish, 1993
2. *Mormonism,* by Davis Bitton, 1994
3. *Ecumenical Christianity,* by Ans Joachim van der Bent, 1994
4. *Terrorism,* by Sean Anderson and Stephen Sloan, 1995
5. *Sikhism,* by W. H. McLeod, 1995
6. *Feminism,* by Janet K. Boles and Diane Long Hoeveler, 1995
7. *Olympic Movement,* by Ian Buchanan and Bill Mallon, 1995
8. *Methodism,* by Charles Yrigoyen Jr. and Susan E. Warrick, 1996
9. *Orthodox Church,* by Michael Prokurat, Alexander Golitzin, and Michael D. Peterson, 1996
10. *Organized Labor,* by James C. Docherty, 1996
11. *Civil Rights Movement,* by Ralph E. Luker, 1997
12. *Catholicism,* by William J. Collinge, 1997
13. *Hinduism,* by Bruce M. Sullivan, 1997
14. *North American Environmentalism,* by Edward R. Wells and Alan Schwartz, 1997
15. *Welfare State,* by Bent Greve, 1998
16. *Socialism,* by James C. Docherty, 1997
17. *Bahá'í Faith,* by Hugh C. Adamson and Philip Hainsworth, 19
18. *Taoism,* by Julian F. Pas in cooperation with Man Kam Leung
19. *Judaism,* by Norman Solomon, 1998
20. *Green Movement,* by Elim Papadakis, 1998
21. *Nietzscheanism,* by Carol Diethe, 1999
22. *Gay Liberation Movement,* by Ronald J. Hunt, 1999
23. *Islamic Fundamentalist Movements in the Arab World, Ira* Ahmad S. Moussalli, 1999
24. *Reformed Churches,* by Robert Benedetto, Darrell L. Gu McKim, 1999
25. *Baptists,* by William H. Brackney, 1999
26. *Cooperative Movement,* by Jack Shaffer, 1999
27. *Reformation and Counter-Reformation,* by Hans J. H
28. *Shakers,* by Holley Gene Duffield, 2000
29. *United States Political Parties,* by Harold F. Bass, J
30. *Heidegger's Philosophy,* by Alfred Denker, 2000
31. *Zionism,* by Rafael Medoff and Chaim I. Waxmar
32. *Mormonism,* by Davis Bitton, 2000
33. *Kierkegaard's Philosophy,* by Julia Watkin, 200

Historical Dictionary
of the Reformation
and Counter-Reformation

Hans J. Hillerbrand

*Historical Dictionaries of Religions, Philosophies,
and Movements, No. 27*

The Scarecrow Press, Inc.
Lanham, Maryland, and London
2000

SCARECROW PRESS, INC.

Published in the United States of America
by Scarecrow Press, Inc.
4720 Boston Way, Lanham, Maryland 20706
http://www.scarecrowpress.com

4 Pleydell Gardens, Folkestone
Kent CT20 2DN, England

British Library Cataloguing in Publication Information Available

Library of Congress Cataloging-in-Publication Data

Hillerbrand, Hans Joachim.
   Historical dictionary of the Reformation and Counter-Reformation /
Hans J. Hillerbrand.
       p.   cm. — (Historical dictionaries of religions, philosophies, and
movements ; no. 27)
   Includes bibliographical references.
   ISBN 0-8108-3673-4 (cl. : alk. paper)
   1. Reformation Dictionaries.   2. Counter-Reformation Dictionaries.
I. Title. II. Series.
BR302.8.H55   2000
270.6—dc21   99–26815
                                                                              CIP

⊖™ The paper used in this publication meets the minimum requirements of
American National Standard for Information Sciences—Permanence of
Paper for Printed Library Materials, ANSI/NISO Z39.48–1992.
Manufactured in the United States of America.

Contents

Editor's Foreword

No matter how much you may relativize, the Reformation was still one of the most dramatic turning points in world history. It propelled countless millions of people toward other directions than they had been following, and even those who continued along the same path at least knew there were alternatives. Otherwise there would have been little need for a Counter-Reformation. These momentous movements concerned not only the people of that time but successive generations as well, usually with less fervor, but with a growing conviction that the new directions were right and natural. Moreover, while the events occurred in Europe, they had an impact on most other parts of the world to some extent. It is hard to come up with many other turning points that affected as many, as much, for as long.

This explains the abiding interest in the Reformation (and Counter-Reformation) and the usefulness of another reference work on the subject. This historical dictionary, while smaller, has the advantage of covering the ground not once but four times, each from a different perspective. The introduction provides a broad historical overview. The dictionary entries present in some detail the crucial persons, places, events, documents, and concepts. The chronology traces the historical progression. The bibliography provides access to a continually renewed literature, delving into many subjects from many vantage points. Because this book was written by one person, it was easier to achieve a balance in the choice of entries and work the various parts into a cohesive whole.

One could hardly imagine a better author for this *Historical Dictionary of the Reformation and Counter-Reformation* than Hans J. Hillerbrand. After receiving his doctorate in Germany, where he occasionally returned as visiting professor, Dr. Hillerbrand spent most of his career in the United States, most recently as chairman of the Department of Religion at Duke University. For over four decades, he has studied, lectured and written about the Reformation. His publications include several dozen articles and a dozen books as well as the editorship of *The Oxford Encyclopedia of the Reformation*, the most substantial work on the subject. During this period, Dr. Hillerbrand has been a member (and president) of the American Society for Reformation Research as well as president of the American Society for Church History and long-standing vice chairman of the Center for Reformation Research. As stated, one could hardly imagine a better author.

Jon Woronoff
Series Editor

Preface

The invitation, three years ago, to write a dictionary of the Reformation and Counter-Reformation provided me with the welcome opportunity to do some careful reflection on what was, and what was not, important in the 16th century. Moreover, the invitation challenged me to augment my own competence and conversance in areas in which I felt less at home than in others. The work on the dictionary thus came to be an informative seminar experience and an immense learning process.

I should record my sentiment that the field of Reformation and Counter-Reformation studies (to use these two traditional terms rather than the substitutes, such as Early Modern Europe or Catholic Reform, that have been proposed) certainly is alive and well. Several journals focus, in one way or another, on the period, and the number of articles and monographs published each year staggers the imagination. Of course, not all was worth publishing, at least from my perspective, but a great deal of what is published assuredly is propelling the scholarly discourse forward and providing new insights. I trust that this dictionary reflects the fact that I have learned a great deal from these publications.

As regards the larger picture of Reformation and Counter-Reformation studies I confess to some uncertainty. The field of historical studies is at present undergoing a paradigm shift in which the traditional dominance of European history is challenged in a number of ways. A number of scholars are arguing that to talk about an "age" or a "period" of the Reformation distorts the broad and important lines of continuity which connect the entire period from the late 14th to the late 17th century. Accordingly, the Reformation is deprived of its distinctiveness. Other scholars find it appropriate to speak of Reformations of the 16th century. These developments –by no means convincing to me—may well effect the future course of scholarship. Whether the field of Reformation studies will be able to retain the important place it had in the past seems to me an altogether open question. Of course, historians are not prophets. And there is no doubt that the period of the Reformation and Counter-Reformation continues to offer excitement and deep insights to those who study it.

I am pleased to acknowledge the welcome help I received from Dr. Karin Brown, who contributed a number of articles to this dictionary. Dr. Brown received her Ph.D. from the City University of New York and has taught at Hunter College. She is the author of *Karl Lueger, the Liberal Years: Democracy, Municipal Reform, and the Struggle for Power in the Vienna City Council, 1875-1882* (New York, 1987). She also contributed more than a dozen articles to the *Oxford Encyclopedia of the Reformation* (New York, 1997).

Hans J. Hillerbrand
Duke University

Introduction

The Reformation of the 16th century used to be seen as one of the pivotal events in European history. Lord Acton, the famous 19th-century British historian, compared the importance of Martin Luther's speech at the diet at Worms in 1521 with Napoleon's defeat at the Battle of Waterloo in 1815, surely a rather extravagant claim. But the 19th century also was the time when the ideas and ideals of the Protestant Reformation were seen as harbingers of modernity, and those disposed to a religious perspective saw the Reformation as the most authentic interpretation of Christianity since the days of the apostolic age. This exuberant perspective was discounted, of course, by Catholic historians whose notion was the diametrically reversed insistence that Protestantism had destroyed a flourishing religious culture. Late medieval Christianity was seen as having a splendid vitality and piety, only to be torn apart by the Protestant Reformation.

Much has been written about the "causes" of the Protestant Reformation of the 16th century, all the way from arguing a despicable state of the Catholic Church in the early 16th century (the favorite explanation of Protestant historians) to the notion that German society found itself in a deep state of crisis early in the 16th century of which the Reformation was an outcome. My own view of the matter is that all of this was so—and yet not so. I am convinced that the Reformation came about through a somewhat serendipitous convergence of a number of factors, some religious and theological, others not. I am also convinced that the early years of the controversy, the years between 1517 and 1522, received a great deal of importance through the figure of Martin Luther, who seemed to be acting just the right way to catapult events in the direction of the unhealable schism of the one Catholic Church. This is not to say that Martin Luther wanted this—certainly not. His role was that of the unwitting actor.

By beginning the story with Martin Luther, I do not mean to reject the notion, nowadays seen as the "cutting edge" of scholarship, that the events of the 16th century and Martin Luther must be placed into a broad historical context, in which the connection between Luther and the Reformation, on the one hand, and late medieval theology and piety, on the other, were far more fluid that used to be acknowledged. There were indeed connections and antecedents, and to look at the broad sweep of two centuries allows insights that It is generally stated that the Reformation had its beginnings with the indulgences proclamation of one John Tetzel and Martin Luther's Ninety-five Theses of October 31, 1517. Luther's theses were meant to invite a theological discussion about the merits of the teaching concerning indulgences (as an outgrowth of Tetzel's teaching). But Luther sent a copy of the theses to Archbishop Albert of Mainz, who in turn informed the Roman curia of the matter asking also that the *processus inhibitorius*, the beginnings of heresy proceedings, be launched to ascertain the orthodoxy of Martin Luther's notions. In the meantime, Luther's theses had begun making the rounds in Germany, and by early 1518 an academic controversy over the theses, and the theological issues they raised, was in the making. Luther contributed fiercely to this debate, but even more importantly, he began to publish small tracts written in the German vernacular, which dealt not so much with esoteric theological topics but with major themes of Christian living—into which he infused, as goes without saying, his own new theological perspective.

By early 1520 three separate developments were clearly in the making: the official proceedings against Luther undertaken in Rome; the theological controversy among the theologians; and an increasingly wide open discussion of topics of Christian faith and spirituality, and other matters of social import, for which Luther's tract was undoubtedly an incisive catalyst. By the summer of 1520 a papal commission had concluded that some 41 sentences culled from Luther's writings were either heretical or offensive to "pious ears." The papal bull *Exsurge domine* gave Luther the opportunity to revoke these sentences within 60 days and report his recantation to Rome within another 60 days or be declared a heretic.

Luther remained adamant. By that time, a new German emperor had been elected, the youthful Charles V (q.v.), and in the context of an increasingly intense debate about what was proper in theology, church, and state, as well as the German territorial rulers' determination to show their importance in the empire in the face of the new emperor, Luther received an invitation to appear before the diet meeting in Worms, on the Rhine, in April 1521. Luther refused to recant and was declared, albeit under dubious legal circumstances, a political outlaw. The intervention of Luther's territorial ruler, Elector Frederick of Saxony, brought Luther unbeknownst to the solitude of the Wartburg in Thuringia, where he was safe from the emperor's forces.

Great agitation was occurring in Germany that went far beyond Luther's own proclamation. A second, more institutional phase of the Reformation began, and the repudiation of monasticism and of the Mass was followed by the inevitable question of what practical consequences should be drawn from this theological judgment. Two schools of thought emerged, one advocating making haste slowly, the other favoring immediate change.

This meant that at a number of places, notably towns and cities, considerable agitation about practical change occurred. In each instance, a forceful clergy proved to be the key figure. By the middle of the 1520s the first actual changes had occurred— closings of monasteries (and the transfer of monastic wealth into the coffers of either the town or the territorial ruler) and the replacement of the Mass by an evangelical communion service.

The Edict of Worms, which had declared Luther an outlaw, had also prohibited any change, but as time passed it turned out that the edict was not worth the parchment it was written on. When the diet met in Speyer in 1526 a surprisingly large number of cities and territories bluntly announced that they were unable to carry out the provisions of the edict. The diet then concluded in its recess that each ruling body should deal with the question of carrying out, or not carrying out, the edict, "as they could answer responsibly before God and the emperor." The diet had a Catholic majority, and this majority clearly meant to stabilize the situation on the basis of the status quo: whatever had been changed in the immediate past was (grudgingly) accepted, but no further changes should occur. The reform-minded rulers and city councils, on the other hand, took the recess to mean something quite different: namely, that they could carry out whatever ecclesiastical and religious policy seemed best in light of their responsibility before "God and the emperor."

Three years later, the Catholic majority, realizing what had been happening, voted to rescind the recess of 1526. The reform-minded estates "protested" this vote and soon thereafter began to be called the "Protestants," meaning the "protesting ones."

Emperor Charles, who had been away from Germany ever since the spring of 1521, was in 1530 preparing to return to Germany in order to preside over a diet to meet at the south German city of Augsburg. Foremost purpose of this diet was to marshal the German estates to provide financial support for raising an army against the Turks. After extensive deliberations at the diet, during the course of which the Lutheran estates presented a statement of their faith, the so-called Augsburg Confession, the majority voted to give the Protestants six months' time to return to the Catholic fold. After that, the Catholics would consider military measures. The fact of the matter was, however, that the emperor needed the support of the Protestants for his military initiative against the Turks, and so in the end the bark proved much worse than the bite.

The remainder of the story of the Reformation in Germany can be quickly told. For the most part it took the form of an endless series of discussions at innumerable diets. At issue was always the legality of the new form of religion. The strength, including military strength, of the Protestants, together with the prolonged absences of Charles V from Germany, meant that for more than two decades no clear solutions seemed possible— neither the legal acceptance of the new Protestant religion nor its radical suppression. Even the emperor's victory in the War of Schmalkald in 1547 altered little, and eventually at the diet at Augsburg in 1555 the coexistence of the Lutheran and Catholic forms of Christianity became a matter of imperial law.

It is a fair characterization to observe that contemporaries found it somewhat difficult to determine the exact nature of the theological disagreement between the two sides. There were obvious differences, such as the Protestant repudiation of monasticism, but even lengthy theological colloquies, convened for the purpose of reconciling the differences, could not bring about ultimate clarity in this regard. Perhaps the explanation must be sought in the fact that neither side was monolithic, but rather that both sides contained what we might call "hard-liners" and "irenicists," and they saw things somewhat differently. Which of these dispositions was running the show at a particular time made a great deal of difference.

But differences existed not only between Catholics and Protestants; they existed within the Protestant camp as well. In fact, one of the major characteristics of the Protestant Reformation is the fact that the movement divided fairly quickly, prompting some scholars to speak of Reformation in the plural, thereby denoting this diversity of Protestant sentiment. It is a judgment call. It depends on whether we want to say that a forest is made up of trees or if trees make up a forest. The fact of the matter is that the various Protestant groupings did all share, by way of a common denominator, the repudiation of the Catholic Church and the papal system.

Still, the story of the Reformation is also the story of several major new religious traditions in Western Christendom. Alongside the Lutheran tradition, there was the tradition first associated with the name of Huldrych Zwingli, the Zurich reformer, whose early death meant that his notions were appropriated and creatively developed a decade later by John Calvin, the reformer of Geneva, whose name has been assigned to the tradition of Calvinism, that branch of Protestantism which has been so influenced over the centuries in the Anglo-Saxon world.

Finally, we must take note of the European dimension of the Reformation. Before it was all over, the agitation of the Reformation had affected all corners of the continent, and in the end most of central and northern Europe had abrogated loyalty to Rome. That is to say, Reformation agitation occurred not only in Germany but in virtually all other European countries as well.

It continues to be a matter of scholarly debate if the catalyst for this European dimension was Martin Luther and the course of events in Germany or if indigenous forces propelled events in various European countries forward in the direction of a Reformation at almost precisely the time this took place in Germany. Understandably, scholars have tended to pronounce their views somewhat in line with their national identity: German scholars have argued that all must be traced back to Martin Luther; French and English scholars have insisted on the autonomous character of Reformation events in these countries. Be that as it may, however, the story of the Reformation (and Counter-Reformation) cannot be written and told without the immediate recognition that the Reformation was a European-wide phenomenon. The precise course and character of events differed. Best known is the story of the English Reformation, since it was so intricately connected with the wish of Henry VIII (q.v.) to secure a male heir for the English throne. English historians have been at pains to point out that more was at stake than a middle-aged male's infatuation with a younger woman, Anne Boleyn, and that the form of Protestantism that became normative in England after Queen Elizabeth I has, no matter what its catalyst, an intriguing integrity.

In other words, the story of the English Reformation has the same measure of flair and drama one can find in the German story. In England it was not until the succession of Elizabeth in 1558 that religious affairs were definitively settled by the formal adoption of a form of religion that her father, Henry VIII, had wanted.

The preoccupation with the rise and emergence of new forms of Christianity must not overlook the foil against which all these developments took place: the Catholic Church. There was a time when it was thought that 16th-century Catholicism was exclusively defined (when it had regained its composure, so to speak) by its reaction against Protestantism. This is nowadays seen as too simple a picture. Currently, scholars hold that there was a richness to Catholic life in the 16th century that is not properly expressed by the term "Counter-Reformation." They point to the reality that Catholic life at the beginning of the 16th century was exceptionally rich, that everywhere the common people clung to their Catholicism, that new monastic orders, always a sign of spiritual vitality in the Catholic Church, emerged quite apart from any discernible impact of the Protestant Reformation (a statement that might even be made about Ignatius of Loyola and the Jesuits!). Understandably, Catholics have not liked the terms "Counter-Reformation," or for that matter "Catholic Reform," since these terms do seem to define 16th century Catholicism all too much in terms of the Protestant Reformation, either as reaction or stimulus.

Nowadays the scholarly perspective is different. The crass difference in perspective between Catholic and Protestant scholars has been significantly softened. It is no longer possible to identify easily a writer's ecclesiastical and theological orientation. Catholic scholars have become understanding of the insights of the Protestant reformers, while Protestant historians have come to concede the vitality that characterized the Catholic Church on the eve of the Reformation. Importantly, however, there have emerged new interpretations and perspectives concerning the 16th century and the Protestant Reformation, which depart dramatically from the traditional perspective. These new perspectives tend to minimize the role of religion in the 16th- century course of events.

The most intriguing of these new interpretations was the postulate of the "early bourgeois revolution" propounded by Marxist historians of the former German Democratic Republic. While the unification of the two Germanys in 1990 caused this Marxist School of Reformation interpretation to disappear, its reverberations have been ongoing in Western scholarship. The basic contention of these Marxist historians—elaborated in the article on the *Early Bourgeois Revolution* in this dictionary— was that German society was undergoing fundamental changes in the late 15th and early 16th centuries and that the changes in the existing social and economic order had to entail a confrontation with the Catholic Church, whose ideology undergirded the existing state of affairs. Martin Luther served as the catalyst for triggering these changes, while the uprising of the German peasants in 1524-25 was the logical conclusion of Martin Luther's proclamation in that now a re-ordering of all of society was demanded. The Reformation proclamation of Luther thus led to the German Peasants' War, and collectively both were the first, or early, bourgeois revolution against the medieval feudal system.

By the same token, the trend in historical scholarship in recent years to emphasize social concerns has also affected scholarship on the Reformation. This has placed interest in popular religion and women in the center of historical research, neglecting theological and religious concerns and emphases. These new perspectives suggest that the 16th-century scene was replete with diverse emphases and that the traditional focus on theological innovation falls short of accounting for the richness of the events of the age. In fact, it has become proper—as in Carter Lindberg's recent textbook—to discard the time-honored label "Reformation" in favor of such terms as "movements of reform" or "Reformations" to denote the diversity and heterogeneity of the course of events.

The first comment to be made about our present understanding of the Reformation is that both church and society were fairly stable toward the end of the 15th and the beginning of the 16th centuries. There is no evidence that would suggest a widespread alienation of people from their church even as it hardly can be argued that European society was in a state of crisis at the time. That is not to suggest that there were no tensions. As at other times, there was a host of issues and problems. Criticism, sometimes quite noisy and strident, of the church, its functionaries, even its teachings was voiced with some regularity. But the evidence is persuasive that people either cared little about the details of church life or that they were willing to accept the church for what it was, despite blemishes— their conduit to eternal salvation.

Everywhere in Europe the church was a most important factor of life. The concordat concluded between the papacy and the French crown in 1516 put the French king virtually in charge of the French church and thus severely limited the power of the church. The kings of Spain and Portugal, who late in the 15th century had looked to the pope as arbiter of their competing claims in the newly discovered Americas, were by the early 16th century determined to resolve disagreements and disputes among themselves, without papal help and intervention. Still, the church stood at the center of society, expressed not only in continuing considerable political influence. In many places throughout Europe churchmen served in the highest echelons of government: the examples of Archbishop Sture in Sweden or Cardinal Wolsey in England come to mind. The church was a formidable landowner. All this meant, of course, that this presence was bound to occasion extensive criticism, not only of church politics and church life, but also in theology.

By the early 16th century a widespread chorus of Humanist criticism of the church had arisen, in some ways anticipating the criticism of the Protestant reformers. The famous controversy surrounding the publication of the *Letters of Obscure Men* was a splendid case in point: here was a biting satire of scholastic theology which was said to have become preoccupied with minutiae of theological subtleties, thereby ignoring the important issues. But, when all is said and done, there can be no doubt that, despite criticism and shortcomings, the Catholic Church entered the 16th century with vigor and self-confidence. There were weaknesses (which even the most loyal of churchmen, such as Pope Adrian VI, never failed to acknowledge), but in the main the Catholic Church possessed devoted servants, conscientious leaders, and loyal adherents. Not for nothing was there no indication of Catholic lack of self-confidence in the years prior to the outbreak of the indulgences controversy.

The major point of tension between the church and the political authorities was the autonomous role the church played in so many respects in society—its clergy were exempt from ordinary criminal jurisdiction, even as education and the care for the poor and the sick were taken to be responsibilities of the church. Understandably this caused resentment, although in some places, notably France, the kings had been successful in amassing the kind of power over the church that was desired. In fact, one may well conjecture that if similar power and authority had been held universally across Europe, the course of the Reformation would have been different.

It is a moot question if this equilibrium in church and society, though one not without tensions, would have provoked some conflagration had it not been for the rash Augustinian professor of theology, Martin Luther, whose Ninety-five Theses of October 1517 set the Reformation in motion. While Luther's theses dealt with theological issues, specifically the as-yet-undefined doctrine of indulgences, and triggered a surprisingly fierce theological controversy, it became quickly evident that more was under way than an esoteric disagreement among theologians. Part of the explanation lies in the fact that Luther took to the pen and published a number of highly popular tracts on themes of the Christian life—such as prayer, marriage, and dying—which seemed to have little to do with the ongoing controversy among the professional theologians. Also, the theological controversy carried the undercurrent of an anti-establishment critique, a revivalist appeal to the way things should be rather than the way they were.

With the insight of hindsight it is possible to detect a number of factors during the years between 1517, the beginnings of the controversy, and 1521, the year of Martin Luther's excommunication, suggesting that the theological disagreement was not likely to be contained. For one, the Catholic Church moved swiftly against Luther—in a way too swiftly. In retrospect, it might have been prudent to demonstrate the same kind of patience with him as has been shown in the 20th century with some of the dissenters from the Catholic mainstream. Both Luther's excommunication and his condemnation as a political outlaw by Emperor Charles V (q.v.) showed signs of haste and sloppiness, which were to haunt the subsequent course of events, since Luther and his followers were able to claim that they had not been given a proper hearing.

The fundamental question, of course, is what this controversy was all about. The Catholic Church provided an answer with stunning speed: by 1520, the church had concluded that Martin Luther was propounding theological heresies. And for the better part of half a century, the two sides marshaled their best theologians to engage in conversation, sometimes irenic, at others quite belligerent, about the contested theological issues. After the dust had settled, and the two sides had accepted the permanence of their disagreements, Protestant theologians (and later scholars too) quickly argued that their theologies were an authentic appropriation of biblical teaching such as had not occurred since the apostolic age. Both their stance, and that of the adamant Catholics who argued that Protestant teachings were well disguised ancient heresies, ignored the reality that some of the Protestant emphases were in fact not new and, what is more, the Catholic Church had been able to live with earlier manifestations in the Middle Ages. Certainly, the notion that two irreconcilable theologies were confronting each other was not a sentiment universally shared in the 16th century. The sharpness of theological distinction came about after the definitive split had already occurred and became part and parcel of the way the

Reformation was understood in the late 16th and early 17th centuries.

It was to be of enormous importance for the course of events that the controversy over the proper understanding of the Christian faith did not remain confined to theology but was promptly understood to have practical ramifications for church life. Some of Luther's followers were determined to undertake ecclesiastical changes in their communities, although the cooperation of the political authorities—city councils or territorial rulers—was necessary to make such determination an accomplished fact. This cooperation occurred at numerous places, making the political authorities the linchpin in the course of the Reformation. Without them, the controversy would have remained a theological squabble. No matter how persuasive the new theology may have been to the people, those holding power had to make formal legal and political decisions in favor of repudiating the Catholic Church.

The Reformation is therefore unthinkable without the pivotal role of the political authorities. Certainly in Germany, the authorities defended, at diet after diet, the ecclesiastical and religious changes they had undertaken in their respective realms and also pressed for legal affirmation of these changes. Thus the Reformation became a political and legal event. The issue was not only if the new theological understanding was heretical, but also if it was legally acceptable to introduce public change in liturgy, worship, and belief. In Germany, this question occupied one diet after the other beginning with Worms 1521. The issue was finally resolved at the diet at Augsburg in 1555. Similar developments took place in all other European countries, some being more, others less affected by theological clamor for change to which the political authorities were called upon to respond. The course of events in England under Henry VIII (q.v.) makes the incisive place of the political forces dramatically clear, even though—by way of a departure from what has just been noted—there was in England no groundswell of agitation for change. In England Henry VIII himself was the agent of change, for reasons not altogether theological (he himself was a staunch theological conservative).

What made for the peculiar phenomenon we call the "success" of the Reformation was a convergence of several factors whose interplay, depending on time and locale, made for the symptomatic course of events. Everywhere a number of factors were operative in the Reformation. There were discussion and controversy over theology, over the practical ramifications of theological affirmations, and over the legality of these practical ramifications. The catalyst was in each instance a theological discussion, though the intensity and nature of this discussion differed from place to place. By no means is it possible to argue that everywhere there was a groundswell of theological or even spiritual agitation, or a popular movement for reform and change that had the markings of a floodtide. While there is, particularly in Germany, clear evidence of popular agitation, of overflowing churches where reform-minded clergy preached, even of iconoclasm and disturbances, one must be very careful indeed not to confuse such agitation with a widespread popular movement.

This crucial role of the political authorities in the Reformation raises the question of motivation. The simplest explanation—the persuasiveness of the new interpretation of the gospel—carried the day for a long time but seems no longer adequate. On the other hand, an equally pointed explanation, namely that the authorities favored the Reformation because of power politics, is not persuasive and convincing either when one examines in detail specific instances of Reformation change. In particular, if categories of class and prurient political and economic interests carried the day, far greater uniformity would have had to be the case with respect to religious change than can be demonstrated. In some cases the Reformation message by itself surely swayed rulers, while in others a power-hungry city council or ruler embraced the new faith without the slightest understanding of the theological implications. What is not possible is a generalization that attempts to put the entire early-16th-century Reformation under one umbrella.

A word needs also be said about the personalities in the course of events. At present, historians are disinclined to pay tribute to the achievements of individuals, heroes as they were called at one time; the disposition to do social history calls for different emphases. Whatever one may say about the historical process in general, one can hardly write the history of the Reformation of the 16th century without acknowledging the role played by key individuals. This is not to say that certain individuals, apart from their surroundings and circumstances, played the role of deus ex machina single-handedly, against all odds. But what must be argued is that certain individuals, of whom Martin Luther is surely the best illustration, seized opportunities and benefited from circumstances that made their contributions pivotal in the end. Luther's use of the German vernacular for many of his publications after 1517 meant that he found a vehicle to create a public consciousness of certain issues far exceeding what might have been possible had he had done what his brethren of the guild of theologians were doing, namely confining their publishing to weighty tomes in Latin. There is no doubt but his German language publications made Luther a household word in Germany by the early 1520s. Moreover, Luther also was a gifted writer, with a knack for picturesque (at times all too picturesque) speech, which had the quality of neatly identifying key issues and questions and then providing the appropriate answers. By the same token, even Luther had to face the bearing of circumstances. If Luther's territorial ruler, Elector Frederick of Saxony, had been of deep Catholic commitment, as was the case with a number of other German territorial rulers of the time, such as Duke George of Saxony, the course of events would have unfolded quite differently. The same observation can surely be made about England, where the weighty figure of Henry VIII overpowered the stage of events. There were forces operative in England that had little to do with the king and his brand of religion, not to mention his marital adventuresomeness. The Anglican tradition, which was eventually promulgated during the rule of Henry's daughter Elizabeth I after 1559, surely had its beginnings in the 1530s: Henry VIII made it clear, even by persecution, what kind of religion was acceptable to him.

What about the popular dimension of the Reformation? It used to be that scholars took for granted that the Reformation proclamation in a dramatic way swayed the majority of the people away from the Catholic Church in the direction of the new evangelical (Protestant) proclamation. A number of path-breaking studies have called this view into question, most recently the work by Eamon Duffy, *The Stripping of the Altars,* which showed how loyal the English people were to their old religion and how tedious and complicated was the acceptance of the new faith. There is no doubt that the reformers set the agenda in the years after 1517 and that the Catholic theological protagonists were very much on the defense for a long time. But the rank and file of the people displayed ambivalence about the new faith.

If religion, then, did play an important role in the course of events, the question must be asked about particulars: what in particular was found so persuasive in the new gospel and interpretation of the Christian faith? It has been suggested that the appeal of Reformation preaching was that it made religion easier for people, removed the welter of rules and regulations from them and made for an easier religion. There is something to that argument, even though it must be kept in mind that before too long the Zwinglian-Calvinist tradition within the Protestant orbit postulated a version of the Christian message which vied with medieval Catholicism in its insistence on doing religion the hard way. The path to salvation in Calvinist Geneva surely was every bit as thorny as it had been in medieval Christianity. But that was a later development and the enthusiasm of those who thronged to the proclamation of "the Word of God," as the reformers liked to describe their preaching, must have had other causes. Surely, one factor was the pristine exuberance with which the reformers propounded their vision of Christian gospel. They were idealists, so to speak, who waxed eloquently about a vision of the Christian faith, not as it was, but as it was supposed to be. It rang with lofty and high ideals.

Did the turbulence of the Reformation make a difference in people's lives, or was it a matter of a "squabble among theologians," as one contemporary noted? This question used to be rather easily answered, at least by Protestant scholars who were persuaded that the message of the Reformation was embraced by the multitudes with an eagerness and enthusiasm akin to the National Basketball Association playoffs. In recent decades, the sentiment has become a bit more muted. We have already noted that there is persuasive evidence for a striking persistence of Catholic sentiment among the common people even in the face of formidable Protestant preaching. It is less clear how to gauge the impact of the various social teachings of the new Protestant bodies-the notion of vocation, for example, which insisted that even lowly and mundane endeavors were divine vocations. Or, if the new Protestant affirmation of marriage as in fact superior to clerical celibacy made a difference in the marriage patterns of men and women.

One thing is clear, however: neither the religiosity of the people nor the formal promulgation of a creed or confession of faith could, by themselves, have altered the ecclesiastical alignment of a territory or city. The German historian Heinz Schilling has argued that the latter part of the 16th century marked the period of "confessionalization," when the German territories undertook to structure of all societal life—education, culture, music, commerce, to some extent even law—on the principles of the confession regnant in the territory. By that time, the Protestant churches had begun to make an impact on popular religion as well as popular culture. A new ethos began to be formed which was to demonstrate a remarkable vitality over the centuries. No observer of 17th-century Germany or France can ignore the dramatic differences between Catholics and Protestants at that time, especially since the most adamant. Protestants, the Calvinists, continued to be in ascendancy.

The Catholic Church used to be seen as marked by perversion and worldliness in the beginning of the 16th century and by its aggressive anti-Protestant stance by the end. This rather lopsided picture has been modified significantly in recent decades. It is clear now that the Catholic Church enjoyed considerable vitality and loyalty at the beginning of the 16th century, that it proved remarkably resilient to Protestant attacks, and that neither the notion that the century was marked by aggressive counter-Reformation nor the idea that it was characterized by a persistent effort at Catholic reform describes the full reality of the Catholic Church in the 16th century. The Catholic Church in the 16th century was mainly characterized by what that church had been for generations—its proclamation of the gospel and its administration of the sacraments. Efforts at reform and combating Protestantism were important but marginal issues. Certainly by the time the Council of Trent (q.v.) convened, the Catholic Church had regained its full self-confidence and proceeded to order its affairs, affirm its teachings, and guide its adherents. The vitality of late 16th century Catholicism has often been related to the vibrant exuberance of the arts of the time—in music no less than in the pictorial arts. Nonetheless, there can be little doubt that the Catholic Church suffered greatly from the Protestant onslaught. All of Northern Europe and large parts of central Europe were no longer associated with the Roman church; Catholicism in Europe became a South European phenomenon.

Recent publications have directed our attention to the reality that religion continued to play a crucially important role in European societies well after the Age of the Reformation. Nothing could be further from the historical reality in Europe than to assume that a steady secularization, that is, turning away from religion, occurred after the 16th century. The "age of confessionalization" meant that far into the 17th century European society underwent a realignment along rigid confessional lines encompassing all areas of life—literature and music no less than philosophy, education, and even law. The Reformation thus, if anything, intensified the formal religiosity of European societies.

Only the Enlightenment and the Industrial Revolution changed this.

Chronology

1500	European towns with a population of over 50,000: Paris, London, Venice, Palermo, Milan, Florence, Bruges, Ghent.
1505	First African slaves sent to America.
1509	John Calvin born.
	April. Henry VIII becomes king of England.
	June. Henry marries Catherine of Aragon.
1512	Martin Luther is awarded doctorate in theology.
1513	Margrave Albert of Brandenburg becomes archbishop and elector of Mainz.
	Machiavelli publishes *Il Principe.*
1515	Thomas Wolsey, archbishop of York, is appointed chancellor in England.
	Battle at Marignano.
1516	Thomas More publishes his *Utopia.*

Erasmus of Rotterdam publishes Greek New Testament.

Death of Ferdinand II; Charles I becomes king of Spain.

Concordat of Bologna between France and papacy.

Bavaria issues the "beer purity law," which stipulates that only hops, barley, water, and yeast may be used as ingredients for beer.

1517   *January.* John Tetzel is appointed general subcommissioner for the sale of the St. Peter's Jubilee indulgence in the diocese of Magdeburg.

October. Martin Luther publishes the Ninety-five Theses.

1518   Martin Luther refuses to recant at Augsburg.

1519   *June.* Election of the Spanish king Charles I as Emperor Charles V.

July. Leipzig disputation between Luther, John Eck, and Andreas Carlstadt.

Philip Melanchthon joins the faculty at Wittenberg.

1520   *September.* Papal bull *Exsurge domine* threatens Luther with excommunication.

November. Bloodbath of Stockholm.

December. Luther burns the papal bull.

1521   *January.* Papal bull *Decet Romanum pontificem* excommunicates Luther.

          April. Luther appears before the German diet at Worms.

          May. Edict of Worms against Luther.

          Luther in hiding in the Wartburg.

          Ignatius of Loyola wounded.

          Philip Melanchthon publishes his *Loci communes.*

          December. Pope Leo X dies.

1522   Election of Pope Adrian VI.

1523   Pope Adrian VI dies. Succession of Clement VII.

          Gustavus Vasa elected king of Sweden; end of Union of Kalmar.

1524-1525 Uprising of the German peasants in Southern and Central Germany.

1525   First adult baptism at Zollikon near Zurich. Beginning of Anabaptist movement.

          Battle at Pavia. Spain defeats France.

          Battle at Frankenhausen ends the uprising of the German peasants. Thomas Müntzer captured and executed.

1526   First diet at Speyer endorses territorial ruler's freedom to decide the execution of the Edict of Worms.

Ottoman victory at Mohacs, Hungary.

1527   King Henry VIII confronts his wife Catherine of Aragon with his judgment that their marriage was in violation of divine law.

Anabaptist meeting at Schleitheim drafts the *Brotherly Union.*

May. Sack of Rome (*sacco di Roma*) by troops of Charles V.

June. Gustavus Vasa introduces the Reform-ation in Sweden.

1529   Second diet at Speyer. Protest of the evangelical estates and rulers against the majority decision to rescind the recess of 1526.

Thomas More chancellor in England.

The Reformation Parliament convenes in England.

Marburg Colloquy between Luther, Zwingli, and others on the real presence of Christ in Communion.

1530   Diet at Augsburg. Submission of the Lutheran Augsburg Confession and its Catholic rebuttal, the Confutation.

1531   Establishment of the League of Schmalkald.

October. Huldrych Zwingli dies at Battle of Kappel.

1532   English Parliament passes the Conditional Re-straint of Annates.

May. Thomas More resigns chancellorship.

July. Peace of Nuremberg.

1533   *January.* Henry VIII marries Anne Boleyn.

September. Elizabeth born to Henry VIII and Anne Boleyn.

Anabaptist majority on the city council in Münster.

1534   English Parliament passes Reformation legislation.

Pope Clement VII dies. Succession of Pope Paul III.

Ignatius of Loyola establishes Society of Jesus in Paris.

1535   Dissolution of the monasteries in England.

Thomas More and Archbishop Fisher executed.

End of Anabaptist rule in Münster.

1536   Anne Boleyn accused of adultery and executed.

Pilgrimage of Grace in England.

Erasmus of Rotterdam dies.

John Calvin arrives in Geneva.

1538   John Calvin expelled from Geneva.

1539   Religious Colloquy at Worms.

Six Articles Act in England.

First Christmas tree in Strasbourg.

1540   Society of Jesus officially recognized.

1542   Charles V signs the *Leyes Nuevas* (New Laws) limiting slavery in the New World.

1543   Nikolaus Copernicus publishes *De revolutionibus orbium caelestium* which challenges the Ptolomaic worldview.

1545   Council of Trent opens.

1546   *February.* Martin Luther dies in Eisleben.

War of Schmalkald.

1547   *January.* Henry VIII dies. Succession of Edward VI.

1548   Augsburg Interim imposed by Charles V.

1549   *Book of Common Prayer.*

Consensus Tigurinus (Zurich Agreement) unites John Calvin and Heinrich Bullinger, Zwingli's successor.

Francis Xavier reaches Japan.

1550   First tobacco in Europe.

1552	Establishment of the Collegium Germanicum in Rome.
1553	Edward VI dies. Succession of Mary Tudor.
1555	*September.* Diet at Augsburg. Promulgation of Peace of Augsburg.
1556	*September.* Abdication of Charles V.
1557	Colloquy at Worms. Last effort at theological conciliation between Catholics and Protestants.
	Pope Paul IV publishes first *Index* of prohibited books.
1558	Mary Tudor dies. Succession of Elizabeth I.
1559	Elizabeth I promulgates religious settlement for England.
	April. Peace of Cateau-Cambrésis between Spain and France.
	Henry II of France dies. Succession of Francis II.
1560	Philip Melanchthon dies.
	Introduction of the Reformation in Scotland.
	King Gustavus Vasa of Sweden dies.
	London issues mandate that poor have a right to social support.

1561	Colloquy at Poissy, France.
	Mary Stuart returns to Scotland and claims right to English throne.
1562	First War of Religion in France.
1563	Adjournment of the Council of Trent.
1564	John Calvin dies.
1565	Pope Pius IV dies. Succession of Pius V in 1566.
	First potatoes reach Europe.
1566	Iconoclasm in the Netherlands.
1567	Spain prohibits use of Arabic language and attire.
1568	Elizabeth I arrests Mary Stuart.
1570	Edict of St. Germain-en-Laye, which gives Huguenots places to worship.
1572	*August 23-24.* St. Bartholomew's Day Massacre.
	Pope Pius V dies. Succession of Gregory XIII.
1574	Jews expelled from Vienna.

1580   Official Lutheran endorsement of the *Book of Concord.*

Michel Montaigne publishes his *Essais.*

1582   *October.* Introduction in Catholic countries of the new (Gregorian) calendar. The next day is October 15. Germany adopts the calendar in 1700, England in 1752.

October. Death of Teresa of Avila.

1585   Pope Gregory XIII dies. Succession of Sixtus V.

First English settlement (at Roanoke Island, North Carolina) in North America

1588   Jesuits establish the *reductiones* (reservations), free of slavery, in Paraguay. They last until 1757.

Defeat of the Spanish Armada.

1598   *April.* Edict of Nantes.

September. Death of Philip II.

Strasbourg church order establishes mandatory schooling for children.

The Dictionary

— A —

ACONTIUS, JACOBUS (c. 1520-1567). Humanist and reformer. Virtually nothing is known about Acontius's early life. In 1557 he turned Protestant and left his native Italy, going to Basel, then to Zurich. In 1559, after the succession of Elizabeth I (q.v.), he moved to England, where he found employment as a military engineer. Aside from an important book on knowledge, *De methodo*, his major work was *Satanae stratagamata* (The Stratagems of Satan), which was published in Basel two years before his death. Frequently reprinted, the book was the most eloquent and formidable plea for religious freedom and toleration in the 16th century.

ACT OF SUPREMACY OF 1534 (26 Henry VIII, c. 1), together with the corollary act of supremacy promulgated by Elizabeth I in 1559 (1 Elizabeth I, c. 1), established the independence of the church in England from the Catholic Church. The act established the king's authority as supreme head of the church in England with the authority to attend to all matters pertaining to the church. Together with further parliamentary statutes, beginning with the Submission of the Clergy in 1532, the act was meant to buttress Henry VIII's (q.v.) case for the annulment of his marriage to Catherine of Aragon.

ADIAPHORISTIC CONTROVERSY. The term comes from the Greek and means "middle things," that is, matters that are in themselves morally neither right or wrong. The adiaphoristic

1

controversy took place within Lutheran (q.v.) ranks in Germany and was triggered by Matthias Flacius (q.v.), since 1544 professor of Hebrew at the University of Wittenberg. For Flacius the two interim solutions to the religious controversy in Germany, the Interims (q.v.) of Augsburg and Leipzig imposed by Emperor Charles V (q.v.) in 1548, were despicable distortions of the gospel rather than adiaphora. Flacius declared that the Lutheran theologians, including Philip Melanchthon (q.v.), who agreed to the Leipzig Interim, had been terrified by cowardly fear. The controversy was not resolved since Flacius and his supporters demanded public penance on the part of the Wittenberg theologians who had agreed to the Interim, which did not occur.

ADMONITION CONTROVERSY. This controversy in the Church of England took its name from a publication by John Field and Thomas Wilcox entitled *An Admonition to the Parliament,* of 1572, in which the two authors argued that the presbyterian form of church government was ordained in the Bible (q.v.). The book made the structure of church government the core of the Puritan opposition to the Elizabethan settlement of religion. The controversy ended in 1577 with the publication of Thomas Cartwright's *The Rest of the Second Replie.* The contention between the two sides was clear: was there in the Bible, specifically the New Testament, a distinct form of church government by which the church had to be ruled? This question was affirmed by the Puritans (q.v.), who argued that according to the Book of Acts the apostolic church in Jerusalem was characterized by a definite governance (by elders or presbyters) which needed to be continued, while the conformists argued that the Bible prescribed no specific form of church government and thus allowed a variety of structures and practices.

ADRIAN VI (1454-1523). Pope. Born in Utrecht and educated by the Brethren of the Common Life, Adriaan Floriszoon Dedel studied at the University of Louvain, where he received his doctorate in theology and both taught and served in administrative positions until 1515. That same year he went to Spain, having been tutor of the future King Charles I (and subsequent Emperor Charles V [q.v.]) since 1507. In Spain Adrian's ecclesiastical career advanced dramatically. He was elevated to Bishop of Tortosa in 1516 and became cardinal the following year. In 1517 he was also appointed co-regent, with Cardinal Jimenez de Cisneros, of Spain and, in 1520, viceroy of Spain. In

January 1522, a year after the death of Pope Leo X (q.v.), Adrian was unanimously elected pope in a conclave that had been deadlocked. His personal piety made him sensitive to issues of church reform. This found expression in a comprehensive acknowledgment of the church's guilt with respect to the tardiness of necessary church reform which Adrian issued soon after his election. His opposition to Martin Luther (q.v.) was unequivocal. Adrian emphatically sought to address a variety of reform measures to curtail abuses in the church but the brevity of his papal rule—he was in Rome for just about a year—meant that his efforts were not graced by lasting and meaningful success.

AMBOISE, CONSPIRACY OF. The death, by accident, of King Henry II (q.v.) in 1559 threw France into what seemed to many a constitutional crisis. The new king was a minor, and the Guise family had promptly seized control of government despite the fact that Antoine of Navarre, as the first prince of blood, could claim some prescriptive rights for a major role in a council of regency which, some argued, should have been constituted for the minor king. Supporters of Navarre came from the provincial gentry whose leader was Jean du Barry, the seigneur of La Renaudie. In February 1560 Renaudie convened a meeting of opponents of the Guise in Nantes in order to plan the removal of the family from power, despite the fact that the lack of constitutionality of the Guise action was not altogether certain. Renaudie's supporters gathered in small groups near Amboise, where the royal court was in residence. Their plan was betrayed, however, and Renaudie and many others lost their lives. The significance of the conspiracy lay in the fact that the French Reformation, which theretofore had been a religious phenomenon, began to combine religion and politics. Moreover, an armed confrontation between the two political factions, which would combine religion and politics, had become a real possibility.

AMSDORF, NIKOLAUS VON (1483-1565). Reformer. Born in Torgau of a noble family, Amsdorf studied at both Leipzig and Wittenberg and became a member of the Wittenberg faculty. He was one of the first of that faculty to embrace Martin Luther's new theology and quickly turned into one of Luther's most ardent supporters. In 1524 he was appointed chief pastor in Magdeburg, where he promptly introduced the Reformation. Amsdorf was among the earliest supporters of the notion that the adherents of the new faith might defend themselves by military means. He advocated the theological legitimacy of armed resistance by the territorial rulers against the emperor and forcefully echoed Luther's notion that the pope was the Antichrist (q.v.). In 1542 the Saxon elector effected Amsdorf's election as bishop of Naumburg-Zeitz, a position in which he encountered considerable conservative opposition.

In 1547, upon the defeat of the League of Schmalkald (q.v.), Amsdorf went into exile and became, after the Augsburg Interim had been promulgated, one of its most adamant critics. This entailed fierce criticism of the accommodating role of Philip Melanchthon (q.v.) and his followers. Amsdorf had engaged in stinging polemics against Lutheran theologians who, in his judgment, were not faithful interpreters of Luther. In continuing this polemic in the early 1550s, Amsdorf became a major representative of the Gnesio-Lutheran (q.v.) faction and a force in Lutheran theology until his death. He moved to Eisenach in 1552, where he helped to publish the first edition of Luther's works.

ANABAPTISM. The term literally means "rebaptism" and thus denotes the fact that the opponents of the Anabaptists saw them as those who had been rebaptized themselves and who generally advocated rebaptism. The Anabaptists, in turn, rejected this characterization, arguing that the baptism received in infancy had not been an authentic biblical baptism. In German, the term "Wiedertäufer" denotes the same element of rebaptism which in English usage gets lost on account of the evasiveness of the suffix "ana". Attempts in scholarship to refer to the 16th-century Anabaptists as "Baptists" or "Baptizers" have generally been unsuccessful because of the evident confusion with the 17th-century English Baptists and the fact that the admittedly scarce English literature from the 16th century does also speak of Anabaptists and Anabaptism. For centuries these Anabaptists had a bad press, so to speak, since history was mainly written by their opponents. They were labeled as "radical," as enthusiasts, and they were neither esteemed personally nor taken seriously in their theology.

There are two opinions with respect to the Anabaptist origins in the 16th century—one that associated the origins of the movement with the activities of Thomas Müntzer (q.v.) with the result that a kinship could easily be posited between the radical and revolutionary activities of Müntzer and the subsequent Anabaptist movement. The other explanation of their origins sees them as having been formed among a group of followers of the Zurich reformer Huldrych Zwingli (q.v.). While the role of Müntzer in the emergence of the Anabaptist movement cannot be underestimated, the movement had its origin in Zurich (though there clearly were other points of Anabaptist sentiment elsewhere). Although never a popular movement, Anabaptism spread, clandestinely and as an underground phenomenon, to South Germany and Austria. Anabaptist congregations and conventicles sprang up throughout these areas. Nowhere, however, did the Anabaptists succeed in enlisting governmental support for their re-interpretation of the Christian religion, with the exception of the northwest German city of Münster (q.v.). There for a brief period of time (1533-35) Anabaptism was the official religion of the community.

The Anabaptist movement never was a homogenous phenomenon, though it remains a matter of scholarly disagreement how extensive this division was and if, accordingly, it is not possible to speak of a "normative" strand of Anabaptism in the 16th century. Clearly, however, there were three major factions within the movement—the Swiss-South German Anabaptists, the Moravian Hutterites (q.v.), and the Dutch-Northwest German Mennonites (q.v.). In a way, this distinction is also a chronological one, with the Swiss-South German Anabaptists constituting the origin of the movement, the Hutterites constituting in the 1530s a major variation thereof, and the North German-Dutch Anabaptists-Mennonites describing, first of all, the consolidation of North German Anabaptism after the debacle at Münster under the leadership of Menno Simons (q.v.). By the time the 16th century ended, a rough organizational consolidation had taken place which subsumed all Anabaptists, with the exception of the Hutterites, under the aegis of the norms enunciated by the followers of Menno Simons.

The absence of a strong organizational entity, however, meant that theological and organizational consolidation were long in coming. As regards Anabaptist belief, the foremost distinction was belief in the administration of baptism (q.v.) to adults who had made a prior confession of their personal faith. Clearly, however, that affirmation had its prior ground in the notion of the church comprised only of those who had made a personal commitment and had attested to their faith by their desire to be baptized. It followed that such belief in Jesus had to manifest itself in a new way of life, in sanctification. In the Mennonite tradition this affirmation found expression late in the 16th century in the notion that a believing spouse had to separate from "bread and board" of the unbelieving spouse. Most Anabaptists were non-resistant, that is, they refused to occupy governmental offices and participate in war.

ANGLICANISM. The Church of England, also known as the Anglican tradition, was one of the four major new ecclesiastical bodies to emerge in the 16th century. While its antecedents and major stimuli reach back to the ecclesiastical changes undertaken during the rules of Henry VIII and Edward VI (qq.v.), the Anglican tradition did not find its definitive embodiment until the religious settlement promulgated by Queen Elizabeth I (q.v.) in 1559.

The essence of the Anglican tradition was its insistence on its catholicity, that is, its ties to the authentic and unperverted Catholic tradition through the centuries prior to the Reformation of the 16th century. This sentiment was already discernible during the rule of Henry VIII. The main efforts at ecclesiastical change under Henry VIII were to remove abuses (the dissolution of the monasteries came under this heading) and to repudiate the authority of the pope but to leave the theological affirmations of the Catholic Church in place. Quite appropriately, the Six Articles Act (q.v.) of 1539 enjoined traditional Catholic doctrine, including clerical celibacy. The religious changes undertaken during Edward VI's reign meant a theological re-orientation in the direction of Protestantism, notably the reduction of the sacraments to two, baptism and the Lord's Supper (qq.v.), and the minimizing of the sacrificial element in the Mass. In the edition of the *Book of Common Prayer* (q.v.), of 1552, there was no longer a clear expression of Christ's real presence in the elements of bread and wine in the Lord's Supper.

Thomas Cranmer (q.v.) drafted a confession of faith for the new church, the Forty-two Articles (q.v.), of 1549. In 1563, upon the Elizabethan Settlement, these Forty-two Articles were revised and turned into the Thirty-nine Articles (q.v.) which have been the doctrinal statement of the Anglican Communion ever since. John Jewel (q.v.) published a systematic theology of Anglicanism in 1562 (*Apologia ecclesiae Anglicanae*), and later in the century Richard Hooker's (q.v.) magisterial *Laws of Ecclesiastical Polity* (1593ff) summarized doctrine and order of the Anglican Church. The theological essence of Anglicanism is its amenability to both Catholic and Protestant theology, what has been called the "middle way," *via media*; its insistence on the historical episcopacy; as well as its commitment to three ecclesiastical offices of bishop, priest, and deacon.

ANTICHRIST. The notion of the Antichrist has a history that goes back to early Christianity. Its scriptural basis is found in various places in the New Testament, in each instance denoting, albeit for most interpreters somewhat vaguely, that preceding the return of Christ an "Antichrist" would appear and subject the church and the faithful to formidable and ruthless persecution. Through the centuries, different specific historical figures were identified as the Antichrist. Preoccupation with the topic of the Antichrist was particularly pronounced at times when eschatological fever ran high. The important contribution of the Protestant Reformation in the story of the Antichrist lies in two areas. For one, the Protestant reformers argued in the forceful identification of the pope as the Antichrist. Martin Luther (q.v.) did so blatantly in his 1520 treatises. He argued cogently that it was generally assumed that the return of Christ, and the concomitant appearance of the Antichrist, would be ushered in by a glorious restoration of the gospel. Inasmuch as such a restoration of the gospel was occurring—in the eyes of Martin Luther and the other reformers—it stood to reason that the Antichrist had to make his appearance as well.

A second contribution of the Protestant reformers was their argument that the Antichrist would not appear as an overt enemy of the Christian church but rather would himself pretend to be the representative of it. In the course of the 16th century the Turks were also identified as the Antichrist, especially by Catholic writers, even though the notion that the Antichrist pretended to be Christian mitigated against this identification. Interest in the topic began to wane—other than for perfunctory pronouncements—in the 1530s, to be revived in England toward the end of the century and especially in the 17th century.

ANTICLERICALISM. Recent scholarship has argued the existence of a pervasive anticlericalism in Europe on the eve of the Reformation and has identified this anticlericalism as a major cause of the Protestant Reformation. Anticlericalism in the context of the Reformation meant not so much criticism of the church as such, or even the specific criticism of the demeanor of the clergy but criticism of the role and place of the clergy in society and the church. This anticlericalism meant opposition against the sundry legal, political, and economic privileges of the clergy in society, such as legal immunity or the exemption of the clergy from ordinary taxation. It also meant criticism of the role of the church in such areas of society as education and the care of the poor. One must be careful not to interpret this anti-clericalism as indicative of judgments about ecclesiastical abuse and perversion. Rather, early 16th-century anticlericalism was unhappiness with the place of the church and its representatives in society. Concomitantly, the role of the priest in the economy of salvation history, the distinction between clergy and laity, with the former the sole vehicles of divine grace, also were part and parcel of this anti-clericalism. The phenomenon of anticlericalism helped explain the attraction, once the Reformation controversy had erupted, of the reformers' notion of the priesthood of all believers.

ANTI-SEMITISM. Rejection and hatred of Jews (q.v.) was an important element of early modern European society, even though the term "Anti-Judaism" rather than Anti-Semitism is more appropriately used: the term "Anti-Semitism" denotes the rejection of Semitic people, when in fact the religion of the Jews was the object of adverse and hostile Christian reaction. Jews had lived a precarious existence in Europe ever since Christianity had become the official religion of the Roman Empire in the fifth century and the compulsory baptism (q.v.) of all citizens, and their children, quickly had become the norm. Through the centuries the Jews, not being baptized, indeed refusing to be baptized, proved to be the quintessential "other" of Christian Europe, and the centuries following the crusades and preceding the Reformation of the 16th century are marked by increasing and chronic anti-Jewish diatribes and pogroms.

Until the time of the crusades, however, relations between Christians and Jews, while strained, were relatively amicable. An analysis of the Christian Anti-Judaic polemic suggests two separable elements: the theological repudiation of Judaism on the grounds that Jews refused to accept Jesus as the promised Messiah of Israel and rejected the other distinctive dogmatic affirmations of Christianity, such as the doctrine of the Trinity. A second element of Anti-Judaism entailed a whole congery of charges of moral and personal wrongdoings raised against Jews, which, so the argument ran, characterized all Jews. Jews were said to kill Christian children in ritual murders, to poison wells, to be responsible for a debased coinage, and to be untrustworthy and dishonest. Obviously, the Anti-Judaic polemic presumed a connection between these two charges but it is important to take note of their distinctive difference. By the early 16th century Jews had been expelled from most European countries, notably, of course, Spain and England. In Germany, virtually all territories had expelled the Jews by the end of the 15th century (this included, for example, Electoral Saxony). Early in the 16th century, Johannes Pfefferkorn, a converted Jew now a Dominican, advocated the burning of the Talmud and other important Jewish books (even though he noted that harsh treatment of Jews would make their conversion to Christianity more difficult). This pronouncement triggered the famous Pfefferkorn-Reuchlin contro-versy, in which Johannes Reuchlin (q.v.), celebrated Humanist and Judaic scholar, took the position that Pfefferkorn's notion was abominable since Jewish books were valuable even to Christians.

ANTI-TRINITARIANISM. As the term denotes, anti-Trinitarianism represented the opposition to the traditional Christian doctrine of the Trinity. The anti-Trinitarians are considered part of the Radical Reformation in that their rejection of traditional Christian dogma was more extensive than that of mainstream Protestant theology; they rejected the doctrinal declarations of the creeds and councils of the early church (Nicaea as well as Chalcedon) and undertook to argue the case about the godhead on the sole basis of scriptural passages. The first manifestations of anti-Trinitarian sentiment in the 16th century came in literary form, notably in Michael Servetus's (q.v.) two treatises *De Trinitatis erroribus* (Errors of the Trinity) of 1531 and *Dialogorum de Trinitate* (Dialogues Concerning the Trinity) of the following year. The universal condemnation of these books caused Servetus to go underground and—other than for the ideas expressed in books— disappear as a participant in Reformation events. There were other Protestant reformers, however, such as the Anabaptist (q.v.) Ludwig Haetzer and the Spiritualist (q.v.) Johannes Campanus, whose writings suggest an uneasiness with the traditional doctrine of the Trinity, without making it a major topic of theological discourse. Interestingly enough, anti-Trinitarian sentiment surfaced in Italy in the middle of the century, where Humanist ideas were mixed with notions taken from pre-Nicene theology. This is not surprising, since both Humanists and reformers wanted to go back to the "sources," and it could be easily argued that fourth-century theology was already perverted. Michael

Servetus surfaced again in the 1550s, with the publication of his *Restitutio Christianismi* (The Restitution of Christianity), which eventually led to his death by burning in Geneva in 1553. The major anti-Trinitarian figures who appear around the middle of the century—the physician Giorgio Biandrata, the jurist Mateo Gribaldi (qq.v.), or the philologist Valentino Gentile—were all from Italy and none of them was a trained theologian. Most of these Italians moved northward to Switzerland and South Germany, where they found no less hostility than they had encountered in Italy.

In Poland anti-Trinitarian sentiment flowered most decisively. Peter of Goniadz used the occasion of a Polish Calvinist synod in 1556 to propound anti-Trinitarian views, which he continued to express in various Calvinist settings during the remainder of the decade. In the 1560s, the topic of the Trinity became the foremost theme in Polish and Lithuanian Calvinism (q.v.)—an indication that the sentiment was no longer confined to a few individuals. Biandrata, who had come to Poland in 1558, quickly came to play a major role in raising the issue. Once again, the contention was that terms not found in Scripture were to be avoided. The theological alternative presented by these critics of the Trinitarian dogma was the notion that God, the Father, the Son, and the Holy Spirit, exist separately, with Son and Holy Spirit subordinate to the Father. The conservative Calvinists rallied against this notion as heresy and separated to form a new Calvinist church, the "major" church, distinguished from the "minor" church of the anti-Trinitarians.

Though the Calvinists attempted to employ governmental help in the suppression of anti-Trinitarian sentiment, the Catholics were unwilling to single out one coterie of heretics while leaving the others alone. Thus, efforts toward governmental suppression of the minor church never gained momentum. During the next decade the Minor (anti-Trinitarian) Church was embroiled in several doctrinal controversies, suggesting that the ease with which the traditional Trinitarian dogma was repudiated was not accompanied by a similar ease in constructing a positive alternative. A number of theological issues were discussed by the anti-Trinitarians—infant baptism, the propriety of a Christian bearing arms and occupying a governmental office, as well as the issue of the preexistence of Christ. The arrival of Fausto Sozzini (q.v.) in Poland in 1579 meant the beginning of a period of theological consolidation in the Minor Church under his aegis. When in 1598 a synod at Lublin affirmed the Christian's bearing of arms, a new chapter in the history of Polish anti-Trinitarianism began.

Under Laelio Sozzini's (q.v.) influence, Anabaptist Unitarianism came to an end, and Socinianism began. Anti–Trinitarianism was also active in Hungary and Transylvania, where the Anabaptist influence was noticeably less than what it was in Poland and Lithuania.

ARMADA. The Spanish fleet that set out to invade England in 1588. In the 1580s, tensions between England and Spain had increased significantly, not only because of Queen Elizabeth I's (q.v.) substantial support of the Low Countries, which were rebelling against Spanish rule in 1585 but also because of the English privateers, "Elizabeth's sea dogs," who had begun to challenge Spain's economic monopoly in the Atlantic and the Americas. Philip II's (q.v.) plan to invade England in 1585 failed but the execution of Mary Stuart in February 1587 aroused him once more to action. Without effective support by the pope, who was interested in seeing Catholicism restored in England but did not wish to see Philip on the English throne, Philip's armada of some 130 ships set sail in July 1588. It ended, whether due to storms or the configuration of the Spanish vessels is still disputed, with the loss of a disastrously large number of Spanish vessels in a military catastrophe for Philip. The defeat of the armada signified the dramatic rise of England's sea power and the disappearance of the danger of a Spanish invasion of England.

ARMINIUS, JACOBUS (1560-1609). Arminius, born in Oudewater to a wealthy Dutch family, studied at Geneva under Theodore Beza (q.v.), married well, and served as a pastor in Amsterdam between 1588 and 1603, when he was appointed professor at the University of Leyden. He developed a liberal Calvinism (q.v.), which turned into a public controversy, when in 1604 he presented theses on predestination (q.v.). Arminius espoused a view which defined predestination essentially as God's foreknowledge of the faith and perseverance of humans. Arminius also affirmed the authority of the magistracy to oversee ecclesiastical affairs.

AUGSBURG CONFESSION. Lutheran statement of faith of 1530. The Augsburg Confession was written by Philip Melanchthon (q.v.) in May 1530 in order to present a comprehensive summary of the new Wittenberg theology at the forthcoming diet to be held at Augsburg. Melanchthon astutely felt the need to differentiate the Wittenberg theology in two ways. On the one hand, the Wittenberg theology had to be distinguished from the seemingly more radical theology of Huldrych Zwingli (q.v.) and other South German theologians (as regards their views of the Lord's Supper [q.v.]) and the fringe movement of the Anabaptists (q.v.). On the other hand, Melanchthon was intent on demonstrating that the Wittenberg theology was a restatement of the ancient theology of the church and that the dissent from the Catholic Church pertained only to the intention to correct certain abuses. The formulations of the Augsburg Confession accordingly were irenic throughout. This represented not only Melanchthon's own temperament (Martin Luther [q.v.], who as outlaw of the empire could not be present at Augsburg, agreed with Melanchthon's document, acknowledging that his own temperament did not allow him to "tread that softly"). At the same time, Elector John Frederick of Saxony wanted a resolution of the religious controversy so that Melanchthon's formulations expressed the Saxon political stance and fit a larger political context as well.

The Augsburg Confession included 28 articles, which are presented in two parts. Articles 1-21 deal with the "eminent articles of the faith" while the remaining seven discuss abuses that must be corrected. Under that heading the confession discusses communion under both kinds, clerical celibacy, the Mass, confession, dietary regulations, monastic vows, and episcopal jurisdiction. Upon its formal presentation at the diet, Emperor Charles V (q.v.) rejected it. Subsequently, the confession gained importance as the theological basis for the League of Schmalkald (q.v.) and, despite its irenic and conciliatory orientation, became the defining doctrinal statement of Lutheranism (q.v.).

AUGSBURG CONFESSION (ALTERED). Lutheran statement of faith. Philip Melanchthon (q.v.) republished the Augsburg Confession (q.v.) in 1540. This new edition contained, in Article 10 on the Lord's Supper (q.v.), an alteration, the significance of which quickly proved to be controversial. The new version read "that with bread and wine the body and blood of Christ are truly offered those who eat at the Lord's table." Depending on how one read this sentence, this constituted a departure from Luther's position (and that of the 1530 version): the phrase "with bread and wine" could be interpreted to mean "alongside bread and wine" so that Christ's presence was not in the elements of bread and wine but rather in a sacramental union with the believer.

This version of the Augsburg Confession is known as the "altered" Augsburg Confession, or by its Latin designation as the *Confessio*

Augustana variata. Initially, Melanchthon's change evoked no adverse reactions on the part of Martin Luther (q.v.) or other Lutheran theologians. None other than John Calvin (q.v.) subscribed to the Altered Confession in 1541. When German Lutheranism (q.v.) at mid-century had to deal with the increasing influence of Calvinism (q.v.) in Germany, the altered Augsburg Confession turned into a major bone of contention in what is known as the Second Communion controversy which pitted Lutherans against Calvinists and crypto-Calvinists, that is, those Lutherans who found the Calvinist interpretation of the Lord's Supper attractive.

AUGSBURG, DIET OF (1530). The diet held in the South German city of Augsburg was convened by Emperor Charles V (q.v.), who had been absent from Germany since 1521. Its major purpose was to deal with three pressing and interrelated issues—the unresolved religious controversy, the designation of Charles's brother Ferdinand as king of the Romans, and the ongoing Turkish threat. The emperor's summons had been surprisingly conciliatory with respect to the religious controversy (considering the fact that the Protestants were, after all, condemned heretics). Charles had indicated that he was prepared to hear "everyone's opinion." Neither among the Protestants nor among the Catholics was there unanimity, nor on the part of the rulers or the theologians, as to the most expeditious course of action.

On both sides there were hard-liners for whom the religious controversy had triggered a definitive and final division, for Catholics since the Protestant positions were demonstrably heretical; for Protestants because of their vision of the gospel. However, on both sides were also conciliatory individuals who were convinced that, with good will and open minds, the disagreements between the two sides would be understood not to be substantial and could be reconciled. In line with the emperor's summons, which stated that he wanted to "hear everyone's opinion," no less than three confessions of faith had been drafted, foremostly that written by Philip Melanchthon (q.v.), subsequently known as the Augsburg Confession (q.v.), which represented the irenic approach to the contested issues in that it went to great lengths to find formulations to minimize the theological differences between the Lutherans (q.v.) and the Catholics. In fact, Melanchthon stated in private conversations at Augsburg that the controversy was only over clerical celibacy, the Communion cup, and the private Mass, in other words, issues that lay more in the realm of church polity and practice than in theology.

Huldrych Zwingli (q.v.) submitted a statement of faith on behalf of Zurich entitled *Fidei ratio,* which was not considered an official document at the diet. The four South German cities of Memmingen, Strasbourg, Lindau, and Constance submitted under the leadership of Strasbourg, a confession of their own (*Confessio Tetrapolitana*) to express their distinctive views regarding the Lord's Supper (q.v.). Their confession was submitted on July 9 but immediately rejected by the diet. The Catholics had refused to submit a statement of their faith— their notion being that theirs was the traditional Catholic faith that needed no new explication.

Strategically, the Augsburg Confession raised the question for the Catholics if the irenic perspective of the confession should be accepted or if a comprehensive Catholic response was needed in order to demonstrate that the Protestants were indeed old-fashioned heretics. In response to the Augsburg Confession Johann Eck (q.v.) revived a set of 404 theses he had drafted earlier and turned them into a rebuttal of Melanchthon's confession, entitled *Confutatio* (q.v.), which the emperor promptly declared to have demonstrated the errors of Melanchthon's document. If the emperor's hope to be able to achieve reconciliation between the two sides had thus proved unsuccessful, there remained the issue of gathering financial and military support from the territorial rulers against the Turks. As far as the Protestants were concerned, the emperor's need for their support strengthened their position. The eventual recess of the diet, formulated much in light of the need of Protestant support, stipulated that the adherents of the Augsburg Confession were given six months to recant, after which time the emperor would consider using military means in order to return them to the Catholic fold.

AUGSBURG, PEACE OF (1555). Emperor Charles V's (q.v.) efforts, after his victory over the League of Schmalkald (q.v.), at the diet at Augsburg (1547-48), were calculated not only to reestablish the Catholic faith in the empire but also to consolidate central (imperial) authority and power in the empire. While there was substantial support for his religious objective, the latter goal understandably evoked the opposition of the territorial rulers, even the Catholic ones. For the first time in decades, the religious controversy ceased to be the overriding issue in German politics. By 1550 the opposition against the emperor had been organized. The key figure was Duke Maurice of Saxony, whose support of Charles in the War of Schmalkald (q.v.) had been a significant factor in the emperor's military success. Maurice, an astute statesman, correctly surmised that the growing opposition against the emperor, if it proved to be successful, would be to his own detriment on account of his previous closeness to the emperor. Maurice promptly put himself at the head of a conspiracy against the emperor to thwart his plans for a political reorganization of the empire. In 1552 the conspirators attacked the emperor, who taken by surprise barely escaped being taken prisoner. The futility of pursuing his political plans became obvious to the emperor as did the awareness that his religious plans, embodied in the Interim (q.v.), were vigorously resisted by the Protestants and ignored by the papacy and the Catholics.

Charles began to realize that the fundamental disagreement on the issue of the parity of the two confessions (q.v.) in the empire (q.v.) and the role of territorial rulers could not be bridged. He began to contemplate his abdication. The religious peace, concluded in July 1552, postponed the final and definitive resolution of the religious question and the territorial ruler's grievances until the next diet. Two years later Charles transferred his imperial responsibilities to his brother Ferdinand (q.v.), who accordingly presided over the diet at Augsburg (February to September, 1555). The estates gathering in Augsburg were concerned, above all, with restoring peace and tranquillity to the empire (q.v.). The sentiment to resolve the religious issue once and for all ruled the day and compelled the estates to seek compromises on the contested issues.

Accordingly, the religious peace was a compromise. It surrendered the notion of a single religion in the empire. The decision was neatly expressed in a famous phrase not found in the peace itself but coined subsequently, "cuius regio, eius religio" ("he who has the rule determines the religion"). It meant that the ruler of a territory or principality had the authority to determine the religion of his subjects. Thus, the Peace of Augsburg vindicated the recess of the diet of Speyer of 1526 (q.v.) which had first placed the execution of the Edict of Worms (q.v.) into the hands of the individual territorial rulers. Germany became legally divided into two religious factions, along territorial boundaries. Only Catholicism and Lutheranism (q.v.) were allowed. The subjects were given the right to emigration. Protestant territories and cities which had accepted the new faith by 1552 were allowed to retain the ecclesiastical property they had secularized. In the imperial free cities, both confessions, Catholic and Lutheran, were allowed to exist side by side. Rulers of ecclesiastical territories who converted to Protestantism had to do so as individuals; their territories were to remain Catholic. Finally, Ferdinand affirmed the right of worship for Lutherans in ecclesiastical territories.

— B —

BAPTISM. One of the seven sacraments (q.v.) of the Catholic Church, baptism was administered by century-old tradition to infants. In the early Reformation baptism was initially not an issue. Even though Martin Luther's (q.v.) redefinition of the sacraments reduced their number from seven to two, baptism was retained by him as a sacrament alongside Communion since it had both a dominical command and a salvatory consequence (as a vehicle of grace). Luther's insistence that faith was a necessary ingredient in the beneficial reception of the sacrament raised the obvious question as to the appropriateness of administering the sacrament of baptism to infants. Not surprisingly, the early 1520s gave evidence of a number of questioners of infant baptism (the Zwickau Prophets, Carlstadt, and Müntzer [qq.v.] come to mind), until uneasiness about the practice turned into its rejection when a group of disciples of Huldrych Zwingli (q.v.) proceeded to perform baptism upon a prior confession of faith in Zollikon, near Zurich, in January 1525, and thereby marked the beginnings of the Anabaptist movement (q.v.).

The Anabaptists insisted that baptism should be administered upon a profession of faith, thus only to those who were capable of such a profession. Moreover, the Anabaptists argued that baptism was not a sacrament, that is, a vehicle of divine grace but rather a memorial, or symbol of the act and covenant of faith, that preceded it. Despite this frontal attack on a rite the Catholic Church had practiced for at least a millennium, the major reformers were unwavering in their affirmation of the traditional practice and theology of infant baptism. Martin Luther used the category of the "faith of infants" to argue that, inasmuch as faith is wrought by God, infants can be as much the recipients of faith as mature adults. For Huldrych Zwingli and John Calvin (q.v.) baptism was seen as symbolic expression of the newborn's incorporation into the Christian community, analogous to the practice of circumcision of newborn males in ancient Israel.

BARNABITES. Catholic monastic order founded in 1530 by Antonio Maria Zaccaria together with two laymen, Giacomo Antonio Morigia and Bartolomeo Ferrari. The order received papal approval in 1533. Its official name is Regular Clerics of Saint Paul; the appellation "Barnabites" comes from the church of St. Barnabas in Milan, with which the new order was intimately associated. The emphasis of the new order was on the theology and spirituality of the Apostle Paul with a strong commitment to work among the poor and marginalized of society. Initially an order only of priests, the Barnabites also had a female parallel, the Angelic Sisters of St. Paul, as well as a lay sodality, the Married Couples of St. Paul. The Barnabites themselves remained a small order, confined to central and northern Italy.

BELLARMINE, ROBERT (1542-1621). Cardinal, Catholic theologian, saint. Born in Montepulciano, Tuscany, Bellarmine joined the Society of Jesus (q.v.) in 1560, was ordained to the priesthood ten years later in 1570, and served as professor of theology at Louvain and Rome. His most important work was a detailed rebuttal of Reformation theology entitled *Disputationes de controversiis Christianae fidei adversus huius temporis haereticos* (Disputation Concerning the Controversies about the Christian Faith against the Heretics of Our Time) and published in 1586. He was also the author of two immensely popular catechisms. In 1599 he was appointed a cardinal. When he was made archbishop of Capua, Bellarmine took up residence in his archdiocese, returning to Rome only to participate in two papal elections. Bellarmine wrote extensively in his later years. He was canonized in 1930 and declared a "doctor of the Church" one year later.

BEZA, THEODORE (1519-1605). Protestant reformer. The future reformer studied the liberal arts and law at Bourges and Orleans but in 1548 abruptly moved to Geneva to meet with John Calvin (q.v.). Between 1552 and 1558 he studied Greek at Lausanne and found time to support the persecuted French Protestants. When, in 1557, Beza drafted a confession of faith calculated to bring the various Protestant factions in Switzerland together, and both Zurich and Bern resoundingly rejected the draft, Calvin offered his support. Beza was asked to head the Genevan Academy and became both a preacher and professor of exegesis in Geneva. His lectures echoed Calvin. After Calvin's death, Beza increasingly became the head of Calvinism (q.v.)

throughout Europe. To support the French Protestants Beza participated both in the Colloquy of Poissy (q.v.) in 1561 and that of St. Germain the year thereafter. At the age of 70, Beza relinquished his public offices and devoted himself to literary activities. During the last three decades of the 16th century Beza undoubtedly was one of the most influential Protestant theologians.

BIANDRATA, GIORGIO (c. 1515-1588/90). Protestant reformer and anti-Trinitarian. Biandrata was born in Saluzzo in the Piedmont. He studied at the University of Pavia and became physician at the royal courts of Poland and Hungary. By 1552 he had returned to Italy, where he quickly aroused the suspicion of the Inquisition (q.v.) for his religious views. This prompted him to move to Geneva in 1556 and to Zurich (q.v.) two years later. In 1560 he returned to Poland, where utilizing connections he had formed during his earlier stay he quickly came to occupy positions of influence. Despite John Calvin's (q.v.) entreaties to his Polish followers that Biandrata held heretical views, Biandrata became the head of the Reformed church in Poland. After 1565 he began to advocate explicitly anti-Trinitarian notions. Biandrata propounded a moderate form of anti-Trinitarianism (q.v.)—his view was that Jesus, despite being created, deserved adoration by the faithful—against the more radical forms of anti-Trinitarianism advocated in Poland.

BIBLE. It was the rallying cry of the reformers that the Bible alone was to be the guide in determining the Christian faith. The Latin phrase for this contention was *sola scriptura (*by Scripture alone). The opposition expressed in this regard was against what the reformers called "human traditions," namely human teachings without Scriptural foundation. In so arguing, the reformers drove a wedge between what in late medieval theology was seen as an inseparable whole—the teaching of Scripture and the church tradition, the latter amplifying and explaining, never distorting the former. It never occurred to the reformers to separate the two. The reformers' stance proved to be a convenient and persuasive hermeneutic tool to attack practices and teachings considered unbiblical. This stress on the Bible as the sole norm of the Christian faith presupposed, of course, the practical availability of the Bible. Gutenberg's invention of movable type in the middle of the 15th century had created the possibility for an efficient and speedy dissemination of printed materials. The flourishing printing industry of the late 15th and early 16th centuries began increasingly to make the Bible available in a way previously not known.

The impetus of the Reformation prompted the translation of the Bible into vernacular tongues, beginning in Germany with Martin Luther's (q.v.) "September Bible" of 1522, a German translation of the New Testament which Luther had begun during his involuntary stay on the Wartburg. Translations of the Bible into other European languages followed, wherever Protestant notions became important. In England, William Tyndal (q.v.) began his English translation far away from home on the European Continent; he suffered the dubious honor of having his translation made official in England, while he himself was burned at the stake as a heretic. For Catholics the quickly emerging diversity of Protestant groupings was proof positive of the need for the explicating role of the church. Moreover, Catholic theologians, beginning with Jacob Latomus in 1522, showed that they had no problem arguing the traditional Catholic doctrine solely on the basis of the Bible. Catholic hesitancy remained, however, with respect both to accepting a text other than that of the Vulgate as authentic and to endorsing vernacular translations of the Bible. While the Catholic Church had no objections in principle, it saw the dangers of unauthorized, private translations as well as uninformed reading of the sacred text.

BLARER, AMBROSIUS (1492-1564), also Blaurer. Protestant reformer. Older brother of Thomas Blarer (q. v.), Ambrosius became a Benedictine monk, then prior. He studied at Tübingen, where he befriended Philip Melanchthon (q.v.). In July 1522 he left the monastery, established contact with Huldrych Zwingli, Johann Oecolampadius, and, since 1528, with Martin Bucer (qq.v.) who greatly influenced his theological development. He was instrumental in introducing the Reformation in Constance and other South German cities. In 1534 Duke Ulrich of Württemberg asked him to assist in the introduction of the Reformation in Württemberg, though four years later the strict Lutherans saw to his expulsion from there. He lived briefly in Augsburg but was expelled and returned to Constance. The defeat of the League of Schmalkald (q.v.) in 1547, and the re-introduction of Catholicism in Constance, made him again a refugee. He moved to Switzerland (q.v.), where he intermittently remained active in ecclesiastical affairs.

BLARER, THOMAS (1499-1570), also Blaurer. Protestant reformer. Younger brother of Ambrosius Blarer (q.v.), Thomas was born in Constance, studied law at Wittenberg, and in 1521 accompanied Martin Luther (q.v.) to Worms. Together with his brother he introduced the Reformation in his home town of Constance. Between 1526 and 1538 Thomas served as mayor of the city. When the plague hit Constance his sister and several close friends were among the victims. The defeat of the League of Schmalkald (q.v.) was for him, as well as for his brother, a catastrophe, even though Thomas initially succeeded in rallying resistance against the emperor. While his brother left for Switzerland (q.v.), Thomas stayed. Constance became Austrian territory and even the religious Peace of Augsburg (q.v.), 1555, did not assure Constance religious freedom. Eventually Thomas moved to Switzerland, where he died near Winterthur in 1570.

BODIN, JEAN (1529/30-1596). Jean Bodin undoubtedly was the most universal of minds in the latter part of the 16th century. His prolific writings—undertaken alongside an active public career—covered the fields of theology, philosophy, and cosmology. Bodin was saturated by Humanistic ideals. The importance of Greek and Roman antiquity was juxtaposed with the intellectual world of Judaism, especially the Kabbalah. His two most important works were the *Colloquium heptaplomeres de rerum sublimium* of 1593, in which representatives of seven religions have a dialogue about true religion, and his *Six livres de la république* of 1576, a massive tome in which Bodin delineated his theory of sovereignty. Both works are difficult to interpret, even though in the *Six livres* Bodin advocated a notion of sovereignty which may be said to have enabled the rise of absolutist theory. As regards Bodin's religious thought it seems that he espoused a kind of Judaizing Neoplatonism.

BOOK OF COMMON PRAYER. The *Book of Common Prayer* was officially adopted in January 1549 by the English Parliament. Its exact title was *The Booke of the Common Prayer and administration of the Sacraments.* Its author was Thomas Cranmer (q.v.), who already in the latter years of the reign of Henry VIII (q.v.) had begun to prepare an English litany, prayers, supplications, and responses to be used in church services. In compiling the *Book of Common Prayer*, Thomas Cranmer drew heavily on existing models—the Sarum (Salisbury

Processional), the Roman Catholic breviary, Martin Luther's (q.v.) *German Mass*. Cranmer's contribution lay in his harmonious merging of these several sources but also, and most importantly, in the beautiful cadences of his language. This language has molded English-speaking Protestantism through the centuries. The prayer book was clearly Protestant in tone and content, and as regards the contested issue of the interpretation of the Lord's Supper (q.v.), its language suggested the real presence of Christ in the sacrament, in other words, a view close both to the traditional Catholic and the Lutheran position. Three years later, the second Edwardian Act of Uniformity introduced a revised edition of the *Book of Common Prayer*. This new edition showed the influence of the continental reformer Martin Bucer (q.v.), then in England, whose several suggestions, accepted by Cranmer, moved the theology of the prayer book into a Calvinist direction. In the new version, priests were referred to as ministers, altars as tables, and communion became a memorial to Christ's death.

For the adamant Scottish reformer John Knox (q.v.), these changes were insufficient. When the new edition of the *Book of Common Prayer* was already in press, Knox exploded with the declaration that to kneel while receiving the sacrament, as the new version of the *Prayer Book* enjoined, was popish idolatry. The Solomonic solution was to add an appendix, the so-called "Black Rubric," which offered a series of explanations (such as kneeling did not mean adoration but was an expression of gratitude). Understandably, the reign of Mary brought the prohibition of the *Book of Common Prayer* but the Elizabethan Act of Uniformity of 1559 re-introduced the *Book of Common Prayer* of 1552 in a somewhat revised form. An antipapal prayer, which spoke of the "tyranny of the bishop of Rome," was omitted—it was hardly politically expedient at the time—as was the "Black Rubric." Importantly, the relevant passages concerning the Lord's Supper from the 1549 and 1552 editions were juxtaposed, which meant a compromise between the Lutheran notion of the real presence and the Zwinglian view of a spiritual presence. The *Book of Common Prayer* has been the liturgical ground of the Anglican communion through the centuries. A major revision took place in 1928.

BORA, CATHERINE VON (1499-1552). Martin Luther's (q.v.) wife. Catherine was born of a noble family and joined a Cistercian convent in 1515. In 1523, under the impact of the Reformation, Catherine and the other nuns in her convent sought to leave the convent, a decision that was facilitated by Martin Luther (q.v.). Since her own family was unwilling to accept her, marriage was the only viable alternative. When it turned out that there were no other marital candidates for Catherine, Luther and Catherine were married on June 13, 1525. The records indicate that Catherine was learned in theological topics and a gifted manager of the Luther household. Six children issued from their marriage (three sons and three daughters), of whom a daughter died at age 13. While the household was reasonably well off during Luther's lifetime, the vicissitudes of the War of Schmalkald (q.v.) brought considerable financial hardship to Catherine after her husband's death in 1546. Catherine died on the way to Torgau in 1552.

BORROMEO, CARLO (1438-1584). Archbishop of Milan and Catholic reformer. Borromeo personified the spiritual and ecclesiastical vitality of Catholicism in the second half of the 16th century. He received his doctorate in theology and law in 1559 and was made cardinal by his uncle, pope Pius IV (q.v.), as whose secretary he functioned, especially during the sessions of the Council of Trent (q.v.), with considerable skill and effectiveness. In the early 1560s Borromeo experienced a spiritual conversion, was ordained to the priesthood and consecrated bishop in 1563, and took up residence as cardinal of Milan in 1565. For the remainder of his life he was a model for Tridentine Catholicism. His personal engagement, his convening numerous provincial and diocesan synods, and his personal visitations throughout his church province were impressive manifestations of Tridentine Catholicism. Borromeo's determined pursuit of reform and enhanced spirituality triggered conflicts with the political authorities, particularly when he excommunicated the Spanish viceroy Requesens who had endorsed certain kinds of public entertainment on a church holiday. Borromeo was canonized in 1610.

BUCER, MARTIN (1491-1551). Protestant reformer. This South German reformer was born at Schlettstadt in the Alsace in 1491 to a modest family. He entered the Dominican order in his hometown, which sent him to the University of Heidelberg in 1517 to pursue theological studies. On the occasion of the Heidelberg disputation in 1518 he encountered Martin Luther (q.v.), who made a lasting and incisive impression on him. Alongside Desiderius Erasmus (q.v.), Luther was the crucial theological influence on Bucer. Efforts in the years immediately following to introduce reform in the Alsace failed;

in 1523 Bucer arrived as a refugee in Strasbourg (q.v.). Here he began to publish evangelical treatises and emerged as an important reform figure in Southwest Germany.

Still a marginal figure at the Marburg Colloquy (q.v.) of 1529, Bucer came into his own as the leading Swiss-South German reformer after Huldrych Zwingli's (q.v.) untimely death in 1531. He experienced the political isolation of Strasbourg and the Zwinglians at the diet at Augsburg (q.v.) in 1530, and in the decade that followed he relentlessly pursued the notion of theological concord between the Wittenberg and the South German reformers. The Wittenberg Concord (q.v.) of 1536 was his achievement: the presence of Christ in bread and wine was expressed in such a way as to allow both Wittenberg and South Germany to accept the formulation. Bucer put his imprint on several church orders, notably in South German towns. When, in the late 1530s, the overall climate of the religious controversy suggested conciliation, Bucer's irenic and conciliatory stance made him the most important figure among the Protestant theologians, not only in Germany but also in Europe.

The defeat of the League of Schmalkald (q.v.) in 1547 forced Strasbourg to accept the Interim (q.v.) and Bucer to emigrate to England in 1549. There he found a kindred spirit in Archbishop Thomas Cranmer (q.v.) and significantly influenced the Edwardian reform of the church. He was appointed professor at Cambridge and received a doctorate in theology. His last work, *De regno Christi*, represented a comprehensive vision of a Christian commonwealth, for it dealt not only with ecclesiastical and theological reform but also with reform of English society. Bucer died on February 28, 1551. During the rule of Queen Mary (q.v.), his remains were disinterred and then burned.

BUGENHAGEN, JOHANNES (1485-1558). Protestant reformer. Bugenhagen began university studies in Greifswald in 1502. Two years later he became principal of a church school in Treptow, and in 1509 he was ordained to the priesthood, without having received theological training. His pedagogical involvement was graced by notable success. Bugenhagen came under the influence of Erasmian Humanism which, in turn, led to an intense preoccupation with the Bible (q.v.). Martin Luther's (q.v.) writings impressed and influenced him, even though he was initially dismayed by their heretical content. In 1521—36 years of age—Bugenhagen moved to Wittenberg and matriculated at the university there. The following year he was one of the first priests to marry. After some unsuccessful efforts by Luther to find a suitable position for Bugenhagen, he was appointed minister of the town church in Wittenberg in 1523.

At that time Bugenhagen began his literary career, which eventually included several exegetical works, such as commentaries on the Psalms, Matthew, and Jeremiah. Importantly, he became heavily involved in organizational matters pertaining to church and school reform in North Germany (Braunschweig, Hamburg, Lübeck). In 1534 Bugenhagen received an invitation from the dukes of Pomerania to introduce the Reformation there. One year later he became a member of the theological faculty in Wittenberg but already in 1537 he responded to the request of the Danish king Christian III, who had called on him to help with the introduction of the Reformation.

In all of his varied organizational involvements Bugenhagen proceeded from his conviction that the church was to be borne by the entire community so that church reform and the introduction of the "gospel" were always to be a communal initiative. During his years in Wittenberg, Bugenhagen played an important role as pastor and counselor/confessor to Luther. Prior to his death in 1558 he sought to perpetuate Luther's theology in the context of the intense doctrinal controversies in Lutheranism (q.v.) after Luther's death.

BULLINGER, HEINRICH (1504-1575). Swiss reformer and theologian. Son of the dean at Bremgarten, a small town near Zurich, Bullinger studied at the University of Cologne, where he received both bachelor's and the master's degrees (1520; 1522). In 1523, already of evangelical conviction, he was appointed teacher at the school of the Cistercian monastery at Kappel. Bullinger succeeded in converting the members of the community to evangelical belief and their acquiescence in the dissolution of the monastery. In 1529 Bullinger succeeded his father as minister at Bremgarten, where he introduced the Reformation.

The political vicissitudes of the War of Kappel (q.v.) in 1531 also turned the fate of the Reformation at Bremgarten, and Bullinger, together with his father and brother, fled to Zurich (q.v.). In December of that year he was appointed *antistes*, or head of the Zurich church, as Huldrych Zwingli's successor by the Zurich city council. His 44 years in Zurich until his death in 1575 encompass the major period of the Protestant Reformation: he outlived not only Luther but also Philip Melanchthon and John Calvin (qq.v.). Early on Bullinger effectively saw to the reaffirmation of the introduction of the Reformation by the Zurich city council against Catholic moves that sought to make Zwingli's unexpected demise the occasion for returning the city to the Catholic fold. Bullinger was responsible for both the first and the second Helvetic Confessions (q.v.) (1536; 1566).

He was a prolific writer. Over one hundred books issued from his pen, Biblical commentaries, a history of the Zurich Reformation, collections of sermons. Greatly influenced by Zwingli's theology, Bullinger nonetheless developed his own distinctive emphases, such as his covenant theology which held that there was a single covenant from Adam to the present. Bullinger had married Anna Adlischweiler, a former nun, in 1529. They had 11 children. Anna died, as did three of their daughters, of the plague in 1565.

— C —

CAJETAN, THOMAS (1469-1534). Catholic theologian and cardinal. Born in the Neapolitan town of Gaeta from which he took his name, Cajetan was a distinguished philosopher and Thomist scholar who took degrees at various Italian universities before entering the Dominican order in 1494. A strong supporter of papal authority, he became general of his order and had been named cardinal when he was appointed papal legate to the Diet of Augsburg (q.v.) in 1518. Here he confronted Martin Luther (q.v.) but failed to win a retraction of Luther's positions on indulgences (q.v.), justification, and papal authority. Cajetan's unavailing arguments were noteworthy for their sober and judicial engagement with the issues dividing the church. He won the respect of Desiderius Erasmus (q.v.) for his erudition and advocacy of ecclesiastical reform. Between 1520 and 1532 he wrote against Luther's views of papal primacy, the Eucharist (q.v.), the Mass, justifying faith, and good works, while urging concessions on the issues of communion under both kinds and clerical marriage. Cajetan devoted his last years to a biblical commentary. His extensive writings formed early modern Catholic thought in philosophy and social ethics as well as theology.

CALVIN, JOHN (1509-1564). French reformer. Jean (John) Calvin was born in the Piccardy region in Northern France, where his father was legal counsellor to the Bishop of Noyon. Calvin studied the liberal arts at Paris and Orleans. The death of his father, who had wished him to study law, allowed him to live as a private scholar. He published a commentary on Seneca in 1532, a work that demonstrates the thoroughness of his schooling in humanistic studies and law. Around that time, Calvin experiencd a conversion to Protestantism, which eventually forced him to leave his native France, though not without having published, in 1536, a summary treatise on the new Protestant faith. Entitled *Institutes of the Christian Religion* (q.v.), it made its young author an increasingly respected figure among the theologians of the Reformation. Planning to move to Germany in order to undertake theological studies, Calvin passed through Geneva (q.v.) in late summer of 1536 and was persuaded by Guillaume Farel (q.v.), who had been instrumental in introducing the Reformation there, to stay. Calvin became a lecturer on the Bible and worked harmoniously with Farel in consolidating the introduction of the new Protestant faith in the city. In 1538 Farel and Calvin experienced a confrontation with the Genevan city council. At issue was whether ordinary or unleavened bread should be used in Communion (q.v.). The two reformers insisted that this was not up to the city council and refused to serve Communion on Easter Sunday. As a result, the two men were expelled from the city. Calvin went to Strasbourg, where he soon became active in church affairs, serving a congregation of French refugees.

The absence of a strong leader among the Genevan clergy prompted the city council, in 1541, to invite Calvin to return. After some hesitancy he returned in 1541. The promulgation of a new church order, the *ordonnances ecclésiastique*, was his work. While it envisioned a close harmonious relationship between the city council and the clergy, it did, on paper, highlight the autonomy of the church. Calvin spent the rest of his life in Geneva. He married Idelette du Bure, the widow of a former Anabaptist but little is known about his personal life. His stern view of Christian morality, coupled with his views on predestination (q.v.), led to constant conflict with the city council and eminent citizens of Geneva. These conflicts subsided only during the last decade of his life, particularly after the spectacular trial of Michael Servetus (q.v.), whose condemnation Calvin endorsed.

Calvin did not become a Genevan citizen until toward the end of his life; Geneva did not become his home, though he labored there and gave all of his talents and energy. He preached extensively (the transcripts of these sermons were destroyed last century), revised the *Institutes* until they became the foremost Protestant systematic theology, participated in the religious colloquies (q.v.) of the late 1530s between Catholics and Protestants, and lived to see his understanding of the Christian religion become normative in many places in Europe, such as France, Scotland, and Poland.

CALVINISM. John Calvin (q.v.), after whom this Protestant tradition takes its name, was himself a reformer of the second generation. As such, together with his temperament, he proved to be more of a systematic theologian than Martin Luther (q.v.). Calvin's *Institutes of the Christian Religion* (q.v.) proved to be the source for the systematic theology of Calvinism. There the notion of the honor of the sovereign god is the defining element of Calvinist theology. *Soli Deo gloria*—to God alone be glory. Such honor of God is the purpose of creation and the salvation of the elect as well as the cause of the damnation of the damned.

Calvin emphasized throughout God's sovereignty over all that happens. This meant, of course, that humans have been eternally predestined either to salvation or damnation. No human striving or effort will make the slightest difference. Justification was by faith alone, effected by the Holy Spirit. Sanctification, the fruit of justification, followed. This was the new birth whose goal it was to restore human likeness to God. Unlike Martin Luther, whose pivotal question was "how do I obtain a gracious God who is gracious to me?" Calvin's question was "how can God's rule among humankind be furthered?" God's universal rule is made concrete in the church, which was the "external means by which God invites us to communion with Christ."

Calvin's understanding of the Lord's Supper (q.v.), particularly the meaning of bread and wine in the event, rejected the notion of the real presence of body and blood (since a body is always locally confined and Jesus' body is after his ascension in heaven). Rather, Calvin advocated the notion that a real communication with the body and blood of Christ takes place: the faithful who receive bread and wine in Communion truly participate in the communion of body and blood of Christ. Also, Calvin stressed, far more so than did Luther, the reality of church discipline in matters where the Lutherans had remained nonchalant. He saw the Bible (q.v.) as containing specific mandates for a large sweep of matters pertaining to church government, the relationship of the church to the public order, etc. In particular, Calvin found the mandates of personal and public morality, which for Luther were part of the orders of creation and thus not expressive of specific

Christian mandates, as explicitly Christian. Accordingly, the consistory in Geneva (q.v.), and other places where the Calvinist ethos carried the day, engaged in a monitoring and surveillance of faith and morals of the people in a way unheard of in Wittenberg.

CANISIUS, PETER (1521-1597). Catholic theologian and churchman. Born in Nijmegen, Holland, Canisius studied at Cologne from 1536 to 1546, having joined the newly founded Society of Jesus (q.v.) in 1543. In 1549, Canisius was appointed professor of theology at the University of Ingolstadt, where he also served as rector of the university. In 1552 he went for two years to Vienna as professor and court preacher. Between 1556 and 1569 he served as the first provincial head of the Jesuits in Germany. The establishment of Jesuit colleges in both Ingolstadt and Vienna was one of the major results of his work during that time. Canisius's efforts were directed toward thwarting the advance of Protestantism in Austria and Bavaria. Since he was also deeply concerned about Catholic reform, tensions broke out between him and his Jesuit superiors in Rome. His lasting literary achievement was his *Summa doctrina christianae* (Summary of Christian Doctrine), 1555, which appeared in a German version the following year. The book was the major pedagogical vehicle for German Catholicism in its efforts to instruct the faithful in the main tenets of the Catholic faith. In Austria, the "Canisius," as the catechism was popularly called, was the official book of theological instruction. Canisius was beatified in 1864 and canonized in 1925.

CAPITO, WOLFGANG (1478?-1541). German theologian, preacher, Humanist scholar, and reformer. Born in Hagenau, near Strasbourg, to a prosperous artisan family, Capito studied at the universities of Ingolstadt, Basel, and Freiburg, earning doctorates in theology as well as in canon and civil law. He was drawn to northern Humanist circles and particularly the teachings of Desiderius Erasmus (q.v.), who in turn admired Capito's scholarly integrity and fluency in Latin, Hebrew, and Greek. In 1515 he was appointed professor and cathedral preacher in Basel, and in 1521 named cathedral preacher and ecclesiastical advisor to Archbishop Albert in Mainz. Capito's early uncertainty over Martin Luther's (q.v.) new theology was resolved after two conversations with Luther and his subsequent move to Strasbourg, where he quickly became a leading figure in the reform movement. Although Capito failed to persuade Erasmus to follow him into the Lutheran camp, he carried his Humanist disciples into the work of reforming not only church life and practice but also the morals, welfare, and education of Strasbourg. Also, in the spirit of Erasmus, he counseled peace and unity within the reform movement, manifesting even a certain understanding for the Anabaptists (q.v.). Leaning to Zwingli's (q.v.) notion of the Lord's Supper (q.v.), Capito nonetheless signed the Wittenberg Concord (q.v.) in 1536 but failed in his efforts to bring the Swiss theologians into agreement with Luther on this issue. Capito published two catechisms, several biblical commentaries and polemical works as well as a translation of Erasmus's *De Concordia*. He died in Strasbourg in 1541 convinced that he had achieved "a brighter understanding."

CAPUCHINS. Catholic monastic order. The Capuchins were a 16th-century offshoot of the Observant Franciscans who, under the leadership of their founder, Mateo de Bascio (1495-1552), were committed to following the rule of St. Francis in all of its severity. Their name is derived from St. Francis's attire, specifically the four-cornered hood, called *cappuccio*. In 1528 the Capuchins received papal approval to have their own superior.

CARLSTADT, ANDREAS BODENSTEIN VON (1480-1541). Protestant reformer. Andreas Bodenstein, known as Carlstadt after his birthplace Carlstadt on the Main River near Frankfurt, studied at the university of Erfurt between 1499 and 1503 and continued his theological studies at Wittenberg where he received the theological doctorate in 1504. In 1510 he became archdeacon of All Saints at Wittenberg, a position which included the responsibility to give theological lectures at the university and to celebrate mass. In 1515, under circumstances that are still not clear, Carlstadt abruptly went to Italy to acquire a doctorate in law. Soon after his return he embraced, in opposition to the scholastic theology which he had taught before, the new Augustinian theology propounded by Martin Luther (q.v.).

In the indulgences controversy (q.v.) Carlstadt quickly became a major figure, and at the Leipzig debate of 1519 many fundamental and controversial theological issues triggered by Luther's Ninety-five Theses were debated between Carlstadt and Johann Eck (q.v.). During Luther's stay on the Wartburg, Carlstadt became the head of the reform movement in Wittenberg, where at Christmas 1521 he celebrated Communion under both kinds. In 1523 he moved to Orlamünde as pastor. By that time, serious theological disagreements with Luther had surfaced. These intensified when Carlstadt began to publish a series of tracts advocating a mystical view of Christianity and, a little later, a radical re-interpretation of the Lord's Supper (q.v.) as not a sacrament (q.v.) but as a memorial to Christ's vicarious death on the cross.

Carlstadt was forced to leave Orlamünde, and he began a restless wandering which put him into the turbulence of the Peasants' War in Rothenburg in South Germany, a brief return to Wittenberg (at the price of a recantation of his dissenting views), and eventually, in 1534, to Basel, where he became a professor at the university. He died of the plague in 1541. Carlstadt's significance is not only that he anticipated early on several of the major theological issues of the Reformation, taking suggestions of Luther to their logical conclusion but also that he was the first to propose an alternate theological position in the movement of reform, indicating that recourse to the Bible (q.v.) as norm of theological reflection did not issue in a uniform position.

CARTWRIGHT, THOMAS (1535-1603). Anglican theologian. Educated at Cambridge, where he received his M.A. in 1560 and became Fellow of Trinity College in 1562. Appointed Lady Margaret professor of divinity in 1569, Cartwright began to preach against the Elizabethan settlement of religion (q.v.). He was promptly deprived of his professorial chair and went to Geneva, returning to England in 1572. After engaging in a fierce war of pamphlets against the use of clerical vestments, serving as catalyst for the Vestiarian Controversy, Cartwright became pastor of the English congregation at Antwerp. His staunch Puritan conviction led to his imprisonment for two years in the 1590s.

CATEAU-CAMBRÉSIS, Treaty of. The treaty of Cateau-Cambrésis was concluded on April 3, 1559 and ended more than half a century of warfare between Spain and France (qq.v.). It settled the relationship between the two countries for decades to come. The provisions of the treaty were that France relinquished any claims to territory in northern Italy (except for five fortified places). France also yielded Savoy and Piedmont. Northern Italy experienced important change in that western Lombardy came to Savoy, while the southern and eastern parts of the area went to the Farneses and Gonzagas. The permanence of the peace was mainly due to the fact that France began to be preoccupied with internal civil strife and war until the end of the century.

CATECHISMS. The extensive Christian catechetical tradition going back to early Christianity refers to the process of instruction in the fundamentals of the faith. In the later Middle Ages, the term "catechism" began to refer to printed summaries used for this instruction. The invention of movable type and the use of the vernacular for these catechisms quickly made them a popular genre of religious literature. Understandably, the Protestant reformers, led by Martin Luther (q.v.), understood the need and desirability for concise instructional materials summarizing the new faith. Luther's own first catechism was published in 1529 under the title *Deudsch Catechismus* (German Catechism). It was meant for the clergy to aid them in their instructional efforts. The catechism contained lengthy expositions of the Ten Commandments, the Apostles' Creed, and the Lord's Prayer, together with an explanation of the two sacraments (baptism and the Lord's Supper [qq.v.]). That same year appeared an abridgment of sorts, the *Der kleine Catechismus* (Small Catechism), also intended for the clergy, though it soon came to be seen as meant for lay people. Luther's publications triggered a wealth of other Lutheran catechisms.

The other Protestant traditions followed suit. The Anabaptist Balthasar Hubmaier (q.v.) published his *Christennliche Leertafel* (Tablet of Christian Teachings) in 1527, while Huldrych Zwingli (q.v.) published his *Eine kurtze christenliche inleitung* (A Brief Christian Introduction) in 1523. In the Calvinist tradition John Calvin's (q.v.) *Le catéchisme de l'Église de Genève* (Catechism for the Church in Geneva), written upon his return to Geneva in 1542, used the question and answer format typical of catechisms to discuss faith, the Apostles' Creed, the law, the Lord's Prayer, and sacraments. In England the first catechism was part of the 1549 edition of *The Book of Common Prayer*, which in turn was expanded in the 1559 version with its section on "wherein is contained a Catechism for Children," essentially the Lord's Prayer, the Ten Commandments, and the Apostles' Creed. Evidently, the Anglican Church had a lower (or more realistic) judgment of what could be expected from the common folk. The 16th century also saw a large number of Catholic catechisms which understandably followed the late medieval pattern of catechisms (for example, the listing of individual sins). The most popular Catholic catechism undoubtedly was the small catechism of Peter Canisius (q.v.) entitled *Parvus catechismus catholicorum* (Small Catholic Catechism), of 1559.

CATHERINE OF ARAGON (1485-1536). Queen of England. Daughter of Ferdinand of Aragon and Isabella of Castile, Catherine was betrothed to Arthur, the eldest son of Henry VII, and came to England (q.v.) to marry him in 1501. Arthur died soon thereafter. When Arthur's younger brother Henry succeeded to the English throne in 1509, Catherine married Henry VIII (q.v.) on the strength of a papal dispensation. Only one child, Mary (q.v.), survived infancy. When Henry in 1527 began to question the validity of their marriage, Catherine adamantly denied that her marriage to Arthur had been consummated, which meant that Henry's rationale for dissolving the marriage was challenged and thus rendered null and void. Catherine's continued refusal prompted Henry to pursue his dramatic policy of cutting the English church from its connections with Rome. Catherine died in a convent.

CATHOLIC REFORM. The term refers to that aspect of Roman Catholicism in the 16th century which is characterized by reform initiatives of whatever sort. Some of these reform initiatives were undertaken, or proposed, well before the Reformation. Early in the century, the Fifth Lateran Council (1512-17) promulgated a number of reform measures, none of which became pertinent since Martin Luther's indulgences controversy (qq.v.) quickly overshadowed the decisions of the council. Luther together with other reformers demanded reform in the church, though far more crucial than matters of practical reform were certain theological clarifications and reformulations, such as the role of authority in the church or the doctrine of justification.

Reform began to be taken seriously by the Catholic Church when the destruction and conquest of Rome by the emperor's forces in 1527, the famous Sack of Rome (q.v.) *(sacco di Roma)*, suggested a divine judgment upon the church. The decrees and canons of the Council of Trent (q.v.) can be seen as the most comprehensive 16th-century Catholic effort at reform, both theologically by delineating in a fairly comprehensive manner the proper Catholic teaching not only regarding the contested topics, such as justification but also regarding matters that had not stood in the center of the theological controversy, such as purgatory, the invocation of the saints, or the veneration of images and relics. The reform measures of the council did not deal with the curia and the papacy (it was considered too hot an iron by the council fathers); the council did deal, however, extensively with the reform of the episcopacy.

Historiographically, the full acknowledgment of Catholic reform as an important element of 16th-century Catholic life is fairly recent. Traditionally, scholars talked about 16th-century Catholicism in terms of the "Counter Reformation," that is, to see 16th-century Catholicism eminently under the perspective of its reaction against the Protestant Reformation. That has been shown to be a delimiting foreshortening of the richness of Catholic life in the 16th-century. By the same token, it is also incorrect to subsume 16th-century Catholicism under the heading of "Catholic" reform. This notion presupposed that the major feature of Catholic life and thought was either a reaction against the Protestant Reformation (Counter-Reformation) or a reaction against perceived Catholic failures and weaknesses (Catholic Reform). It must be noted that there was much of continuing Catholic vitality and life for which neither the term "reform" nor "Counter-Reformation" suffice.

CECIL, WILLIAM (1520-1598). British statesman. Born of a gentry family in Lincolnshire, Cecil studied at Cambridge and, during the reign of King Edward VI (q.v.), rose to become, first, private secretary to the Duke of Somerset, then secretary of state during the rule of the Duke of Northumberland. Cecil stayed aloof from governmental affairs during the reign of Mary but with the succession of Elizabeth I (q.v.) resumed the position of secretary of state in 1558. He relinquished that position in 1572 to become Lord Treasurer. While challenged in the late 1560s and early 1570s by conservative forces, Cecil never lost the queen's confidence, making him in many ways the pivotal figure in her reign. Without personal ambitions, Cecil showed himself Elizabeth's devoted servant. As regards his religious conviction Cecil clearly was a Protestant, perhaps even a moderate Puritan (q.v.).

CHAMBRE ARDENTE. French "burning chamber" or "fire chamber," a special criminal court established by the French king Henry II (q.v.) in 1547 for the "extermination of the so-called reformed religion". The appellation was that given by Protestants due to the zeal of the court to sentence convicted Protestant heretics to the executioner's fire. It is estimated that some 37 Protestants were executed because of sentences passed by the court. The court was abolished in 1550.

CHARLES V (1500-1558). Emperor. Born on February 24, 1500 in the Spanish Netherlands, offspring of the union between Emperor Maximilian I's son Philip and Ferdinand of Aragon's daughter Joanna of Castile. Charles learned French as his mother tongue, spending his youth in the rich and brilliant culture of the Burgundian court, with its stilted ceremonies and conventions but also its astute diplomacy that sought to maintain peaceful relations with both France and England (q.v.). Raised by his aunt Margaret, regent of Burgundy after his father's death in 1506, Charles had two influential mentors: Guillaume Chievres de Croy, the Burgundian chamberlain, later Charles's chief minister, and Adrian of Utrecht, his spiritual advisor, later Pope Adrian VI (q.v.). These two men molded his political and religious world view, particularly the notion that the imperial crown represented a spiritual sovereignty over all of Christendom, as Charlemagne, Charles's namesake, had once been able to realize.

The death of Ferdinand of Aragon, who upon Philip's death in 1506 had exercised the regency in the united Spain of Aragon and Castile, led to Charles's succession as king in 1516. With his grandfather Maximilian's death in 1520 Charles acquired the possession of the Habsburg (q.v.) hereditary lands, notably Austria and the Low Countries (q.v.) and the Franche-Comté, and became an obvious choice for the imperial crown. In June 1519 Charles was unanimously elected emperor of the Holy Roman Empire (q.v.) of the German Nation. One year later he was crowned king which, now with papal endorsement, allowed him to carry the imperial title as well, even though he was not actually crowned emperor until 1530 in Bologna.

Charles's reign as emperor of the Holy Roman Empire spanned a full generation (1519-1556). Even under ordinary circumstances, it would have been difficult to govern such a vast and divergent expanse of possessions. Charles paid little attention to his Habsburg possessions, which he entrusted to his brother Ferdinand in 1521, and to the Burgundian lands. Having married Isabella, the sister of the Portuguese king, Charles devoted much attention to Spain (q.v.), where initially he was viewed as a foreigner. Aided in no small measure by the emerging Spanish colonial empire, the country began to enjoy considerable prosperity. The religious controversy of the Reformation largely bypassed the Iberian peninsula; relations with the church remained harmonious.

Two rivalries overshadowed Charles's rule. One was the Protestant Reformation. When the religious controversy first reached the German diet, at Worms, in 1521, Charles left little doubt that he held no sympathy for Martin Luther (q.v.). The Edict of Worms (q.v.), which outlawed Luther and his followers, bears Charles's stamp. By the same token, the course Charles sought to steer in order to resolve the religious controversy was a moderate one, more Erasmian in nature than reflecting the stance of the papacy. This disagreement divided the two foremost leaders of the Catholic cause and involved Charles in a running conflict with a succession of popes. Charles had sought the convening of a general council to address matters of ecclesiastical abuse and reform, and also to bring about a reconciliation between the two sides. When, in the early 1540s he realized the obstinacy of the Protestants, he waged the War of Schmalkald against the League of Schmalkald (qq.v.). However, upon the successful conclusion of the war, Charles mistakenly attempted both to impose a religious settlement upon the Protestants and a more centralized structure of government upon the German territorial rulers. Not surprisingly, he failed.

By the time the diet convened in Augsburg (q.v.) in 1555, it was clear that Charles had failed definitively in his goal to restore unity to the church in the empire. The rivalry between Spain and France (q.v.), which Charles inherited from his father, similarly occupied his entire rule. At issue was the hegemony either of the house of Habsburg or the French house of Valois. The rivalry meant that in the decade of the 1520s, so crucial for the advance of the German Reformation, Charles was preoccupied with this political concern which was at the time a far more critical issue for him than the restoration of religious unanimity. Tellingly, Charles did not attend the Augsburg diet in 1555, for the diet meant the failure both of Charles's plans for a reform of governance in the empire and of his efforts to restore religious uniformity. A lifetime of convictions and commitments were repudiated by the diet.

Shortly after the adjournment of the diet, Charles abdicated. In October 1555 he turned the governance of the Low Countries over to his son Philip II (q.v.), who in January of the following year also received Spain, the Spanish overseas possessions, and Naples, while Ferdinand continued to exercise rule over the Habsburg hereditary lands. In December 1556 Charles abdicated as emperor, succeeded by Ferdinand who held the office until his death in 1564. Charles himself moved to Spain, where at the small town of San Yuste, some 100 miles west of Madrid, he had a mansion built for himself adjacent to a monastery. Legend has it that Charles spent his time at San Yuste seeking to make his numerous clocks run the same. In fact, he stayed in close touch with the political world of Europe until his death on September 21, 1558. Like no emperor after him, Charles saw his imperial role as that of the universal guardian of the Catholic faith. Also, like few emperors before or after him, Charles saw the imperial office not simply confined to Germany but as representative of all of Christendom. Both notions influenced his imperial rule from beginning to end: Charles saw himself as successor to Charlemagne with a realm extending from the Americas in the West to Hungary in the East, surely the greatest accumulation of possessions since the days of the great medieval emperor. Consequently, Charles's attention was not solely, and not even primarily, focused on Germany and the religious controversy there. He saw himself as the protector of Christendom against the Ottoman onslaught.

CHURCH MUSIC. The 16th century saw a remarkable vitality of sacred music, initially on the part of the Protestant Reformation, after the Council of Trent (q.v.) also in the Catholic Church. In the early 16th century church music revolved essentially around the Mass, with the Gregorian chant (or Latin plainsong) occupying the central place. Martin Luther (q.v.) initially retained much of this tradition, though with important modifications. While Luther found the use of Latin altogether acceptable, the emphasis on communication with the laity (q.v.) prompted, in his *German Mass* of 1526, the introduction of the vernacular German hymn which came to be the central part of Lutheran and Protestant worship and church music. Luther himself wrote several hymns.

A host of composers proceeded to give these hymns polyphonic settings. In England (q.v.), the *Book of Common Prayer* (q.v.) also retained the essential structure of the Latin Mass, though with the obvious modifications that bespoke the new theological understanding. Its major achievement, aside from use of the English vernacular, was the eloquence and elegance of its language. The prayer book did not provide for congregational singing. During Queen Elizabeth's (q.v.) reign the anthem was added to the service; it was generally sung by choirs or soloists. Huldrych Zwingli (q.v.) took a dim view of church music even as he broke more categorically with the structure of the Mass. The Reformed-Calvinist (q.v.) tradition was characterized by a simple service of worship in which the hymns were frequently metrical paraphrases of the Psalms. For the Catholic tradition the Council of

Trent was a milestone in that, with the proviso of textual intelligibility, polyphony was declared to be acceptable church music, thus ending the dominance of monophonic music. The fact that Italian music dominated Europe for the better part of two centuries also left its legacy on Italian sacred music. (See also HYMNALS).

CHURCH ORDERS. The establishment and formation of Protestant churches separate from the Roman Catholic church meant that the new Protestant churches had to promulgate orders dealing with the structures and practices of the new churches. This included such topics as the calling of a minister and the structure of congregational offices. The first church order growing out of the Reformation was drafted at the Homburg synod in Hesse (1526) but was never put into practice. Initially, the promulgation of church orders was intimately connected with the practice of visitations (q.v.) in which commissions of clergy and laity sought to take the pulse of a local congregation.

The Protestant church orders of the 16th century were promulgated by secular authorities (territorial rulers or city councils) and had as their objective to replace canon law or augment those portions of canon law that had been found acceptable with the new vision of the gospel. Historically, the beginnings of Protestant church orders can be found in the provisions of the first diet of Speyer (q.v.) in 1526. Its stipulation, that each ruler should deal with the Edict of Worms (q.v.) as he could answer before God and the emperor, was taken to mean by supporters of the Reformation that it was now possible to order ecclesiastical and theological matters freely in their jurisdictions. This interpretation constituted the beginnings of what came to be called the territorial church government, the organizational structure of the churches along territorial, that is, political lines. A number of cities which had introduced religious changes had taken such initiatives well before 1526 (Zurich, Strasbourg, Nuremberg). Electoral Saxony had undertaken a first visitation in 1525. In 1526 followed the beginnings of a systematic visitation in Electoral Saxony, supported in 1527 by Philip Melanchthon's (q.v.) instructions, formalized as *Unterricht der Visitoren* (Instruction for Visitors) of the following year. In a way, this development represented a continuation of late medieval tendencies in that the papacy had in the 15th century sought to utilize the help of secular authorities to strengthen autocratic papal power against the episcopacy.

The content of the Protestant church orders included instructions for the liturgy and administration of the sacraments (q.v.); doctrinal matters; education; the education, examination and ordination of clergy, appointment of teachers; administration of church property; issues of remuneration of the clergy; the care for the poor; and the general supervision of ecclesiastical affairs. There were some 30 Protestant church orders in the 16th century which can be grouped into three or four families, denoting the influence of the reformers Johannes Bugenhagen and Martin Bucer (qq.v.) and that of the church orders of Brandenburg and Württemberg.

The most important non-Lutheran church order was the Genevan church order, written by John Calvin (q.v.), in 1541—the *Ordonnances Ecclésiastique*. In it, the identification of four church offices, that of pastor, deacon, elder, and teacher, so important for the Calvinist/Reformed tradition was delineated as was the "consistory," a body comprised of pastors and secular representatives to monitor faith and morals of the faithful. The French *Discipline Ecclésiastique* of 1559, was influential also in the Low Countries (q.v.) and the Lower Rhine. In England, Thomas Cranmer (qq.v.) prepared a separate liturgy (the *Book of Common Prayer*, eventually in three important editions of 1549, 1552, and 1559); his efforts to revise canon law, and thereby deal with the numerous nonliturgical issues of church life, remained unsuccessful. In Scotland (q.v.), the *Book of Discipline* was issued in 1560, the year the Reformation was officially introduced there, to be followed by the *Book of Common Order* in 1564.

CLEMENT VII (1478-1534). Pope. Born Giulio de' Medici to an important Florentine family, Clement was an illegitimate child. In 1513 his cousin Pope Leo X (q.v.) appointed him archbishop of Florence. After his birth had been legitimized and he was ordained to the priesthood, Clement became a pivotal figure in the administration of the Roman curia. Elected supreme pontiff upon the death of Adrian VI (q.v.), Clement was pope for over a decade. He paid much attention to international politics, concluding an alliance with France (q.v.) in 1525 and participating in the League of Cognac (q.v.) the following year. In 1527 Clement suffered the humiliation of the Sack of Rome (q.v.) by the forces of Emperor Charles V (q.v.), and he himself was Charles's prisoner for over half a year. In 1529 Charles and Clement reconciled, in some measure because Clement hoped that Charles would use his influence to restore the Medicis to power in Florence. In 1530 Clement crowned Charles Roman emperor and vaguely promised to convene a general council, one of Charles's major objectives to resolve the religious controversy in Germany. Clement had no deep convictions about urgent reform, though he supported various new initiatives in the church, such as the Theatines and the Capuchins (qq.v.). However, Clement evidently had an irenic approach to the religious controversy. In 1530 he appeared to be willing to endorse clerical marriage and the Communion cup for the laity (q.v.) if the Protestants would surrender their positions on the other contested issues.

Personally industrious and of impeccable behavior, Clement's reign spanned the time during which the incipient cause and course of the Reformation petrified, and Clement played an important role in it. During his pontificate occurred not only the turning away of Sweden (q.v.) from the Catholic fold but that of England (q.v.) as well. Clement was too involved in political machinations to render a definitive judgment in Henry VIII's (q.v.) "great matter," the so-called divorce, and his inability to make a decision (in Henry's favor, of course) caused the split. Moreover, Clement did not share Emperor Charles's urgent sense of the necessity to convene a general council to deal with the disputed religious issues so that almost a generation passed before such a council convened at Trent (q.v.).

CLERGY, EDUCATION OF. 1. Protestant Clergy. In view of the widespread anticlericalism and low opinion of the Catholic priesthood in the early 16th century the education of clergy speedily became a matter of importance once it had become clear by the middle of the 1520s that a organizational break with the Catholic Church was in the making. The first step was to assess the qualifications of the incumbent clergy in the context of a general visitation (q.v.). The church visitations, first carried out in Electoral Saxony in 1526, were to assess the state of affairs of the congregation and also the level of conscientious competence on the part of the clergy. In 1529, Philip Melanchthon (q.v.) published his *Instructions for Visitors* which were meant as an initial program of reform for the clergy.

The new Protestant message placed much greater demands on the clergy than had been the case with Catholic clergy before the Reformation, notably the task of preaching. The need for formal theological training of a new type of clergy became quickly evident to the leading Protestant reformers. One of the characteristics of the introduction of the Reformation in a territory or city was the establishment of academies for the training of future clergy.

2. Catholic Clergy. The major stimulus for intensified clerical education in the Catholic Church was provided by the 22nd session of the Council of Trent (q.v.) in September 1562 when the council fathers adopted the decree "de vita et honestate clericorum" (concerning the lives and integrity of the clergy) and one year later, in July 1563, the decree "de seminarorum erectione et regimine" (concerning the establishment and structure of seminaries). The often casual provisions for the education of the clergy in the late Middle Ages were replaced with fairly specific mandates of high standards. These decrees stipulated the establishment of seminaries in episcopal dioceses in which, beginning at age 12, students would be instructed in all theological disciplines. A large number of seminaries were established, with pivotal ones in Rome, to train clergy for the various countries: in Germany at Eichstädt and Würzburg, in Belgium at Douai (q.v.) to train clergy for Protestant England (q.v.). Unlike the new Protestant seminaries (academies and universities) which were generally established by the political authorities, Catholic universities tended to be creations of the church.

CLERGY, REGULAR. The term is used for all clergy who have made monastic vows (and who, accordingly, have a commitment to a "rule"), though in the narrow sense the term applies especially to the members of the new monastic orders which were formed in the 16th and 17th centuries in order to stimulate reform in the Catholic Church, such as the Theatines (1524), the Barnabites (1530) (qq.v.), and others.

COCHLAEUS, JOHANNES (1479-1552). Catholic theologian and anti-Lutheran polemicist. Born in Wendelstein, he studied in Cologne and Ferrara, where he received a doctorate in theology in 1517. He was ordained a priest in Rome, returning to Germany in 1519. Although, as proponent of reform in the Catholic Church, he was initially inclined to see a comrade-in-arms in Martin Luther (q.v.), Cochlaeus turned against the reformer by 1520. The following year he served as advisor to the Catholic legate Aleander at the Diet of Worms (q.v.) and became a leading spokesman for Catholics at subsequent German diets and colloquies. Cochlaeus was an uncompromising champion of the Catholic church, and his polemical writings left a permanent mark on Catholic perceptions of the Reformation in general and Luther in particular. He castigated Luther not only as a heretic who was leading the German people astray but also as a muddled thinker whose inconsistencies muffled the theological basis of the Reformation. Luther and other Protestant leaders were condemned for repudiating their monastic vows. Catholic teaching, by contrast, derived its singular authority from its coherence and continuity as well as the sanctity of those who had guided the faithful through the centuries. Cochlaeus was not highly esteemed by the church he defended so vigorously. He did not attend the Council of Trent (q.v.) or see an edition of his collected works. He was buried in Breslau (Vratislava), where he had spent the last 13 years of his life.

COGNAC, LEAGUE OF. The decisive defeat of the French by Emperor Charles V (q.v.) in the battle of Pavia (February 24, 1525), in which Francis I (q.v.) became the emperor's prisoner, led to the peace of Madrid (January 14, 1526). In it France (q.v.) had to agree to all of the emperor's demands: the forfeiture of Naples, Milan, and Genoa as well as of Flanders and Artois. Francis I protested the peace, which had been made possible by his imprisonment, and soon thereafter all the anti-Habsburg forces coalesced. It included Francis I, Venice, Florence, and the papacy, and the alliance was signed on May 22, 1526. It became known as the League of Cognac.

COLET, JOHN (1466-1519). English humanist and churchman. After receiving his education at Oxford, Colet traveled extensively in France and Italy, where he was lastingly influenced by Marsilio Ficino's Neoplatonic reading of the Apostle Paul. He was appointed to a professorship at Oxford in 1496 and soon became a friend of Thomas More and Desiderius Erasmus (qq.v.), whom he directed to the study of the Bible (q.v.). In 1504 he became dean of St. Paul's in London. Using his generous parental inheritance he founded the St. Paul's School in 1512. Two years later the bishop of London charged him with heresy, clearly triggered by Colet's criticism of church abuses among which he included both celibacy and auricular confession. He was sentenced to death but pardoned by King Henry VIII (q.v.).

COLIGNY, GASPARD DE (1519-1572). French Huguenot (q.v.) leader. Scion of one of the foremost noble families in France (q.v.), Gaspard de Coligny found his calling in the military. He was appointed commanding officer of the French infantry in 1547, governor of the Ile de France and Piccardy in 1551, and Admiral of France one year later. In August 1557 he was taken prisoner at St. Quentin by the Spanish and was released when the treaty of Cateau-Cambrésis (q.v.) was signed in April 1559. During his imprisonment, first near Brugges, then at Gent, Coligny was converted to Calvinism (q.v.). After his release he promptly assumed a respected leadership position among the French Protestants, was responsible for the concessions made to them by the estates general at Orléans in 1560, and helped initiate the colloquy at Poissy (q.v.) in 1561. When the French wars of religion began in 1562, Coligny was the obvious leader of the Huguenots. He was instrumental in concluding the Peace of St. Germain-en-Laye of 1570, which gave the Huguenots religious and civic equality.

Coligny thought that Catholics and Protestants could live side by side in France, and he was convinced that the king, Charles IX, and his mother, Catherine de' Medici, shared his sentiment. He took the proposed marriage of Henry of Navarre (q.v.), a Protestant, and Margaret of Valois, sister of Charles IX, as a further indication of common perspective, not knowing that Catherine de' Medici, who was troubled by Coligny's seemingly increasing influence over the king, had plotted his assassination. A first assassination effort on August 22, 1572, failed, but two days later Coligny was the first of the many victims of the St. Bartholomew's Day Massacre (q.v.).

COLLOQUIES, RELIGIOUS. The notion that intellectual and theological disagreements could be resolved through debate and discussion was a fundamental assumption during the 16th century. Accordingly, the age of the Reformation is characterized by a large number of colloquies held between disagreeing factions in order to arrive at agreement. These colloquies can be subsumed under several categories. Some were between Protestants and Catholics—such as Leipzig (q.v.), Worms, and Poissy—some among Protestants—the Second Zurich disputation, Marburg (q.v.)—some between mainstream Protestants and Anabaptists (q.v.) (Bern).

All of these colloquies were convened by political authorities who, in some instances, also took on themselves the authority to pronounce on the outcome of the colloquy or debate. Most of the colloquies took place in the incipient phase of the Reformation in a given place (Leipzig, Zurich) and were meant to guide the political authorities in their decision making concerning the disputed religious issues. A set of colloquies took place in Germany in the late 1530s. They represented a final effort of Catholics and Protestants to effect conciliation between the two sides. Emperor Charles V (q.v.) faced, by the late 1530s, the reality of an unresolved religious controversy in Germany that had been going on for over 20 years. His own initiatives seemed thwarted by the apparent unwillingness of several popes, beginning with Clement VII (q.v.) to convene a general council to deal with the reforms in the church. Charles was determined to find a resolution of the religious controversy in Germany on his own initiative. The Truce of Nice (1538) removed one major obstacle: for 10 years the chronic conflict with France (q.v.) would not be the distraction, both psychological and military, as it had been ever since the beginning of his rule. His constant military clashes with France had precluded any forceful action against the German Protestants. The Peace of Frankfurt, of April 1539, in turn provided the appropriate irenic climate. It gave the adherents of the Augsburg Confession (q.v.) a six months' period of toleration during which no religious suits would be heard by the imperial cameral court nor any military solution of the religious controversy be attempted. In turn, the Protestants agreed to discuss possible subsidies for military action against the Turks.

The main point of the peace was to find time for a thorough theological colloquy between the two sides. After an abortive gathering at Hagenau, where no agreement could be reached on procedural matters, substantive discussions got under way at Worms. Secret negations between Martin Bucer (q.v.) and Johann Gropper brought virtual agreement between the two. Then the discussions continued at the diet at Regensburg. Strikingly, agreement was reached in the matter of justification, to be sure with a compromise formula but disagreement prevailed with respect to virtually all other topics (the Mass, the church, the authority of councils, confession). Thus, the outcome of the colloquies was failure. A bit more than a decade later, the Peace of Augsburg (q.v.) seemed to make further colloquies unnecessary. However, since the rhetoric of the peace had spoken of an eventual reunion, a number of theological colloquies were held after 1555: at Worms in September 1557; at Baden in 1589; in Emmendingen in 1590; in Regensburg in 1601. Outside Germany, important colloquies took place in Poissy (q.v.), France, in 1561 (between Catholics and Huguenots) and in Thorn, Poland, in 1645.

COMMUNION. See **EUCHARIST; LORD'S SUPPER.**

COMMUNISM. This modern term is used to refer to historical discourses and developments which focus on the absence, complete or partial, of private property. In the 16th century Thomas More's (q.v.) *Utopia* depicted, clearly echoing notions from classical antiquity, a commonwealth in which there was no private property. When Thomas Müntzer (q.v.) was interrogated at the end of the German Peasants' War (q.v.), he quoted language from the New Testament Book of Acts that "among Christians all things should be held in common." No practical consequences ensued from this cryptic pronouncement until in the mid-1530s the Anabaptists (q.v.) in Münster did in fact introduce communism. The customary explanation for this rather dramatic step is that the economic necessities of the siege of the city, combined with the reading of the New Testament, prompted that turn. Just about the same time, Austrian Anabaptists under the leadership of Jakob Hutter (q.v.) had migrated to Moravia to find toleration for their beliefs. Settling in communities, these Hutterites (q.v.) were at once characterized by a communal sharing of goods.

CONCORD, BOOK OF. The endorsement of the Formula of Concord (q.v.) by an overwhelming majority of Lutheran (q.v.) theologians and territorial rulers suggested that this concurrence be formally recorded. The endorsement took place in June 1580, half a century after the presentation of the Augsburg Confession (q.v.) at the diet at Augsburg (q.v.) in 1530. For the presentation of what was called the *Book of Concord*, several documents were added to the formula: the three ecumenical creeds and several previous Lutheran confessions (the *Augsburg Confession*, the *Apology of the Augsburg Confession*, the *Articles of Schmalkald*, and Luther's *Small* and *Large Catechisms*). The formula, together with these additions, is known as the *Book of Concord*.

CONCORD, FORMULA OF. The numerous and divisive theological controversies within Lutheranism after Martin Luther's (qq.v.) death continued unabated even after Philip Melanchthon's (q.v.) death in 1560. Essentially, the faction of the Gnesio-Lutherans (q.v.) stood against the Philippists (q.v.), neither of whom seemed able to budge from their positions as to who was the authentic heir of Luther. It took the intervention of Lutheran territorial rulers to bring about doctrinal unity among the Lutherans in the second half of the 16th century. First, the churches of Swabia and Lower Saxony signed the Swabian-Saxon Formula of Concord in 1575. The following year, this formula was revised into the *Torgau Book*, which was subscribed by additional theologians. Suggestions for changes were received and the resulting document became the *Solida Declaratio* of the subsequent *Book of Concord* (q.v.). At that point, subscriptions were solicited from Lutheran rulers. The overwhelming majority of Lutherans (three electors, 20 princes, 24 counts, 38 imperial free cities, and some 8,000 teachers) signed the formula.

The formula has two major sections, the *"Epitome"* and the *"Solida Declaratio."* Both treat the same topics under 12 headings, the former in somewhat loose and general, the latter in crisp argumentation. The extremist positions that had been advocated in the course of the several intra-Lutheran controversies were repudiated, and a compromise formula was offered for each of the contested issues. The topics treated in the document reflect the theological controversies within Lutheranism (original sin; free will; justification; good works; law and gospel; the "third use" of the law; the Lord's Supper [q.v.]; the person of Christ; Christ's descent into hell; adiaphora [the middle things]; predestination; and the sectarians).

The formula is a superb illustration of the change that affected all of Protestantism toward the end of the century: the Christian faith is defined doctrinally. The Formula of Concord may be said to have achieved theological uniformity in Lutheranism. While the charges of crypto-Calvinism (q.v.) against some Lutheran theologians continued after 1580, the formula set forth the acceptable and universally accepted spectrum of Lutheran theology. It thus marked the beginning of the Lutheran Church as it developed in the subsequent centuries. While the extremist position of some of Melanchthon's own Philippist followers and disciples were repudiated by the formula, it was nonetheless Melanchthon's spirit of irenic conciliation that carried the day.

CONFESSIONALIZATION. This term recently introduced into historical scholarship refers to a European-wide development toward the end of the 16th century, when European societies underwent far-reaching changes in the course of which all aspects of society were subjected to the perspective of the regnant confession (q.v.). This period of confessionalization is considered to have been part of a lengthy period of transition from the medieval world to modernity beginning in the late 14th century and ending in the 18th. This confessionalization affected all of the religious traditions, Catholic no less than Protestant, and had its beginning in the 1570s. It meant that all facets of a commonwealth, literature, music, philosophy, architecture, to some extent even law, were reformed to express the regnant confession.

CONFESSIONS. In the 16th century the term "confession" was used in a twofold sense. First of all, confession meant the ecclesiastical bodies (Catholic, Lutheran, Calvinist) which were characterized (thus the label) by different distinctive confessions. Secondly, confession meant statements of faith of which several were promulgated in the course of the 16th century. Understandably, most of the confessions of the 16th century were Protestant and were intended to set forth one's own distinctive theological position in contrast to traditional Catholic dogma.

Some Protestant confessions, however, notably the Lutheran Augsburg Confession or the English Six Articles (qq.v.), intended not so much to show their distinctiveness as their essential agreement with Catholic teaching. Overwhelmingly, however, the Protestant confessions of the 16th century meant to demonstrate the distinctiveness of one's own theology both vis-à-vis Catholicism and the other Protestant traditions.

In the Lutheran tradition the notable confessions were, in addition to the Augsburg Confession, the Schmalkald Articles and the Formula of Concord (qq.v.). In the Calvinist/Reformed tradition, the important documents are the Consensus Tigurinus, the Gallic Confession (or Confession of Faith of La Rochelle), the two Helvetic Confessions (of 1536 and 1566), and the Belgic Confession (of 1561). In England (q.v.), the Forty-two Articles, subsequently modified into the Thirty-nine Articles (q.v.), formed the confessional core of the Anglican Church. For the Anabaptists the *Brotherly Union*, or Schleitheim Confession (q.v.), of 1527, assumed a widespread but not universally normative character, while among the Hutterites Peter Riedemann's *Account of our Religion,* while a personal document, took on the status of a confessional document. Among the anti-Trinitarians (q.v.) of the 16th and early 17th centuries the *Racovian Catechism* (q.v.) may be said to be the eminent confessional document. The characteristic feature of the Protestant confessions was the extensive use of biblical references to support the theological points made. While it is difficult to offer an evaluation, it would seem that the Augsburg Confession, together with its Apology, was the most important confessional statement coming from the 16th century in that it was accepted as normative by all Lutheran churches.

CONFUTATION. Despite their initial misgivings over presenting a statement of Catholic doctrine, which was deemed self-evident and not in need of additional explication, at the diet at Augsburg (q.v.) (1530), Catholics found it prudent in the end to submit an assessment of the Lutheran Augsburg Confession (q.v.). After a draft prepared by a group of 20 theologians had proved to be too cumbersome, Johann Eck (q.v.) was asked to prepare a Catholic response to the Augsburg Confession. Formally, therefore, the Catholics submitted a response to the Lutheran (q.v.) statement, not a statement of their own. Using his own previous anti-Reformation writings, Eck submitted a work of 351 pages to the emperor on July 12. Emperor Charles V (q.v.) found the document too long and too polemical, whereupon Eck cut it by two-thirds, confining himself to addressing issues raised in the Augsburg Confession. His statement received the designation "Confutatio" and, upon its formal presentation to the diet, Charles declared that it persuasively demonstrated the errors of the Augsburg Confession. An important document in the sequence of theological discussions in the Reformation, the *Confutation* does not represent a comprehensive Catholic response to the contested theological issues since the Augsburg Confession did not comprehensively delineate the Lutheran perspective either.

CONSENSUS TIGURINUS (Zurich Agreement). The Consensus Tigurinus was concluded in 1549 between John Calvin and Heinrich Bullinger, Huldrych Zwingli's (qq.v.) successor in Zurich (q.v.). In substance the document is a compromise between the Zwinglian position which saw the Lord's Supper (q.v.) as a symbolic memorial of Christ's death and Calvin's position which affirmed the sacrament's conveying of spiritual gifts to the partaking believer. The Consensus rejected the Lutheran notion of a real presence of Christ in the elements of bread and wine. While it left open some issues, which subsequently became topics of heated controversy between Zurich and Geneva (q.v.), the Consensus was the basis for a Reformed doctrine of the sacrament of the altar.

CONTARINI, GASPARO (1483-1542). Venetian diplomat, cardinal, and papal legate. Born in Venice to a patrician family, Contarini studied philosophy and theology at the University of Padua and as a young man made a conscious choice for a secular as against a monastic vocation. He also came to affirm that Christ's sacrifice rather than good works justified humans and was therefore sympathetic to the Lutheran Reformation short of breaking with the Catholic Church. He wrote a number of treatises on ecclesiastical and political topics and served the Republic of Venice in important diplomatic posts, first as ambassador to Emperor Charles V (q.v.) from 1521 to 1525.

From 1528 to 1531 he was Venetian envoy to Pope Clement VII. His treatise *Confutatio articulorum seu quaestionum Lutheranorum* (Refutation of the Articles and Questions of Lutherans) was a response to the Augsburg Confession, enjoining moderation toward the Protestants and holding out hope for a resolution of the religious conflict. Contarini's defense of papal power, *De potestate pontificis* (Concerning the Powers of the Pope), led to his appointment as cardinal in 1535. Upon entering the priesthood in 1537, he became a vocal critic of church abuses, advocating in particular reform of the curia. Contarini's last major appointment was as papal legate to the Colloquy of Regensburg in 1541. Contarini's conciliatory approach proved unsuccessful. He died the following year in Bologna.

CONTROVERSIES, THEOLOGICAL, IN LUTHERANISM. Martin Luther's (q.v.) failure to write a cohesive systematic theology meant that his theological insights could be given a number of different interpretations. Some of these divergent interpretations surfaced during Luther's lifetime, though Luther's authority—and, surprisingly, his willingness to accept differences of opinion—kept things under control. After his death, however, several controversies broke out into the open, all of them triggered by the reality that Luther's colleague Philip Melanchthon (q.v.) came to emphasize certain aspects of Luther's theology which other Lutheran theologians considered to be falsifications and aberrations. Moreover, Melanchthon's seeming willingness to accept the Interim (q.v.) of 1548 discredited him in the eyes of many Lutheran theologians. Melanchthon's role was reduced to that of the leader of the Philippists (q.v.), those Lutheran theologians who shared Melanchthon's theological perspective and saw him as the authentic heir and successor to Luther. These theological conflicts commanded the attention of the Lutheran tradition and sapped its strength to deal with resurgent Catholicism and the dynamic Calvinism (q.v.) of the second half of the 16th century. The major controversies were the adiaphoristic, the majoristic, the antinomian, and the synergistic controversies. The adiaphoristic controversy (q.v.) focused on the question of morally (and theologically) neutral "middle things," while the remaining controversies all pertained to different perspectives of what takes place when an individual is justified and saved.

COPERNICUS, NIKOLAUS (1473-1543). Astronomer. Copernicus, about whose life not much is known, was a canon in Frauenburg, East Prussia. His significance lies in his work *De revolutionibus orbium caelestium* (Concerning the Revolutions of the Heavenly Bodies), on which he had been working for a long time, postponing its publication. In his book, Copernicus rejected the Ptolemaic worldview, which had the planets and the sun revolve around the earth and instead proposed a heliocentric system. Copernicus's revisionism was more than a new astronomical insight. Importantly, the Ptolemaic system sustained the Christian notion of the centrality of the human drama of redemption in the universe even as it seemed to correspond to the plain meaning of certain biblical texts. Copernicus's argumentation was entirely astronomical but its implications were far-reaching.

The publication of Copernicus's work was accompanied by a preface from the pen of the Lutheran reformer Andreas Osiander, who characterized (and thereby understated) Copernicus's intent by insisting that a scholar must be free to propose hypotheses. Both theologians, and especially, astronomers sharply criticized Copernicus's work, and it was only a century later that Galileo and Johannes Kepler added both observation and calculation that turned Copernicus's hypothesis into an acknowledged scholarly fact. The theological discussion about Copernicus, and later Galileo, focused on the question if the new astronomical insights were compatible with the passage in the Book of Joshua (1:12ff) where Joshua commands the sun to stand still. It was not until the discoveries of Kepler and Galileo in the 17th century that the issue of the viability of the Ptolemaic system came sharply out into the open and thereby laid the cornerstone for the conflict between traditional Christian theology and the new science.

COUNTER-REFORMATION. This term, given widespread parlance by the famous 19th-century German historian Leopold von Ranke, was first used by him to denote the period in European history following the period of the Reformation, roughly the century between 1550 and the mid-1700s. Ranke meant to indicate that this one hundred year period was characterized by an aggressive Catholic effort to counter the Protestant Reformation. It was epitomized by the founding of the Jesuits, the Council of Trent, or the tempers of such Catholic rulers as Philip II (qq.v.) of Spain. Subsequently, the term came to denote also the mentality of the Catholic Church in its response to the Protestant Reformation. The term was used for a long period to describe 16th-century Catholicism as eminently characterized by its efforts, especiallly in the latter part of the 16th century, to repudiate the Protestant Reformation. It was replaced by the term "Catholic Reform" (q.v.), which was to indicate that 16th-century Catholicism was not only characterized by its efforts to counter the effects of the Protestant Reformation but also by a rich variety of internal reform measures of its own. More recently, the suggestion has been made that even the term "reform" should be abandoned in that most of Catholic life in the 16th century remained untouched both by the Protestant Reformation and efforts to repudiate it, nor was the Catholic Church during that century characterized by an inordinate effort at reform. This line of reasoning led to the suggestion of the use of the utterly neutral term "Roman Catholicism in early modern Europe".

COVERDALE, MILES (1488-1568). Reformer. Born in Yorkshire, Coverdale studied at Cambridge as an Augustinian monk. He was part of the group that met at the Cambridge White Horse Tavern to discuss the new theological ideas that were propounded in Germany (q.v.). In 1528 he left for the Continent, translated theological tracts, and by 1535 had translated (mainly from German and Latin versions) the Bible (q.v.) into English. Subsequently, Coverdale engaged in various publishing activities, both on the Continent and, briefly, in England (q.v.). He enjoyed supportive patrons—Thomas Cromwell (q.v.) and the duke of Somerset. In 1551 he was appointed bishop of Exeter where he served until Edward VI's (q.v.) death in 1553. He returned once again to the Continent, where he contributed to the Geneva Bible. After Elizabeth's (q.v.) succession, Coverdale returned to England, assisted in the consecration of Archbishop Parker, received the D.D. degree from Cambridge, though he was never (probably because of his Puritan [q.v.] leanings) restored to his episcopal see.

CRANACH, LUKAS, the younger (1515-1586). Painter. Son of the painter Lukas Cranach the elder, Lukas was the only son not to die in childhood. Following in the artistic footsteps of his father, he became one of the most important portrait painters of the German Renaissance. He is particularly known for his portraits of the Wittenberg theologians and other eminent personages.

CRANMER, THOMAS (1489-1556). English Reformer and theologian. Cranmer received his university training in Cambridge, where he received the doctorate in theology in 1526. While not initially involved in the agitation for ecclesiastical reform in England (q.v.) in the 1520s, Cranmer joined the effort to secure the annulment of Henry VIII's (q.v.) marriage to Catherine of Aragon (q.v.) in 1529. This assignment took him away from the academic surroundings of Cambridge.

While in Germany on a diplomatic mission in the king's "great matter" to Charles V (q.v.), he married the niece of the Nuremberg reformer Andreas Osiander (q.v.) in 1532. In Germany he received word that Henry had chosen him to be the new archbishop of Canterbury. Later Cranmer stated that he dallied in Germany so as to escape the actual appointment but he was consecrated early in 1533. That same year he presided over the ecclesiastical court which pronounced the king's marriage with Catherine invalid and subsequently officiated at Henry's wedding to Anne Boleyn. During the remainder of Henry's rule Cranmer showed himself to be a loyal servant of the king—granting annulments of the king's marriages to Anne Boleyn and Anne of Cleves, as well as accepting the staunchly conservative Six Articles Act (q.v.) of 1539.

During the rule of Edward VI (q.v.), Cranmer became the heart of religious change and reform in England. He was the architect of *The Book of Common Prayer* (q.v.), as well as the collection of official sermons, *The Book of Homilies*, he oversaw the drafting of the Forty-two Articles and launched an abortive attempt to adapt canon law to the new conditions in England. The succession of Mary Tudor (q.v.) brought his arrest and conviction for treason (Cranmer had supported the attempt to put Jane Grey on the English throne) in November 1553. In 1555 he was tried for heresy. Despite signing no less than six progressively more abject recantations of his involvement in English religious change, Cranmer was burned at the stake on March 21, 1556, not without having recanted all his recantations.

Cranmer's complicity in the whims of Henry's varied religious changes triggered much criticism, even moral outrage, though his shifting positions can easily be explained by noting his high view of royal authority as an agency of God's will. His views on the Eucharist (q.v.) evolved slowly. After lengthily holding to the (Lutheran) view of a real presence of Christ in the Communion elements, he embraced, by the late 1540s, after complicated negotiations, a view of a spiritual presence of Christ in the elements of bread and wine. Cranmer was immensely learned, though his contribution to the Anglican (q.v.) tradition lies not so much in theology as in his genius for formal prose, so splendidly embodied in *The Book of Common Prayer*.

CROMWELL, THOMAS (c. 1485-1540). English Chancellor. Cromwell's father was an alehouse keeper in Wimbledon, and Thomas, for the first two decades of his life, pursued various commercial interests in London. By 1514 he was in the service of Cardinal Wolsey (q.v.), whose fall from the king's grace he survived in 1529. An advantageous marriage brought Cromwell economic security and well-placed connections which facilitated his rise to political prominence. After Wolsey's fall from power in 1529, Cromwell rose rapidly in the service of Henry VIII (q.v.), engineering the king's divorce from Catherine of Aragon (q.v.) and legislating the separation of the English church from Rome and the establishment of royal supremacy. The explanation lies not only in Cromwell's masterful mind and hard work but also in his ability to conceptualize a new manner of government for England (q.v.), namely to see Parliament as the embodiment, in consort with the king, of power in England.

The English Reformation, which was reform by parliamentary statute, was Cromwell's design. From the mid-1530s onward, Cromwell also served as the king's vice-gerent. This meant that he ran ecclesiastical no less than political affairs. As the king's chief minister in church and state, Cromwell also initiated reforms in government and presided over the dissolution of the English monasteries, a policy he had begun under Cardinal Wolsey. He was instrumental in the publication of an official English Bible (q.v.) based on the work of Miles Coverdale and William Tyndale (qq.v.), and was created earl of Essex in 1540. Cromwell's vast accumulation of wealth and power as well as his overt Protestant sympathies created enemies among the religious conservatives and the higher-born but less favored. They took advantage of Henry's failed marriage to Anne of Cleves and a misconceived attempt to ally England with Protestant Europe (both of which Cromwell had initiated) to turn the king against his chief minister. Cromwell was arrested on charges of heresy and treason and executed without a trial on July 28, 1540.

CRYPTO-CALVINISM. In the early 1550s John Calvin's (q.v.) theology was in the process of becoming vastly influential in Protestant areas. It also began to make inroads in Germany, particularly since the Zurich Consensus (Consensus Tigurinus) (q.v.) had brought about a conciliation between Heinrich Bullinger (q.v.) and Calvin in the understanding of the Lord's Supper (q.v.). Facing this dynamic and aggressive Calvinism, Joachim Westphal, a Hamburg Lutheran pastor, took to the pen to publish his *Farrago* as a kind of wake-up call to his Lutheran compatriots in 1552 against the subtle intrusion of Calvinist thinking into Lutheranism (q.v.). Fiercer publications followed, and before too long a formidable controversy was under way. Unlike the communion controversy of the 1520s, this new controversy was not merely between Lutherans and Calvinists but also within Lutheran ranks. There were Lutheran theologians who found the Calvinist teaching attractive and were bothered by the emerging Lutheran orthodoxy and doctrine of ubiquity. For those Lutherans who were suspected of secretly harboring Calvinist notions, the term "crypto-Calvinist" became standard. The term began to be widely used after Philip Melanchthon's (q.v.) death in 1560.

— D —

DEATH PENALTY. The Christian tradition exhibits an intriguing ambivalence, at least in the early centuries of the Christian church, with respect to the question of the morality of the death penalty, the question being if a Christian could, in fact, participate in carrying out an execution. This ambivalence found expression in the high Middle Ages in the notion that the church cannot be part of the death penalty but that government may use it by virtue of its divine office. The justification for the death penalty was seen in the necessity of protecting society, which argument was also used in order to justify the death penalty for heretics. The Reformation echoed this traditional sentiment, including the use of capital punishment for what was labeled public heresy, except that the Anabaptists and some anti-Trinitarians (qq.v.) argued that, while government had the right to use the sword, no Christians may have anything to do with such exercise.

DENCK, HANS (c. 1500-1527). Anabaptist (q.v.) theologian. This early South German Anabaptist leader must have received a solid Humanist (q.v.) education in his youth, for when he became a public figure in the mid-1520s he displayed evidence of impressive learning. Unfortunately, nothing is known about his early background. He served as school teacher in Nuremberg (1524-25). He was expelled from the city for his unorthodox theological views that became public in conjunction with the affair of the so-called "three godless painters" in Nuremberg who seemingly held pantheistic notions.

Denck was influenced by a convergence of the medieval mysticism of Johannes Tauler and the *German Theology* and the thought of Andreas Carlstadt and Thomas Müntzer (qq.v.). This led him to join the emerging Anabaptist movement, since adult baptism (q.v.) was to him the outward symbol of the inner regeneration that had taken place in the individual. Denck emphasized an inwardly received revelation, in true spiritualist fashion, which meant that all externals, including the Bible (q.v.), were only of secondary significance. Denck joined another Anabaptist, Ludwig Haetzer, who was of a similar disposition, in translating some of the prophetic books of the Old Testament into German (the so-called *Worms Prophets* after the place of publication). Denck participated in the so-called "Martyrs Synod" which took place in Augsburg in 1527, which received that appellation since most of the participants were subsequently apprehended as heretics and sentenced to death. Denck himself died of the plague that same year.

DENMARK. Late in the 14th century, Queen Margaret I (r. 1387-1397) effected the Union of Kalmar which united most of northern Europe under Danish leadership (1397). Her successor Erik (r. 1397-1439) continued the policy of seeking the independence of the crown from papal interference. In 1464 King Christian I (r. 1448-81) obtained the right to nominate, and thereby effectively determine, all candidates for ecclesiastical posts in the lands of the Union of Kalmar. The establishment of a Danish university at Copenhagen received papal approbation at the same time.

The Reformation in Denmark was triggered by the same combination of political, economic, and religious factors as elsewhere in Europe. At the beginning stood an uprising against Christian II (r.

1513-23) who had allied himself with the burghers in the towns against the high nobility and the clergy. Christian's brutal policies in Sweden (q.v.) led to an uprising. The appointment of a new archbishop of Lund became entangled in the Danish-Swedish conflict, with the result that during the first phase of the Reformation no canonically installed archbishop was in office there. In 1523 Christian was expelled from Denmark, attempted to return but was imprisoned until his death in 1559. Concerns about Christian's openness toward the Lutheran (q.v.) "heresy" were part of the picture, and his successor Frederick I (1523-33) had to pledge his loyalty to the Catholic religion. Frederick used the tensions between the nobility and the higher clergy to obtain in 1526 and 1527 at diets at Odense considerable economic concessions from the clergy. He also tolerated evangelical preachers and rejected papal approval for episcopal appointments. His goal was a reformed Catholic national church in Denmark, even though there was evidence of Lutheran sympathies on his part.

At his death uncertainty about a successor prompted the royal council to postpone the election. The powerful city of Lübeck supported the return of Christian II, while the Catholic nobility endorsed Frederick's son Christian of Schleswig-Holstein. A civil war broke out, at the end of which Christian proved victorious. As Christian III he ruled from 1534 to 1559. He arrested the Catholic bishops, holding them responsible for the conflict, and confiscated their ecclesiastical property. The recess of the diet of 1536 endorsed the appointment of evangelical superintendents who soon took the traditional designation of bishop. In September of 1537 the Reformation was officially introduced in Denmark with the help of Johannes Bugenhagen (q.v.), who ordained the new superintendents. A new church order (*Kirkeordinans*) was introduced and the University of Copenhagen revitalized. While Christian forcefully introduced the Reformation, he pursued a flexible foreign policy which allowed him to conclude a friendship treaty with Charles V (q.v.) in 1544 and remain neutral in the War of Schmalkald (q.v.). The leaders of the Danish Reformation were Peder Palladius (1503-1560) and Hans Tausen (1494-1561). (See also SWEDEN.)

DIET. The Holy Roman Empire (q.v.), symbolically headed by a non-hereditary but elected emperor, had as its representative assembly the diet. It was convened by the emperor and generally discussed issues affecting the empire as a whole, such as coinage, the Turkish threat, or—after 1519—the Reformation. However, the territorial estates viewed themselves as sovereign rulers which fact, together with the absence of a written constitution, meant that major procedural questions pertaining to the diet, for example, if majority decisions were binding on all the estates, remained unresolved. Since the non-German rulers of the empire rarely attended the sessions of the diet, the diet tended to be less a deliberative body of the entire empire than of Germany (q.v.).

The diet consisted of three chambers or colleges. The seven electors formed their own chamber (the king of Bohemia actually attended the sessions only to participate in the election of the new emperor). The eminence and importance of the electors made their deliberations the most important ones of the diet. Secondly, the princes' chamber was comprised of both secular and ecclesiastical rulers, the latter heavily represented by archbishops, bishops, abbots, etc. The third chamber was comprised of the free imperial cities which owed their allegiance directly to the emperor. They depended, in theory, on the emperor's protection. Since the Reformation was a matter transcending the individual territories, every diet, beginning with Worms (q.v.) in 1521, had the religious controversy on its agenda. Three important diets stand out: Worms, 1521, when the demand of the estates forced the emperor to give the condemned heretic Martin Luther (q.v.) a hearing; the diet at Augsburg in 1555 (q.v.), which resolved the religious controversy; and—most importantly—the diet at Speyer in 1526 (q.v.) which was the occasion for a dramatic enhancement of the authority and power of the territorial rulers (over against the empire and emperor) in that the recess stipulated that until a general council each estate could act in matters of religion as could be justified before God and emperor. While the religious division ran deep after 1521, note must be taken that the diet accomplished a great deal in the course of the 16th century, not the least the adoption of a new criminal code for the empire, the *Carolina*, in 1530. Far more so than other European countries at the time, the German diet functioned well.

DISCOVERIES OF THE NEW WORLD. Christopher Columbus's landfall in America in 1492 set in motion a grandiose European effort to explore and settle the vast lands that lay beyond the Atlantic Ocean. Even if, for convenience sake, the traditional term "discovery" is used, it must be clear that it was not so much the fact that Europeans "discovered" faraway lands which made for the dramatic quality of the happening. Rather, the importance of the discoveries lay in the radically new legal notion that these discovered lands had no masters and thus could be placed under the rule of European monarchs. The discussion among legal experts, such as Las Casas and Francisco de Vitoria (q.v.), focused on this issue.

It is too simplistic, however, to see the aggrandizement of power as the sole motive in the European expansion. There were other forces, such as the desire for conquest, for booty, for profit. So was the crusading ideal which suggested that an easy westward route to China and India would allow the conquest of the Holy Land from the East. Spain (q.v.) and Portugal were geopolitically the obvious major countries with regard to a westward expansion of Europe, and a fierce competition began between the two in the second half of the 15th century. Repeatedly, beginning with the papal bull *Inter caetera* of May 1493, the pope was called upon to act as arbiter in disagreements and conciliate the two countries. However, when in 1529, Spain and Portugal concluded the treaty of Sargasso, they did so without any papal involvement and without any recourse to the notion of a crusade or missionary activity. This clearly demonstrated that papal influence had become symbolic at best. Spanish theologians argued that the new world was God's gift for Spain, that Spain was the chosen people of the new covenant even as the Israelites had been the chosen people of the old covenant. The Spanish conquest of lands in the Americas followed a strict legal pattern. It is noteworthy that the Spanish possessions in the new world were not at all seen as colonies but rather as part of the Spanish empire.

DISPUTATIONS. Formal disputations were an important feature in medieval intellectual life. Quite appropriately, the Reformation of the 16th century may be said to have begun with an academic disputation—Martin Luther's (q.v.) Ninety-five Theses, which were meant as a call for an academic discussion of the practice of indulgences (q.v.) in the church. The underlying presumption of academic disputations was that "truth" was given and could be recovered through a dialectic process of raising and answering questions, by the juxtaposition of assertion and repudiation. Accordingly, numerous disputations were held in the course of the Reformation, and one can distinguish a number of different kinds of disputations. There were those disputations which were held in a given locale in order to aid the political authorities to form a judgment on the contested religious issues (Zurich 1523 and Nuremberg 1525).

Other disputations sought to clarify contested theological issues without immediate and direct practical bearing. These could be held between Catholics and reformers, such as in Leipzig, 1519, or among reformers, such as in Marburg (q.v.), 1529, or at Bern, 1538, in the latter a disputation between mainstream Zwinglian reformers and Anabaptists (q.v.). Though the emperor prohibited theological disputations concerning the Christian religion (in the Edict of Burgos of July 1524), the disputations continued way into the century. The significance of the disputations lies undoubtedly in the fact that they provided the rationalization for the introduction of the Reformation in specific locales. All the same, it seems clear that the participants were not so much committed to achieving agreement, which the medieval understanding of disputations should have compelled them to find, as to demonstrate the superiority of their own position. (See also COLLOQUIES, RELIGIOUS.)

DIVORCE. The medieval church had categorically rejected the notion of divorce since persons marrying were sacramentally united whether or not their union was consummated. At the same time, a range of considerations, developed out of an understanding that marriage (q.v.) possessed moral and societal significance, prompted the development of the so-called marital impediments, conditions that made a marriage invalid. Understandably, the notion of impediments meant that despite a strict prohibition of divorce, marriage could be dissolved if the proper impedimenta were found to have rendered a "marriage" as invalid from the beginning. According to the canon law teaching of the medieval church, a proper marriage could not be divorced. The basis for this position lay less in the sacramental character of marriage (which only applied to baptized Christians) than in the principles of natural law. Canon Law stipulated a surprisingly large number of impediments to a proper marriage (such as relationship affinities; youth; impotence; etc.). The church could provide dispensation from certain impediments though not from those demanded by natural law.

Divorce was only possible in a non-consummated marriage under a few carefully defined circumstances (such as when one spouse decided to take monastic vows). If divorce was, for all intents and purposes, not possible, the dissolution of an invalid marriage was another matter. This entailed an ecclesiastical determination that an impediment had existed when the marriage was entered into. These principles were dramatically put to the test when Henry VIII (q.v.) of England sought to "divorce" his wife Catherine of Aragon (q.v.). Again, the term "divorce" is inaccurate; Henry sought an annulment of marriage on the grounds that an impediment had existed when Catherine and he entered into matrimony. Accordingly, the papal dispensation which had allowed him to marry Catherine was invalid (because it was based on inaccurate information). This had to do with the fact that canon law derived from a passage in Deuteronomy the conclusion that one could not marry one's brother's widow.

In Henry's case, the question hinged on the consummation of the marriage between Catherine and his brother Arthur. Henry argued that it had been consummated; thus, the papal dispensation was invalid. Interestingly enough, all of the Protestant reformers whose opinions were sought in the matter concluded that Henry's marriage was valid. While the specific reasoning differed, the common denominator of the opinion of the reformers was the rejection of the complicated system of papal dispensations.

The understanding of the reformers was that there were simple biblical stipulations with respect to marital impediments. The fact that the Catholic Church had made them complicated was yet another indication of papal abuse. The reformers also argued that there was a biblical mandate for divorce in cases of adultery. Moreover, since the reformers rejected the sacramental character of marriage, it was possible for them to allow an important role for civic mandates and courts.

Zurich (q.v.) established the first so-called marriage court in which—as in similar institutions in other Protestant territories—the clergy retained an important, albeit not sole voice. The Catholic notion that a "divorce" of a consummated marriage (on account of one spouse being non-Christian) only allowed a separation from bed and board was picked up by the Anabaptists (q.v.) for whom, even though the term "sacrament" (q.v.) was rejected, human marriage was a replica of the marriage between the believer and Christ. Accordingly, an unbelieving spouse affected this spiritual marriage, and a strong faction among the Anabaptist/Mennonites (q.v.) in North Germany and Holland advocated in the second half of the 16th century that the believing spouse should separate from bed and board of the unbelieving spouse.

DORT, SYNOD OF. A national synod of the Reformed Church in the United Provinces convened at Dordrecht (Dort) on November 13, 1618, and remained in session until May 29, 1618, to resolve various doctrinal controversies. Representatives came not only from the United Provinces but also from Reformed churches in Germany, Switzerland, England, and Scotland (qq.v.). The synod declared the Heidelberg Catechism (q.v.) to be the authoritative statement of the Reformed faith. It affirmed the doctrine of predestination (q.v.), though not in its supralapsarian form (i.e., God predestined salvation and damnation even before the fall of Adam and Eve). The synod reached no agreement on a uniform order of worship. The Remonstrants (q.v.) were condemned as heretics.

DOUAI. A city in Belgium, Douai became a center of English Catholicism in the second half of the 16th century. In 1568 a college (seminary) was established in Douai, which was strategically located in relationship to England (q.v.), and by the end of the century a steady string of Douai-trained priests had come to England. Thereby, English Catholicism, an underground movement, retained its vitality in the face of Elizabeth I's (q.v.) settlement of religion far longer than might have been expected. Since many of the priests trained in Douai were imprisoned and even executed in England, the college also engaged in publishing materials of their martyrdom. An English translation of the Bible (q.v.), translated from the Vulgate, appeared in 1582 and 1609. It is known as the "Douai" version.

— E —

EARLY BOURGEOIS REVOLUTION. This thesis, formulated by Marxist historians of the former German Democratic Republic (East Germany) in the 1960s, held that the Protestant Reformation was an integral part of the first, or early, bourgeois revolution against the medieval feudal economic system, which received its fatal blow from the French Revolution in 1789. It argued that German society was in a crisis in the early 16th century since new economic wealth and power were being created apart from the traditional, land-oriented feudal system but that the holders of this new economic power lacked political power. Since the Catholic Church and its theology provided the ideological underpinning for the medieval feudal system, any attack against that system had to be directed against that church.

The concept of the early bourgeois revolution distinguishes between two phases—the "people's reformation" between 1517 and 1524, characterized by the leadership of Martin Luther (q.v.), and the German Peasants' War (q.v.), under the leadership of Thomas Müntzer (q.v.), who sought to undertake a revolutionary alteration of the existing order. While non-Marxist historiography has failed to accept this thesis, its impact—through its emphasis on the social and economic setting of the Reformation, and the tensions which existed there early in the 16th century—has been far-reaching in western Reformation scholarship as well.

ECCLESIASTICAL ORDINANCES. Immediately after his return to Geneva (q.v.) in September 1541 John Calvin (q.v.) drafted a new church order for the city which was adopted by the city council in November of that year. These *Ordonnances Ecclésiastiques* (Ecclesiastical Ordinances) were modeled after the Strasbourg church order with which Calvin had become familiar during his stay there.

The ordinances stipulated four ecclesiastical offices: pastors, teachers, elders, and deacons. The responsibility of the pastors was to preach the Word of God and to administer the sacraments. The pastors of the three municipal churches and of the surrounding villages made up the *"vénérable compagnie des pasteurs"* (the venerable company of pastors) which was to meet weekly to study the Bible (q.v.) and consult with one another. The task of the teachers (called "doctors") was to provide instruction to theological students and the laity (q.v.). The elders' responsibility was to oversee the congregation in general, which task included the monitoring of the lives of the congregation. Together with the pastors the elders comprised the consistory. The elders were both nominated and appointed by the city council. Meeting weekly, the consistory examined those who through gossipmongery, drunkenness, immorality, card playing, etc. strayed from the path of proper behavior. The deacons were responsible for caring for the poor and the sick.

The essential feature of this configuration of ecclesiastical offices, as envisioned by John Calvin, was both the emphasis on the importance of education, as expressed by the office of the doctors, and the monitoring of the lives of the faithful. Importantly, however, such surveillance was not a single-handed pursuit of the clergy. Since the elders were appointed by the city council, the body politic—representing the congregation—played a major role in the function of the consistory and its activities. In short, church and society collaborated. While the pastors, by virtue of their learning and office, were undoubtedly the moral center of the consistory, the city council, by appointing the majority of the members of the consistory, could see to it that political considerations outweighed religious ones whenever the two found themselves at odds. (See also CHURCH ORDERS.)

ECK, JOHANN (1486-1543). Catholic theologian. Johann Maier, known as Johann Eck for his birthplace Eck in Swabia, studied at the universities of Heidelberg, Tübingen, Cologne, and Freiburg. He received the doctorate in theology in Freiburg in 1510. That same year he moved to the University at Ingolstadt, where he remained until his death. Eck was ordained to the priesthood in 1508 and throughout his university career intermittently served an Ingolstadt parish church. Open to university reform Eck quickly became a prolific writer on a variety of subjects—economics, logic, predestination (q.v.).

He became involved in the controversy surrounding Martin Luther's (q.v.) Ninety-five Theses when he was asked to share his reactions to Luther's document. While he claimed that his jottings, which were pointedly negative, had not been meant for publication, they were published and thereby Eck was drawn into the public controversy. He was the main spokesman for traditional theology at the Leipzig debate even as he subsequently proved to be the driving force behind seeing Luther excommunicated in 1521. At crucial stages thereafter, such as at Augsburg (q.v.) in 1530, when he was the author of the *Confutation* (q.v.), the Catholic response to the Lutheran Augsburg Confession (q.v.), or at Regensburg in 1541, when he denounced the *Book of Regensburg*, Eck adamantly insisted that the teachings of the reformers were traditional heresies disguised as novelties. More than anybody else, Eck set the theological direction on the Reformation polemic. His own theology was a restatement of the consensus of medieval theology.

EDWARD VI (1537-1553). English king. Edward was the son of Henry VIII's (q.v.) third wife, Jane Seymour, and Henry's only male heir to the English throne. Well educated, fluent in four languages, Edward succeeded his father in January 1547 at the age of nine. During his minority, which was to end at his 18th birthday, royal power was to be exercised by a council of regency. In actual fact, however, power lay in the hands of Edward's uncle Edward Seymour, Duke of Somerset, and (after 1549) in John Dudley, eventually Duke of

Northumberland. Edward did not himself formulate and exercise royal authority; English policy, especially religious policy, during the six years of his reign (1547-53), lay in the hands of Seymour and Dudley, who introduced Protestantism into England. Thus, Edwardian reform— from the dissolution of the chantries and the introduction of the *Book of Common Prayer* and of the Forty-two Articles (qq.v.) to the aborted effort to revise canon law—was the work of men, such as Thomas Cranmer (q.v.), who had the youthful king's confidence but carried out their own objectives and goals.

ELECTORS. The Golden Bull of 1356 formalized the election procedure for the emperor by vesting the election in the seven "electors" (*Kurfürsten*). They were, respectively, the rulers of Electoral Saxony; the archbishops of Cologne, Mainz, and Trier; the margrave of Brandenburg; the count palatine of the Rhine; and the king of Bohemia. Rulers of powerful territories, their influence was particularly important when it came time to elect a new emperor. The archbishop of Mainz, who was the chancellor of the Holy Roman Empire (q.v.), convened the other electors in Frankfurt in order to elect a new emperor. The ruler so elected was officially king of the Romans and emperor, though in theory the imperial coronation was performed by the pope in Rome.

ELIZABETH I (1533-1603). English queen. Daughter of Henry VIII (q.v.) and Anne Boleyn, Elizabeth was born in 1533, not too long after Henry and Anne had married. When by 1536 her mother had failed to give the king a son, she was executed; Henry promptly married Jane Seymour and Parliament declared Elizabeth illegitimate. Elizabeth received an unusually broad education which enabled her, for example, to translate Marguerite d'Angouleme's *Mirror for Sinful Souls* in her teens. During the reign of her half-sister Mary, Elizabeth conformed outwardly to the restored Catholic faith but her half-sister's suspicions brought about her confinement in the Tower of London for an extended period of time.

Upon her succession to the throne in 1558, Elizabeth quickly turned to the matter of a religious settlement, since it was obvious that the Catholicism which her half-sister had reintroduced in England (q.v.) could not be continued. Elizabeth herself was illegitimate in the eyes of the Catholic Church, and Mary's religious policies had evoked much opposition among the English people. A relatively tranquil international scene allowed Elizabeth to turn to a religious settlement at home. It was promulgated by Parliament in the spring of 1559 and entailed a clear compromise. Not only did it not embrace the adamant Calvinism (q.v.) that many of the Marian Exiles (q.v.) demanded; it also, by juxtaposing sections from the conservative prayer book of 1549 and the more liberal book of 1552, wavered between the restoration of religion as it had formally existed at the end of Henry's reign and as it had at the end of Edward VI's (q.v.) reign, the one all but Catholic in name, the other decidedly Protestant.

It is not exactly clear what lay behind the settlement; different theories have been advanced—that the adamant Protestants in Parliament forced Elizabeth to go beyond the 1549 *Book of Common Prayer*, or that the Catholics in the House of Lords forced her to accept the 1549 version, While the country expected further religious changes to follow the 1559 settlement, nothing of that sort happened. Most of the provisions subsequently dealt with were of a conservative nature: many saints' days were restored and clerical marriage was not officially sanctioned. It has been suggested that Elizabeth's toleration of Catholics had political rationale. England needed the support of Spain against France (qq.v.), and Elizabeth could ill afford to alienate Philip II (q.v.) by harsh measures against Catholics in England. Philip indeed showed himself sensitive in that he succeeded in using his influence with the papacy in forestalling Elizabeth's excommunication until 1570.

Elizabeth never married, even though during the first half of her reign there seemed to be nonstop negotiations for a suitable husband. Philip II in particular, widower of sorts of Mary Tudor, was more than a willing suitor. Each marital candidacy failed in the end, probably because Elizabeth never intended to marry in the first place. The queen had the fortune of a wise advisor, William Cecil (q.v.) (since 1571 Lord Burghley), one of the most astute statesmen of the entire 16th century, who had no personal ambitions and served his queen wisely. Politically, Elizabeth had to face the implications of her excommunication by the pope in 1570 that freed all English people from their loyalty to the queen. Philip II, urged for years by the pope to take military action against England, dallied, early on hoping that he could follow his marriage with Mary Tudor by marrying Elizabeth.

When an alliance between France and Spain materialized in 1583, Philip moved to action—and from that time onward to the end of her reign Elizabeth found herself at war with Spain. As is so well known, the greatest danger came to England in 1588, when the Spanish armada (q.v.) set out for England. Its defeat by the English (and bad weather) meant that the most formidable danger to the realm disappeared. At the end of her reign, England was rapidly emerging as Europe's foremost sea power. Religiously, much has been written about Elizabeth. Some have suggested that she was what the French called "politique" (q.v.), someone who was English first, and a religious person second. It seems more accurate to note that she was a religious person of conservative theological orientation. (See also ELIZABETHAN SETTLEMENT.)

ELIZABETHAN SETTLEMENT. When, after Elizabeth I's (q.v.) succession to the throne in 1558, Parliament convened in January 1559, religious issues were foremost on the agenda. Elizabeth wanted to restore the supremacy of the crown over the church, and accordingly a bill was submitted to Parliament. This bill ran into opposition in the House of Lords, where the conservative bishops, all appointed during Mary's reign, exerted strong pressure. While there has been much controversy over the course of events in the spring of 1559 (and Elizabeth's true intentions with respect to a religious settlement), it appears that the queen wanted to return England (q.v.) to the state of affairs at the end of her half-brother Edward VI's (q.v.) reign in 1553, that is, a fairly Protestant settlement. An Act of Supremacy re-established royal supremacy, with the exception of substituting "supreme governor" for "supreme head," canceled the Marian laws of heresy which had reintroduced the medieval heresy laws in England. An Act of Uniformity reintroduced the 1552 version of the *Book of Common Prayer* (q.v.), though with changed wording with regard to the Lord's Supper (q.v.) so as to denote the real presence of Christ in the elements of bread and wine. The settlement also included a number of minor stipulations, largely financial in nature, the consequence of which, however, was to further impoverish the church. The settlement was bitterly attacked by the bishops, all of whom had been fervent supporters of Queen Mary (q.v.). Elizabeth, about whose religious faith scholars have quarreled endlessly, was determined to consider the settlement as final. She would allow no further discussion in Parliament. And despite chronic attacks from what soon were called the Puritans (q.v.), the settlement remained unchanged.

EMPIRE, HOLY ROMAN. The Holy Roman Empire was a complex federation of a large number of utterly diverse entities—territories, ecclesiastical prelates, counts, lords, imperial cities as well as knights, villages, and also areas which were part of the empire but did not participate in the diet (q.v.). The three major structures of the empire were the diet, the imperial cameral court, and the emperor. The empire, for which in rough approximation the term Germany (q.v.) is used as a synonym, comprised not only present-day Germany but also present-day Holland, Belgium, the eastern third of France, Switzerland, Northern Italy, and Austria (q.v.). It was thus considerably larger than Germany, though most of the empire was comprised of lands where a German dialect was spoken. The use of the appellation "holy" and "Roman" was meant to signify that the empire was a kind of universal monarchy of Christendom, transcending individual states, a parallel to the universality of the Roman church.

Formally, the empire was comprised of three types of legal entities. First, imperial free cities, whose numbers changed over time but may be said to have been around 80 at the beginning of the 16th century. These cities enjoyed the immediate protection of the emperor. Secondly, there were the secular territories; and, lastly, the ecclesiastical territories, which were governed by princes of the church. It was to be of major significance for the subsequent course of events that the empire did not follow the development occurring in most other European countries at the time, namely a trend toward centralized authority. If anything, the development in the empire went in the opposite direction, affording ever greater power and authority to the territorial rulers.

The titular head of the empire was an elected king who also carried the title Roman emperor, being crowned by the pope. Unlike France or England (qq.v.), in Germany the rule was not hereditary but an elective office. The so-called "Golden Bull" of 1356 vested the power to elect the emperor in the seven "electors" (q.v.). After 1438 the succession of emperors came without exception from the house of Habsburg (q.v.). It is not beside the point to note that imperial elections were uniformly accompanied by so-called election agreements (*Wahlkapitulation*), which formalized the new emperor's concessions to territorial rulers. Moreover, elections were routinely bought with bribes, meaning that the new emperor always found himself in a twofold dependency—to the territorial rulers to whom he had to make concessions in the election agreement and to those who advanced him the moneys to finance the election. Real power was available to the emperor only through his own hereditary possessions which, of course, in the case of the Habsburgs were substantial—in the case of Emperor Charles V (q.v.) combining possessions in Spain (q.v.), Burgundy, the Low Countries (q.v.), and Austria. In the course of the 16th century the center of power shifted dramatically to the territorial rulers, and the fact that the empire became legally divided, with the Peace of Augsburg (q.v.), into two religious groupings did its share to minimize the significance of the overarching entity, the empire.

EMSER, HIERONYMUS (1478-1527). Catholic polemicist. Born near Ulm in South Germany and having studied at Basel and Tübingen, as well as Leipzig, Emser was ordained to the priesthood before spending two years as secretary to Cardinal Peraudi as he traveled through Germany. He became the chaplain of Duke George of Saxony in 1505 but gave up that position in 1511 to pursue Humanistic studies. After the Leipzig debate (q.v.) of 1519 Emser became one of the most ardent anti-Lutheran polemicists. With the support of Duke George and the papal nuncio Aleander, he launched a series of polemical works attacking Martin Luther (q.v.) and other reformers, such as Andreas Bodenstein Carlstadt and Huldrych Zwingli (qq.v.). Luther responded in kind, taking a cue from the ibex in Emser's coat of arms to refer to him as "the goat." His topics covered the major points of the theological controversy—the Mass, priesthood, Scripture. In 1527, shortly before his death, his German translation of the New Testament was published. It proved to be immensely popular among Catholics, seeing over 60 editions.

ENGLAND. England entered the 16th century under the rule of Henry VII, who had ascended the throne in 1485 after his successful conclusion of the War of the Roses. Henry's rule was characterized by an astute centralization of power which included a frontal attack on the barons who potentially threatened royal authority; an equally astute foreign policy, cemented by the marriage of his daughter to James IV of Scotland and his oldest son Arthur to Catherine of Aragon (q.v.); and frugal expenditures, which made for a well-filled royal treasury and a stable country whose problems were of the past. The death of Henry's son Arthur in 1502, one year after his betrothal to Catherine, placed the younger son Henry in line of succession. Henry succeeded to the throne in 1509 and, with papal dispensation, married Catherine. The diplomatic gains from such a union had not changed since Catherine's betrothal to Arthur.

Unlike his father, Henry VIII (q.v.) threw himself with gusto into various foreign involvements, none of which proved to be particularly successful. Henry's chief advisor came to be Thomas Wolsey (q.v.), who had managed Henry's military expedition against France (q.v.) in 1513 and been the negotiator of the peace with France the following year. An unsuccessful and unpopular war against France, which began in 1522, forced Henry VIII to convene Parliament for financial support. Parliament balked, an indication for Henry that his rule was not as secure as he might have assumed. When, in 1525, Wolsey sought to raise the "amicable grant" for the king's foreign initiatives, a de facto tax not authorized by Parliament, widespread opposition and even uprisings followed.

Despite his increasing lack of popularity, Wolsey continued to have the king's confidence and exercise both the highest ecclesiastical and political office in the land. Undoubtedly, a major reason was that in 1527 the king began to seek a papal annulment of his marriage with Catherine, and Wolsey had to be the crucial figure to negotiate the annulment with the pope. Two years later, however, it became clear that Wolsey had been unsuccessful in his efforts. He was promptly dismissed from office and replaced by Thomas More (q.v.), who received the king's concession that he would not be involved in what was called "the king's great matter." Two new advisors, Thomas Cromwell and Thomas Cranmer (qq.v.), appeared on the scene—both were to dominate the 1530s—and they suggested to the king that the matter be tried in the king's courts in England, a strategy which, little by little, the king undertook to pursue.

First, however, came a strategy of intimidation of church and clergy. Henry convened Parliament in 1529 and had Parliament denounce a number of ecclesiastical abuses, notably the shortcomings in the administration of the ecclesiastical courts. Undoubtedly, this was to be an indication to the pope that the king might well go the way of the Lutheran princes in Germany (q.v.). The following year charges (the technical term was "praemunire") were filed against the entire English clergy for complicity with Wolsey's legatine authority and their acceptance of a foreign authority, the pope. The English clergy responded by making a major financial gift to the king (supposedly in gratitude for his defense of the Catholic faith against Lutheran heresy) but Henry insisted that the clergy acknowledge his status as "protector and supreme head" of the English church and clergy. This the clergy eventually acknowledged with the meaningful, yet evasive addendum "so far as the law of Christ allows." The final attempt to blackmail, or cajole, the pope into agreeing to the king's request came in early 1532, when Parliament, now reconvened, passed the Conditional Restraint of Annates, which prohibited the payment of annates—a tax in the amount of one annual income by new incumbents of ecclesiastical offices—to Rome. Parliament also declared its grievance over the fact that important regulations and laws pertaining to the English church were made in Rome, whereupon the clergy agreed in the "submission of the clergy" that it would seek henceforth royal assent for all new constitutions, canons, and ordinances.

Thomas More, realizing the revolution that had occurred in the English church, resigned his position as lord chancellor. Thomas Cromwell took his place not only with administrative competence but also with a bold conceptual interpretation of what lay at the heart of the matter: that the king was the sovereign of an "empire" and as such possessed supreme authority in both church and state and that Parliament was the physical manifestation of the English people. Its voice, conjoined with that of the king, was of paramount importance. In rapid sequence Parliament passed a series of bills—notably the Restraint of Appeals, which prohibited appeals from the decisions of English courts to Rome; the Supremacy Act, which declared the supreme "headship" of the English king over the English church; the Succession Act, which legitimized future offspring from what was now Henry's legitimate marriage to Anne Boleyn; and the High Treason Act, which made any overt denial of the king's titles, such as that of "supreme head of the church in England," high treason punishable by death. Actually, these parliamentary statutes defined the king's role in the English church not unlike that of Lutheran territorial rulers in Germany without, of course, having undertaken the kind of ecclesiastical and religious reforms that had occurred in Germany. Most English churchmen and laity (q.v.) submitted to the changes, with the exception of a few, notably Thomas More and Bishop John Fisher (q.v.), whose eventual execution demonstrated that Henry was sensitive to the persistent Catholic sentiment in the land.

Until the end of his reign in 1547, Henry sought to walk the tightrope between Catholicism, on the one hand, and newly emerging Protestantism, on the other. Religiously, however, the king was conservative, indeed a good Catholic. He had become involved in the Reformation controversy with a vigorous defense, in part undoubtedly written by none other than Thomas More, of the traditional Catholic understanding of the seven sacraments. This literary venture earned him the title "defender of the faith" by the pope, a title which English sovereigns have claimed ever since, despite England's break with Rome in the 1530s.

Henry's foremost concern was the repudiation of papal legal power in England and a measure of ecclesiastical reform in England that was based on the Erasmian understanding. Not surprisingly, given that turbulent age, Henry was concerned about the role played by religion in sustaining law and order. Yet despite Henry's conservative orientation, significant changes did take place in England. In 1536 Parliament ordered the dissolution of the smaller monasteries; three years later the larger monasteries were dissolved as well. In both instances, the king was the beneficiary of the enormous wealth held by the monasteries (on the eve of the Reformation the church was the largest landholder in England) but Henry astutely passed, either as outright gift or at attractive prices, a great portion of these monastic lands to loyal supporters. When the ecclesiastical changes seemed to favor the spread of Protestant notions in England, Henry had Parliament pass the Six Articles Act (q.v.) in 1539 whose six points, notably clerical celibacy and the Mass, expressed traditional Catholic sentiment.

Henry's death, in January 1547, meant the succession of his nine-year-old son Edward VI (q.v.) but power was exercised by a council of regency in which Edward Seymour, the Duke of Somerset, quickly came to play the pivotal role. And even though the council and Somerset did not wish for any religious changes, by this time Protestant sentiment in Parliament was strong enough to force the gradual dismantling of Henry VIII's religious policies. In 1549 Parliament passed an Act of Uniformity which not only introduced the *Book of Common Prayer* (q.v.) but also prohibited all other forms of worship in England (which meant, of course, the prohibition of both the traditional Catholic Mass and the less liturgical Calvinist services). Other changes followed, as did an uprising in Norfolk (Robert Kett's Rebellion), which had to be suppressed with brutal force. At the same time, Thomas Cranmer (q.v.) drafted a confession of faith for the English church, the Forty-Two Articles (q.v.), which showed both Lutheran and Calvinist influence.

The untimely death of King Edward VI meant the succession of his half-sister Mary, daughter of Catherine of Aragon, a turn of events her father Henry VIII had so desperately striven to avoid. While a person of deep personal piety, integrity, and noble ideals, Mary was only concerned about the restoration of Catholicism in England. A few months after her succession, Parliament met and passed several bills repealing virtually all of the ecclesiastical legislation that had been passed under her half-brother Edward. While agreeable, Parliament still balked at various points, such as the restoration of monastic lands, or that of papal supremacy, indicating that by that time, at any rate, Protestant sentiment at least in Parliament was strong. In November 1554 Parliament expressed itself repentant of the schism, while in January of the following year the rest of Henry's ecclesiastical legislation, from the Statute of Appeals to the Supremacy Act, were repealed. Mary accompanied the reintroduction of Catholicism with a strident persecution of Protestant sentiment in the land. The most illustrious victim was Thomas Cranmer, who was burned at Oxford in 1556.

It turned out, all the same, that Mary's restoration of Catholicism was not at all accompanied by harmonious relations with the papacy: Pope Paul IV insisted that the confiscated church lands be restored to the church and then declared war on England; Reginald Pole (q.v.), who had been elevated to be archbishop of Canterbury, was cited to appear in Rome under the suspicion of heresy. The succession of Elizabeth I (q.v.) in 1558, daughter of Anne Boleyn, meant not only a return to some form of Protestant religion in the country but also—as matters turned out—a surprisingly long rule: Elizabeth died in 1603, after a rule of some 45 years. The fickleness of events that accompanied the brief rules of her half-brother Edward and half-sister Mary gave way to a long-term rule and long-term policies. While only 25 years of age when she became queen, Elizabeth clearly understood the objectives of English policy—to keep England aloof from dependency on Continental powers, to develop the economic resources of the country, and to resolve the religious diversity in the land. The Elizabethan settlement (q.v.) of religion, which Parliament promulgated at her urging in 1559 with the Act of Supremacy and the Act of Uniformity repealed the ecclesiastical legislation of Mary, gave Elizabeth the title of "supreme governor of this realm, as well in all spiritual or ecclesiastical things or causes, as temporal," reintroduced the *Book of Common Prayer*, with a careful juxtaposition of the wording of the 1549 and 1552 editions concerning the Lord's Supper.

In 1563 the Thirty-nine Articles (q.v.), a revision of Cranmer's original Forty-two Articles, were approved by convocation and endorsed by the queen. The articles now stood theologically midway between Lutheranism and Calvinism (qq.v.). They were thus moderate in tone, allowed for divergent emphases, and undoubtedly enjoyed the support of a majority of the English people. Nonetheless, the failure to embrace a more committed form of Protestantism made for deep unhappiness among some, especially those who had spent the Marian years in exile on the Continent, where they had occasion to observe, in Calvinist locales, a comprehensively reformed religion, one devoid of clerical vestments, images, crucifixes, and church music. These adamant reformers, known as the Marian exiles (q.v.), urged a more comprehensive settlement but Elizabeth steadfastly refused. By 1564 it was evident that further change was unlikely, and the controversy broke out into the open, interestingly enough over the issues of clerical vestments. Other controversies followed, and when it was all over, the Puritan controversy had engrossed, with differing issues, England for the better part of a century. Still, it is Elizabeth's legacy to have given the Church of England the form which it has had ever since. Moreover, when she died, England was well on its way to economic prosperity and international power. (See also ANGLICANISM; PURITANISM.)

EPISCOPACY. A lengthy development in the Middle Ages gave the bishops of the church the power and authority of teaching, ordination, and jurisdiction over their respective dioceses. In particular this meant that the bishop had the responsibility to celebrate the Mass on Sundays and feast days, to reside in his diocese, to undertake an annual visitation (q.v.) of his diocese, and to present a report every five years to the Holy See about the condition of the diocese. The privileges of the bishop included the purple attire, episcopal ring, and pectoral cross. The Reformation significantly weakened the place of the bishop in favor of a greater importance bestowed on the parish clergy, now by Protestants called pastors. The administrative responsibilities formerly carried out by the bishop were taken over in most Protestant churches by functionaries who held such titles as inspector, superintendent, or general superintendent. The office of bishop was retained in the Scandinavian countries, in England, and in Bohemia and Hungary. Much of the former episcopal authority was assumed in Germany and Switzerland (qq.v.) by the secular authorities, and significantly so in Protestant lands.

ERASMUS, DESIDERIUS, OF ROTTERDAM (c. 1469-1536).

Humanist. The great Humanist was born in Rotterdam and received his first schooling in Deventer and Herzogenbusch, where he was influenced by the Modern Devotion, a late medieval movement of emphasizing spiritual living. After joining a monastery near Gouda he entered the service of the bishop of Cambrai, whom he was to accompany on a trip to Italy; this secured his release from having to observe the monastic rule. This was to last his lifetime. Erasmus pursued studies at the University of Paris, where he received a bachelor degree in theology in 1498. During a stay at Oxford he was in contact (1499) with the great English Humanists of the day, John Colet and Thomas More (qq.v.), and he learned to share their enthusiasm for Cicero, Socrates, and the Apostle Paul.

Erasmus's literary career began shortly after the turn of the century with the publication of the *Adagia*, a collection of proverbs, and the *Enchiridion militis Christiani* in 1502. The *Enchiridion* (the Handbook of the Christian Soldier), a summary of the Christian faith written for a soldier, gave him European-wide fame and reputation in that it offered a summary of the Christian faith in terms of a new understanding of lay spirituality. In 1505 Erasmus published Lorenzo Valla's annotations on the New Testament, and an extended stay in Italy (1506-09) afforded him the opportunity for further study of the ancients. A second stay in England (q.v.) (1509-14) followed. He served as professor of Greek at Cambridge but neither teaching nor the students were much to his liking. During his stay he completed his *Encomium Moriae*, the famous *Praise of Folly* (1509). Between 1515 and 1521 he sojourned briefly in Brussels, Louvain, and England. In 1518 appeared his *Colloquia familiaria*, on the face of things simple exercises in Latin style but in content brutal and sarcastic attacks against religious and ecclesiastical practices, such as monasticism (q.v.), veneration of the saints, pilgrimages, and fasting.

These sharp attacks on church practices, together with the new enunciation of the Christian faith, which was a far cry from scholastic theology, prompted many to see Erasmus as the real mentor behind Martin Luther's (q.v.) attack on indulgences (q.v.) in 1517. Most of Erasmus's efforts and energies were devoted to editorial and editing work: he engaged in a formidable editing effort to bring out new editions of the church fathers (Ambrose, Augustine, Basil, Chrysostom, Ireneaus, Origin). In 1516 appeared his greatly disputed Greek edition of the New Testament, which not only included his annotations on biblical passages but also offered the variant readings of the text of the

Latin Vulgate. Importantly, the preface to the reader argued for Scripture as the sole ground for the Christian faith and advocated the translation of Scripture into the vernacular languages. The indulgences controversy and the incipient Reformation saw Erasmus, much to the surprise of many Humanists, standing on the sidelines, first mildly in support of Luther, then, albeit with equal evasiveness, critical of him.

Urged by friends to take a stand, he published his major treatise against Luther in 1524—the *De libero arbitrio* (Concerning Free Will), which Luther countered with his equally formidable *De servo arbitrio* (The Bondage of the Will). This exchange, which focused on the question of the human ability to freely do the good, which was denied by Luther and affirmed by Erasmus, marked the separation of Humanist notions of reform and Martin Luther's reinterpretation of the Christian gospel. Continuing his prolific program of writing and editing, such as a handbook on preaching, Erasmus lived in Basel in the 1520s. When that city became Protestant, he moved northward to Freiburg, where he died in 1536.

Erasmus was arguably the major intellectual figure in the early 16th century. His impact on his time—and especially on the Reformation—must be sought for one in his editions of the New Testament and of the ancient fathers. This provided the Protestant Reformation with the tools that allowed the reformers to advocate their notion of Scripture as the sole norm and authority of the Christian faith. With the exception of Martin Luther, the other major reformers were all Humanists, and they had imbibed, in one way or another, Erasmus's understanding of the Christian faith.

More importantly, however, Erasmus enunciated a new vision of the Christian faith which was at odds with both that of the Protestant Reformation and that of traditional Catholicism, so much so as a matter of fact that Erasmus's name appeared repeatedly on lists of prohibited books issued by the Catholic Church. Erasmus's understanding of the Christian religion was that of what he called the "philosophy of Christ." By that he meant not only to convey that the deepest truths of Scripture were in fact not exclusively confined to Scripture but were to be found elsewhere as well, such as in Greek philosophy. Erasmus also understood Christianity as the mandate to follow the moral law of Jesus in the Gospels. Thus, an important ethical norm characterized Erasmus's understanding of the Christian faith; the absence of dogmatic and theological preoccupation made the Erasmian understanding a very attractive one once Europe had tired of the incessant doctrinal disputes among the theologians. (See also HUMANISM.)

ERASTIANISM. The term is derived from Thomas Lüber, Latinized Erastus (1524-1583), a physician who also possessed keen theological interests. Erastus became embroiled in a theological controversy in the late 1560s over the issue of church discipline. Erastus maintained that the secular authorities, like the kings of ancient Israel, had authority over both the civic and the religious communities. The church was for Erastus synonymous with society. Erastianism thus refers to a philosophy which sees the church as part of society and subordinate to it. At the same time, Erastianism, which flowered in England (q.v.) during and after Elizabeth I's (q.v.) reign, took a low view of ecclesiastical authority.

ESCHATOLOGY. The term refers to the teaching of the "last things," that is, the happenings at the end of the world. Eschatology assumes, in other words, that the world will not continue forever but that it has a specific end even as it had a specific beginning. Eschatology means preoccupation with such theological and biblical topics as the Second Coming of Christ for the final judgment, the nature of his coming, either calmly or in great turbulence, or the end of the world. Related is the term "apocalypticism," which sees the present as in a deep crisis and expects the imminent triumph of good over evil.

Apocalypticism is eschatology transferred into the present, with all of the drama and excitement depicted in certain biblical passages. Early Christianity expected the end to be imminent. This is the overriding tenor of much of the New Testament. While with the passing of time the expectation of an imminent end disappeared, Christian theology continued to ponder the various issues related to it. Periods of intense eschatological (and thus apocalyptic) expectation alternated with times during which little attention was paid to the end. Undoubtedly, the way theologians experienced their own time—as time of crisis or of calm— played a pivotal role in making eschatological thinking important.

The early 16th century was characterized by a widespread expectation that the end was near. This meant that theologians and others were able to see certain biblical passages about the end as describing their own time. Since the triumph of the gospel was considered to be a hallmark of the end times, the general eschatological atmosphere undoubtedly helped further the cause and course of the

Reformation. It was characteristic of Martin Luther's (q.v.) eschatology that it focused on the Apostle Paul and intimately connected the teaching about the end times with the affirmations concerning justification and christology. Luther's eschatology was thus existential eschatology: the experience of God's wrath and grace in the encounter with Christ were not simply systematic theological reflections. Luther experienced the fires of hell in his conscience. The other reformers more or less echoed Luther's thinking; John Calvin's (q.v.) emphasis on predestination meant that eschatology could not play an important role in his theology.

In the Radical Reformation (q.v.) different emphases came to the fore. In particular, the influence of Melchior Hofmann (q.v.) meant that the cosmic dimension found in the Apocalypse received great attention. If medieval theology emphasized the individual—eschatology centered on the individual's "end," namely death—and Luther combined this existential experience with an emphasis on the cosmic order of things, it is clear that the Anabaptists tended to focus only on the latter. Thus, Hofmann was certain that he had correctly calculated the end, namely the time of Christ's return. The development of Münster Anabaptism (qq.v.) must be seen in that context. For the Münster Anabaptists, restoration of the gospel, that mandatory characteristic of the final days, meant the restoration of their gospel. In the wake of the debacle of Münster, Anabaptism de-emphasized all eschatological elements.

EUCHARIST. No less than five divergent interpretations of the Eucharist—variously known also as the Lord's Supper (q.v.) or Communion—can be found in the 16th century. In each of these interpretations, the point of departure was not so much the New Testament exhortation to perpetuate Jesus' last meal with his disciples, as the precise nature of this perpetuation. The question pertained to the significance and meaning of Jesus' words of institution ("This is my body . . . this is my blood").

The medieval Catholic view, known as transubstantiation, differentiated between "substance" and "accident," the essence and the appearance of a thing, and it held that the officiating priest transformed the "substance" of bread and wine into the true body and blood of Christ, even though the "accidents," i. e., the appearances of bread and wine, remain. The several reinterpretations in the 16th century offered different views of the words of institution. Martin Luther (q.v.), and the Lutheran (q.v.) tradition, rejected the use of non-biblical terms (the use of the terms "substance" and "accidents") in theology but otherwise affirmed that the body and blood of Christ were truly present in the two elements. This meant a literal interpretation of the words of institution.

This view was challenged, first by a Dutch physician, Cornelisz Hoen, then by the Zurich reformer Huldrych Zwingli (q.v.), who asserted that the words of institution should be interpreted symbolically: Jesus meant to convey to his disciples that bread and wine symbolized, or signified, his body and blood. All the same, Zwingli affirmed a spiritual presence of Christ in the elements. This view was subsequently modified by John Calvin (q.v.), who held that the believers united with Christ, who was spiritually present in the communion elements. A third Protestant perspective was offered by the Anabaptists (q.v.) who held that Communion was a memorial in which the believers commemorated the death of Jesus. Unlike the Catholics and the Lutherans, for whom the Eucharist was a sacrament, that is, a vehicle of divine grace, the Anabaptists saw the event simply as a commemoration. The words of institution were interpreted symbolically. Finally, note must be made of a view which failed to attract followers: it was propounded by Andreas Carlstadt (q.v.), who argued that in speaking the words of institution Jesus had actually pointed at himself. This meant, of course, a symbolic interpretation, essentially a variant of the perspective held by the Anabaptists (q.v.) but failed to be widely persuasive, particularly since Carlstadt could offer no satisfactory explanation, as to where Jesus had pointed when saying "This is my blood."

Closely related to the divergence in the interpretation of the words of institution there also existed differences with regard to the meaning of the event. Both Catholics and Lutherans affirmed the sacramental character of the event: they saw bread and wine, that is the body and blood of Christ so offered, as tangible vehicles offering forgiveness of sins to the believer. The other theological traditions in the 16th century saw the event essentially as commemorative, even though the Calvinist-Reformed (q.v.) tradition attained great spiritual depth through its notion of a spiritual communion of the believer with the risen Christ. The different interpretations of the Lord's Supper offered by the several Protestant reformers constituted the major reason for the several divisions of 16th-century Protestantism. While there were other differences between Lutherans and Calvinists, for example, it was the divergence over the issue of Communion, that was the most intense.

— F —

FAITH. In medieval Catholic theology sophisticated distinctions had evolved with respect to the various definitions and aspects of faith, thus, for example, the distinction between "implicit" and "explicit" faith. The former was the faith of untrained laypersons who, without fully understanding theological details, believed the various teachings of the church. "Explicit" faith, in turn, was the informed and "explicit" belief in the teachings of the Catholic Church. Importantly, medieval theology drew a distinction between "unformed" and "formed" faith, which in turn rested on a parallel distinction between the righteousness of Christ and the righteousness of God. Christian life was a move from the one to the other. The righteousness of Christ, which was appropriated in baptism (q.v.) and penance as well as the "implicit" faith, enabled the Christian to do those meritorious works that were necessary to become righteous and thereby meet the demands of God's righteousness. Faith was thus formed by love.

The central importance of the doctrine of justification for the Protestant reformers meant that the understanding of faith occupied a pivotal place in the various Protestant theologies. For Martin Luther (q.v.) faith appropriated the divine promise of the forgiveness and of love of the sinner, even though that promise was all but impossible to fathom in view of the profundity of human sin and rebellion against God. Thus, for Luther, faith was trust. It was christocentric in that what the believers trusted was God's promise that the righteousness of Christ was imputed to the believers. Importantly, such faith entailed the believer's certainty of salvation. For Luther the equation was a simple one. All the believer had to do was to trust in God's promise of forgiveness and salvation. Trust in this promise meant certainty.

The other major reformers, such as Huldrych Zwingli and John Calvin (qq.v.), echoed in many ways Luther's notions. Differences arose among them, and among individual Lutheran (q.v.) reformers, with respect to the question of the relationship of faith and love, that is, what are the consequences of possessing such salutary faith? Did it lead to a life of love and good works? In this regard the Zwinglian-Calvinist tradition was intent to argue that faith needed structure and that the law of Scripture was important even in the life of faith. Luther, on the other hand, saw the life lived in faith in terms of spontaneity: faith was active in love. With the assurance that comes from trusting God's promises, the believer will spontaneously and joyfully serve the neighbor.

FAMILY. As goes without saying, in the 16th century the family was both a sociological and a theological phenomenon. As a sociological phenomenon, the family was the fundamental unit of 16th-century society. While family members were seen as having sets of mutual obligations with each member having assigned duties and responsibilities, the fundamental structure was patriarchal. Fathers ruled, and the father's rule was to assure the spiritual and material prosperity of the family and household. Even though the family thus stood at the center of society, late medieval society was also characterized by a high rate of celibacy and a relatively late age of marriage, especially for men. Whether this was a cause for lower fertility and smaller family size continues to be debated. With means of birth control primitive at best (essentially the use of *coitus interruptus*), children tended to be born to couples in a roughly two-year cycle.

Infant and childhood mortality were high in early modern Europe, and family size, which varied widely, was smaller than the facticity of births at regular two-year intervals might indicate. Scholars have argued that the premodern family, facing high infant mortality and risks of childbearing, shielded itself from the almost constant grief of losing children in childbed or infancy by remaining detached from their children. Still, there is also abundant evidence from the 16th century that there existed strong and intense emotional ties between spouses as well as between parents and children. Parents suffered and experienced the loss of a child with the same emotional intensity as we would find in the 20th century.

Theologically, the 16th century was heir to the medieval notion of marriage (q.v.), praised as a noble calling to continue the human race but found it inferior to the virtue of celibacy. The Protestant reformers countered with the emphatic assertion that celibacy was a special gift of God only for the very few and was not a superior virtue. God had instituted marriage to fulfill a noble and important function. Families were the place for the orderly exercise of human sexuality, the nurturing propagation of children, and—in Christian families—the nurturing of the Christian faith. The "holy household" took the place of monastery and convent. This dramatically positive view of the family became an important hallmark of the Protestant faith in the 16th century. (See also DIVORCE.)

FAREL, GUILLAUME (1489-1565). Born in southeastern France, Farel studied in Paris, became a teacher, and moved to Basel in 1523.

Further peregrinations took him to Strasbourg, Lausanne, Neufchatel, and Geneva (q.v.), always for the purpose of preaching the new gospel of the Reformation. Farel returned to Geneva several times in 1535, and he was instrumental in the introduction of the Reformation in the city in May 1536. When, less than two months later, John Calvin (q.v.), who had recently gained modest attention through the publication of a summary statement of the Protestant faith, the *Institutes of the Christian Religion* (q.v.), passed through Geneva on his way to Strasbourg, Farel persuaded him to stay. Two years later a conflict between Farel and Calvin and the Genevan city council led to their banishment from the city. Farel became pastor at Neufchatel, where he stayed for 27 years until his death in 1565. While Farel wrote extensively—some 15 books came from his pen—his historical significance lies less in these somewhat verbose and unoriginal writings than his practical churchmanship. In particular, the course of the Reformation in France (q.v.) was greatly influenced by him.

FERDINAND I (1503-1564). German emperor. Ferdinand, brother of Charles V (q.v.), was born in Salamanca, Spain, second son of Philip of Austria and Joan of Castile. In 1521 he moved to Austria to assume the rule of the German Habsburg (q.v.) possessions as per an agreement with his brother Charles. In 1526 Ferdinand was elected king of Hungary and Bohemia. Ferdinand not only ruled the Austrian hereditary lands of the Habsburgs during the first half century of the Reformation, he also represented his brother Charles on several occasions at German diets (q.v.). Ferdinand was an adamant opponent of Protestantism, even though he could be quite pragmatic and was open to the need for reform in the Catholic Church. He was a major force behind the Peace of Augsburg (q.v.) in 1555.

FISHER, JOHN (1469-1535). English bishop and cardinal. After studies at Cambridge, Fisher became spiritual advisor to Margaret Beaufort, the mother of King Henry VII. This position enhanced his influence and career—at his urging Lady Margaret founded two colleges at Cambridge, Christ's and St. John's, even as he became bishop of Rochester in 1504. Open to the new Humanist notions, Fisher saw to an invitation to Desiderius Erasmus (q.v.) to come to Cambridge, which in turn led to the acceptance of Humanist ideas and ideals there. Still, surprisingly Fisher published a polemical work against the French Humanist theologian Jacques Lefevre d'Etaples in

1519, which showed his essentially conservative disposition. Two years later he launched an attack on Martin Luther (q.v.) in which he showed that Luther's heretical views on Scripture and faith were the basis for his other heretical notions. In 1523 this critique was published under the title *Confutatio*; it was one of the most influential anti-Protestant writings of the early Reformation. Further polemical writings against other reformers, such as Johann Oecolampadius (q.v.) in 1527, followed.

These polemical writings made Fisher a determined, if not altogether original, polemicist for the old faith. While holding to an Augustinian view of justification by grace, Fisher's other theological affirmations were conventionally Catholic. From 1527 onward, Fisher became embroiled in King Henry VIII's (q.v.) effort to seek an annulment of his marriage to Catherine of Aragon (q.v.). In Fisher's mind there was no doubt that the marriage (q.v.) was valid. When it became evident that the king's position on his marriage had the corollary of seeking royal control over the English church, Fisher became one of the king's most prominent opponents. In 1534 he was condemned to life imprisonment. His refusal to swear the oath of succession sent him to the Tower of London, and his denial of the royal supremacy made him guilty of high treason. When word reached England (q.v.) that Pope Paul III (q.v.) had elevated him to cardinal, Fisher was executed on June 22, 1535. Fisher was canonized in 1935.

FLACIUS ILLYRICUS, MATTHIAS (1520-1575). Lutheran theologian. Born near Trieste in what is now Croatia, Flacius, whose Croatian name was Vlacic, pursued Humanistic studies in Venice, Basel, and Tübingen and came to the University of Wittenberg (q.v.) in 1541. His pivotal experience was his conversion in which the Lutheran understanding of justification and *"sola fide"* played pivotal roles. In 1544 he was appointed professor of Hebrew at Wittenberg. When Charles V (q.v.) imposed the Interim (q.v.) on the Protestant territories after his success in the War of Schmalkald (q.v.) and Philip Melanchthon (q.v.) advocated a policy of accommodation, Flacius emerged as the foremost protagonist who found the Interim and any accommodation to it an abomination. In 1549 he moved to Magdeburg, working in printshops to earn his livelihood and continue his literary and theological polemic. After Charles's religious policy had failed, and the Interim ceased to be a pertinent issue, Flacius turned to two major projects—a comprehensive church history, known as the

Magdeburg Centuries, and a scriptural hermeneutic, the *Clavis scipturae sacrae* (The Key to Holy Scripture). In addition he continued his polemical writings as head of the Gnesio-Lutheran (q.v.) party, which was persuaded that Melanchthon and his followers were perverting Martin Luther's (q.v.) authentic message.

Flacius was involved in all the intra-Lutheran controversies (q.v.) which beset German Lutheranism (q.v.) after Luther's death—the majoristic, the antinomian, the synergistic, and the Osiandrian controversies. In the synergistic controversy Flacius asserted in 1560 that original sin had become the substance of humans through Adam's fall, a position that grew out of Flacius's notion that humans were totally incapable of contributing anything to their salvation. In 1557 Flacius became professor at the new university of Jena but soon left for Regensburg, where he sought to establish a university committed to his interpretation and understanding of Luther's theology. After brief stays in Antwerp and Strasbourg, Flacius moved to Frankfurt, where he died in March 1575. Flacius was an incessant polemicist, both in tone and in substance. While some of his positions, such as on original sin, were extremist aberrations, he deserves credit for his pointed defense of what he perceived as Luther's legacy and also for his *Magdeburg Centuries,* which, while subtly conveying the perspective of Lutheran orthodoxy (q.v.), was a major landmark in the development of the scholarly study of church history.

FORTY-TWO ARTICLES. More precisely known as the "Articles of Religion," the Forty-two Articles grew out of Thomas Cranmer's (q.v.) effort in 1548 to produce a confession (q.v.) of faith that would unite the reformers both on the Continent and in England (q.v.). The articles were published in 1549 under the title "articles agreed on by the bishops and other learned men, in the synod at London," a misnomer, since no such synod had endorsed, or even discussed, Cranmer's articles. Unlike some of the Continental Protestant confessions, the Forty-two Articles did not restate the whole of Christian theology but rather, much in keeping with the tenor of the Reformation in England, only those doctrines, accretions in practice, and perversions of authority that had characterized the medieval church and needed to be corrected.

Deemed heretical during the rule of Mary Tudor (q.v.), the Forty-two Articles were revived under Elizabeth I (q.v.) in 1562, when a text of the articles that had been greatly revised by Matthew Parker was presented to convocation. The articles on grace, blasphemy against the Holy Spirit, the moral law, and the Millenarian heretics had been deleted, and four new articles (on the Holy Spirit; good works; the wicked receiving the Lord's Supper [q.v.]; and Communion under both kinds) added. Convocation weighed in by deleting three articles dealing with the Anabaptists (q.v.) (which were considered no longer a relevant issue), which reduced the number to 39. When the queen endorsed the articles in 1563, further changes were made, as was also the case in 1571, when Bishop John Jewel (q.v.) put the articles into their final form. Traditionally, the articles were included in the *Book of Common Prayer* (q.v.).

FOXE, JOHN (1517-1587). English Humanist author and martyrologist. Born in Lincolnshire, Foxe studied at Oxford, where he acquired a solid Humanist education, making him conversant with Hebrew, Greek, and Latin. Foxe became a private tutor and spent the years of Mary Tudor's (q.v.) reign on the Continent as a committed Protestant. He settled at Basel, where his interest in ecclesiastical history prompted the publication of a church history, *Commentarii rerum in ecclesia gestarum* (The Books of the Events in the Church) in 1554 and an expanded version, which carried the narrative forward to the reign of Mary. Supplied by relevant materials from friends, he augmented the story of the English church after 1532 and published a volume of some 1,800 pages entitled *Actes and Monuments of these Latter and Perilous Days*. Further editions followed: that of 1570 was twice the length of the 1563 edition. Editions followed in 1576 and 1583, with the definitive edition appearing in 1596, nine year's after the author's death. Foxe never rose to be a public figure and, despite the immense popularity of his *Book of Martyrs*, barely eked out a living. (See also MARTYROLOGIES.)

FRANCE. Politically, France enjoyed a considerable measure of territorial and administrative centralization in the later Middle Ages, which gave the kings (who came from the house of Valois between 1328 and 1498, and the houses of Orleans and Angouleme until 1589) firm control over the country. The king had the right of taxation, , which, as the chief source of royal income, made him independent of the Estates General. Late in the 15th century, Charles VIII ventured to turn the country into the foremost European power and in 1494 invaded Italy. While he scored some successes, in the end he was driven back to France by Ferdinand of Spain (q.v.). This marked the beginning of the conflict between Spain and France over the control of Italy which did not end until the middle of the 16th century.

In France a unique relationship existed between the church and the French crown by the end of the Middle Ages, giving the crown rather unprecedented power in ecclesiastical affairs. The Pragmatic Sanction of Bourges, signed in 1438, established several important ecclesiastical privileges for the French crown, such as the collection of papal taxes and the appointment of major ecclesiastical officials. The sanction was much disputed in the decades that followed so that the Fifth Lateran Council declared it to be null and void. However, at the same time (1516) the new Concordat of Bologna, while allowing the papal collection of annates and the French king's recognition of papal supremacy over general councils, vested in the king the right to nominate the candidates for vacant archbishoprics, bishoprics, and abbacies. Practically, this meant that these appointments lay in the hands of the king.

The rule of Francis I (1515-47) (q.v.) was overshadowed not only by the continuing struggle with Spain over the possession of Italy, in the course of which Francis did the unthinkable—he allied himself with the Ottoman Empire—but also by the first manifestations of Reformation sentiment in the country. A Humanist circle in Meaux, mentored by Jacques Lefevre d'Etaples, had affirmed Erasmian notions both of a new Christian spirituality and the need for ecclesiastical reforms. The influx of Lutheran (q.v.) ideas into the country in the early 1520s triggered the outright and confrontational expression of new theological ideas. While Francis I was himself a religious moderate, of the Erasmian variety, his conflict with Charles V (q.v.) over Italy forced him to look for allies. Pope Clement VII (q.v.) was an obvious choice, especially when, after the Battle at Pavia in 1525, Francis was himself taken prisoner by Charles. Moreover, the Reformation agitation disturbed domestic peace in the land, at a time when the conflict with Spain made it important for the country to be tranquil.

Francis's death in 1547 and the succession of Henry II (q.v.) made for a more determined suppression of Protestant sentiment. Henry, in contrast to his father's empathy for an Erasmian form of Christianity, was convinced that the Protestants were a mortal danger for the realm. He established a new judiciary body, the *chambre ardente* ("fire court") (q.v.), whose function it was to suppress heresy. The Edict of

Chateaubriand of 1551 intensified the suppression of Protestantism. With the support of the German Protestants Henry was able to expand the French borders to the east, by winning Metz, Toul, and Verdun but the conflict with Spain remained unresolved. Financial and military problems forced Henry to conclude the treaty of Cateau-Cambrésis (q.v.) in April 1559, which ended over half a century of intermittent French-Spanish conflict and war.

A few months later Henry died unexpectedly. The heir to the throne was Francis II, 15 years of age. Francis's youth should have raised the question of regency for the minor king. The question was never discussed, for Charles Cardinal of Lorraine, of the house of Guise, summarily took over the reigns of government. This move evoked the opposition of the noble family of the Bourbons, princes of the blood. Political enmity and jealousy mingled with religious disagreement. Two factions emerged, the Catholics supporting the Guises, while the Huguenots (q.v.), as the French Protestants now were called, supported the Bourbons. This meant a growing intrusion of political considerations into the religious controversy. In 1560 the conspiracy of Amboise (q.v.) constituted the first outright political effort on part of Protestant sympathizers and Protestants, namely to seize the minor king Francis and do away with the growing influence of the Guises in French affairs. The death of Francis II in 1560 meant the succession of Charles IX, nine years of age, whose mother, Catherine de' Medicis, naturally assumed the regency for her son until the end of his reign in 1574. An edict of January 1562 at St. Germain-en-Laye gave the Huguenots the right to public worship. It was the intention of this edict to restore peace between the two religious factions.

When, in March 1562, Duke Francis of Guise massacred members of a Huguenot congregation at Vassy, and left little doubt that he would see to it that the January Edict of Toleration would be revoked, the first of the wars of religion, which intermittently lasted until 1598, broke out in France. Neither the Catholics nor the Huguenots were militarily strong enough to inflict a decisive defeat upon the other, nor did the Huguenots command, despite their support in the nobility, a large enough cadre of supporters among the French people to make them a major force.

The first eight years of fighting ended in 1570 with the Edict of St. Germain-en-Laye, which granted the Huguenots amnesty and also granted them such impressive concessions, including extensive rights to worship and hold four fortified cities, that the Catholics were determined to undo the recognition of the Huguenots. The St. Bartholomew's Day massacre (q.v.) of August 24, 1572, in which Admiral Coligny (q.v.), the political leader of the Huguenots, was murdered, as were several thousands of other Protestant leaders both in Paris and in the provinces, triggered the resumption of hostilities between the two factions. This coincided with the succession of Henry III (r. 1574-89) (q.v.). Another peace, of Beaulieu (May 1576), gave the Huguenots complete religious freedom in France, though it exempted Paris from this concession.

By that time two new factions emerged in France. One was a group of antimonarchic tracts and writers, notably François Hotman (q.v.), whose *Franco-Gallia*, 1573, not only affirmed the right of resistance against a lawless king but also noted the originally elective character of the royal office which bound the king to a covenantal agreement with the Estates General—and opposition to him in case he failed to follow the covenant. The anonymous *Vindiciae contra tyrannos* (Defense against the Tyrants) developed the notion of a right of resistance against a tyrannical king even more forcefully. Secondly, there were the "politiques" (q.v.), those French, both Catholic and Protestant, who were tired of the primacy of religious issues and controversies in the realm. They were determined to put the common good and the unity of the realm above matters of religion. Jean Bodin (q.v.), whose *Six Books on the Republic* (1576) developed a theory of sovereignty that was to be lastingly influential, was the most outstanding representative of this group of thinkers.

The situation became more complicated when in 1576 Catholic nobles formed the Catholic League, since they had concluded that the king could not be relied upon to defend the Catholic faith. A meeting of the Estates General, overwhelmingly Catholic in its sentiment, voted to have Catholicism as the sole religion in the realm. The Peace of Bergerac (1577) gave the Huguenots freedom of conscience but limited their public worship to those places where the authorities permitted it. The retreat from the stipulations of the Peace of Beaulieu had begun. The last war of religion broke out in 1585, and once again demonstrated the confusion of religion and politics in France. King Henry III was childless and, after the death of his younger brother, the last of the line of the Valois, Henry of Navarre stood next in the line of succession. Navarre was leader of the Huguenots, thus hardly acceptable to a country still overwhelmingly Catholic and also not to the pope. The war of "the three Henries" followed (Henry III, Henry of

Navarre, and Henry of Guise). Initially, Henry of Guise had the upper hand. He entered Paris in May 1588 with the intention of making himself king in place of the unpopular Henry III. Henry III, in turn, resented the power of the Guise and ordered the assassination of Duke Henry of Guise and Cardinal Louis of Guise. With a semblance of retribution, Henry was himself assassinated in 1589. Henry of Navarre now became king and took the title of Henry IV (q.v.). While formally the head of the Huguenots, he was hardly a religious person, a politician and statesman first.

In July 1593 Henry IV abjured his Protestant beliefs and converted to Catholicism, uttering according to tradition the words "Paris is well worth a mass." His conversion to Catholicism was less a traitorous denial of the Protestant faith than it was a wise political move. Henry realized that there was no way that the country could be pacified under a Protestant king. A lengthy struggle was necessary before Henry finally controlled the country. In April 1598 Henry took the decisive step of resolving the religious controversy which had beset the country since the 1520s and had brought bloodshed and ruin to the land ever since the 1560s: the Edict of Nantes (q.v.) granted freedom of worship to the Protestants, allowing them to worship where they had done so in 1596 and 1597. Elsewhere, however, Protestant worship was restricted. Governmental offices were to be open to Catholics and Protestants alike. The Protestants also received a number of fortified places.

Thus, the 16th century and the Reformation ended in France. Protestantism had never been strong enough numerically (it probably comprised no more than 10 percent of the French population) to be victorious, apart from a royal intervention. The Edict of Nantes provided about as much to the Protestants as they could hope for. The monarchy had suffered disastrously but for the remainder of his reign, until he was assassinated by a deranged Catholic fanatic in 1610, Henry laid the groundwork for divine-right absolutism, which made the king supreme in France, and France preeminent in Europe. (See also HUGUENOTS; POLITIQUES; POISSY, COLLOQUY OF.)

FRANCIS I (1494-1547). King of France. Son of Charles of Angoulême and Louise of Savoy, Francis succeeded to the royal throne in 1515. Immensely gifted, Francis lacked the capacity of intense and serious involvement in the affairs of state, was superficial and irresponsible, and was often subject to the influence of his advisors (and mistresses). Francis was unusually enlightened toward the new ideals of the Renaissance and showed in the main an exceptional toleration toward Protestants. His self-image prompted not only major building projects, such as the Louvre in Paris but also ambitious foreign goals, such as French domination of northern Italy. The victorious battle at Marignano in 1515 gave Francis a firm hold on Milan and northern Italy. The following year he concluded a concordat with the papacy which gave the French king almost unprecedented power and authority over the French church. Francis's predilection for foreign affairs meant that no major innovations occurred during his reign. Royal power became more absolute, and the nobility turned into a court nobility dependent on the king for financial support and status.

FRANCK, SEBASTIAN (1499-1542). Author. Born in Donauwörth in South Germany, Franck entered the priesthood but early on encountered Martin Luther (q.v.) and by the mid-1520s had become an ardent partisan of the Wittenberg reformer. He served as pastor in a village near Nuremberg. By 1529, however, he found himself dismayed by what his pastoral experience told him about the absence of any moral impact of the Lutheran Reformation, and he resigned his position. From then on, living in Nuremberg, Strasbourg, Ulm, and Basel, earning his livelihood as soap-maker and printer, Franck published some 20 writings dealing with a variety of religious and historical topics. He translated Desiderius Erasmus's (q.v.) *Praise of Folly* into German, published a collection of proverbs (also following in Erasmus's footsteps), and compiled the *Paradoxa*, a collection of 280 incompatible statements. His foremost work was his *Chronica, Zeytbuch und Geschichtsbibel* (Chronicle and Book of the Tomes and History). This was a universal history which included a telling section, in alphabetical order, on "heretics," which under the guise of objectivity left the reader with the awareness that heresy was not an objective reality but always in the eyes of the beholder. Franck's theological works display an otherworldly spiritualism which eschewed all external manifestations of religion and found comfort in the consciousness of an invisible community of all suffering children of God. Franck died in Basel. (See also RADICAL REFORMATION; SPIRITUALISM.)

FREDERICK III, OF SAXONY (1463-1525). Saxon elector (q.v.). Known as "the Wise," Frederick succeeded to the rule of Electoral Saxony in 1486. Intent on enhancing the power of his territory,

Frederick at first scored certain successes but after the turn of the century his weaknesses became obvious and he suffered a series of setbacks. While Saxony was a wealthy territory, and Frederick himself clever and conscientious, it was small and relatively unimportant. Thus Frederick's possibilities of playing a larger role in German and European affairs were exceedingly limited. It is to Frederick's credit that, when his name was mentioned as a candidate for the imperial crown, he categorically demurred. Frederick's great cause of fame is, of course, the protection he afforded Martin Luther (q.v.), professor at the University of Wittenberg (q.v.), which the elector had founded.

There is no clarity as to why Frederick variously supported Luther, from his insistence that Luther be given a hearing in Germany instead of Rome in 1518 to his hiding Luther on the Wartburg in 1521. No doubt, without Frederick's protecting hand, Luther might well not have survived beyond 1521. Rivalry with the archbishop of Mainz, who was a Hohenzollern, or pride in his university have been cited as reasons, as have been Frederick's sense of fairness and his religious convictions. Frederick died in the heat of the uprising of the German peasants in the Peasants' War (q.v.) in the spring of 1525, which he ominously saw as a sign of divine judgment, after having received Communion under both kinds on his deathbed.

FROBEN, JOHANN (c. 1460-1527). Printer. Froben learned the art of printing in Nuremberg, then moved to Basel, where he acquired citizenship in 1490 and became a member of the printers' guild in 1492 and again in 1522. His first published book was a Latin Bible, which he printed in 1491. Working in cooperation with other printers, especially Johannes Amerbach, Froben steadily gained influence and importance. After 1513 he became the foremost Basel printer, known for the exactness of his printing and the beauty of his fonts. In 1514 Desiderius Erasmus (q.v.) came to Basel to meet Froben, and from that time on the two men were connected by a close friendship. In 1516 Froben published Erasmus's New Testament in the original Greek. With two exceptions, Froben only published in Latin, Greek, and Hebrew. When the impact of the Reformation began to effect the printing business, Froben, undoubtedly under Erasmus's influence, stayed aloof from printing Reformation materials. During the early years of the Reformation Froben published numerous editions of various church fathers, classical authors, and grammars. Over 500 titles have been associated with Froben. (See also HUMANISM; PRINTING.)

FUGGER, JAKOB (1459-1525). Merchant. Originally planning an ecclesiastical career, Fugger left the monastery in 1478 and joined his brother's trading company. After an apprenticeship in Venice, he returned to his hometown Augsburg, expanding the family business of trading, especially in textiles, by investing in silver and copper mining in the Tyrol. He modernized the business, established trading outposts throughout Europe, and organized an extensive intelligence network. Fugger had his own representative at the curia and not only handled the financial aspects of the indulgences (q.v.) sale in Germany but also financed the massive bribes used to assure the election of Charles V (q.v.) as emperor. Fugger vigorously opposed Martin Luther (q.v.) and the new religious teaching. Luther's hearing in 1518 in Augsburg by Cardinal Cajetan took place in Fugger's house. On his deathbed Jakob Fugger reaffirmed his faith in the Catholic church.

— G —

GAISMAIER, MICHAEL (c. 1491-1532). Peasant leader. While virtually nothing is known about Gaismaier's youth, his position as secretary to the governor of South Tyrol allows the conjecture of legal training at a university. Drawn into the maelstrom of peasant unrest against the bishop of Brixen in 1525, Gaismaier quickly assumed the leadership role in the uprising. He helped draw up a list of grievances which reveal the influence of the Reformation. When the uprising had been squelched, Gaismaier fled to Zurich (q.v.) where he drafted his *Landesordnung*, a blueprint for an ideal Christian society. There was to be no social distinction in this society, and the "godly" character of this society was to be scrupulously maintained. After an abortive attempt in 1526 to stage another uprising in the Tyrol, Gaismaier fled to northern Italy, where he was assassinated in 1532. (See also PEASANTS' WAR).

GALLIC CONFESSION. This confession of French Huguenots (q.v.) was adopted at the first national synod of the Reformed (q.v.) churches in France in May 1559. Its 40 articles place the French Reformed church very much into the context of the time, that is, pointed opposition to all forms of Catholicism and also Protestant radicalism. The confession includes a typically Calvinist (q.v.) section on "discipline for the ministry" in which the three offices of pastor, elder, and deacon are identified as biblically required. Modifications of the confession were made throughout the 16th century; late in the 17th century it began to decline in importance.

GARDINER, STEPHEN (c. 1497-1555). English bishop. Gardiner studied and taught at Cambridge University, rising to become master of Trinity Hall. Cardinal Wolsey (q.v.) saw to his appointment in the royal household, where he became deeply involved in King Henry VIII's (q.v.) attempt to secure a papal annulment of his marriage. In 1529 Gardiner was appointed the king's principal secretary and in 1531 he became bishop of Winchester. His stance in the ecclesiastical changes in England (q.v.) in the 1530s was to accept the break with Rome, however reluctantly but to act determinedly to prevent the victory of Protestantism in England. His *De vera obedientia* (Concerning True Obedience) of 1535 argued the case for the king's "headship" in both church and state. The final years of Henry's rule were marked by several publications on topics of traditional theological belief and by his rivalry with Archbishop Thomas Cranmer (q.v.). Under Edward VI's (q.v.) rule, England's steady advance to Protestantism caused Gardiner to be imprisoned twice and to be deprived of his see. While he accepted the *Book of Common Prayer* (q.v.), he defiantly took issue with Cranmer over traditional eucharistic theology, which Cranmer increasingly abandoned. With Mary Tudor's (q.v.) succession in 1553, Gardiner became Lord Chancellor, though with Philip II's (q.v.) increasing influence, Gardiner's importance waned. He presided over the trial of the leaders of English Protestantism but died before the full force of the Marian persecutions had come about.

GENEVA. This town on the westernmost end of Lake Leman in the southeast corner of Switzerland had been the seat of an important bishopric ever since the early Middle Ages. By the early 15th century it had reached the substantial size of 5,000 inhabitants. Increasingly, however, the dukes of Savoy wrested rights from the Genevan bishops, even though the bishopric continued to be significant. In the middle of the 15th century the bishop of Geneva oversaw some 453 parishes and was entitled as imperial ruler to participate in the deliberations of the German diet (q.v.).

The 16th century brought the coming of the Reformation to Geneva. This was associated with the preaching of Guillaume Farel (q.v.) and the city's desire for political autonomy and strengthened economic ties with those cantons that had turned Protestant. A small group of Genevan citizens succeeded in attaining control of the Genevan city council, expelling the representatives of the bishop, of the duke of Savoy, and of many clergy. Formally the Reformation was introduced through several mandates of the Genevan city council: the celebration of the mass was prohibited in August 1535, while the mandate introducing the Reformation in Geneva was issued on May 21, 1536. John Calvin (q.v.), who had passed through Geneva on his way to Germany, was detained by Farel to assist in the consolidation of the work of ecclesiastical reform. He began his biblical lectures early September 1536.

Farel and Calvin set out to draft a church order (q.v.) for Geneva but a conflict with the city council led to their expulsion in April 1538. Calvin was asked to return to the city in 1541 in order to guide the effort of reforming the Genevan church. The Genevan church order, the *Ordonnances Ecclésiastiques* (q.v.) of November 1541, was his work. This church order was revised by Calvin in 1561 and by his successor Theodore Beza (q.v.) in 1576. It ordered not only the life of the Reformed church in Geneva but also of Reformed (Calvinist) churches throughout Europe. Until the end of the 18th century, the Genevan city council played an enormously important role in ecclesiastical affairs in the city. Calvin established the Genevan academy in 1559 with its *schola privata* and its *schola publica*, the former a preparatory school, the latter a university in which, however, only theology was taught for some time. The academy thus proved to be the training ground for Calvinist clergy from throughout Europe.

After Calvin's death in 1564 and the succession of Beza, Geneva suffered numerous setbacks: the decline of its ally Bern, financial difficulties, and determined efforts of the dukes of Savoy to subdue the city. A war between Savoy and Geneva from 1589 to 1593 further weakened Geneva. Savoy made a last attempt to subdue Geneva in 1602 but remained unsuccessful.

GERMANY. For the 16th century the term "Germany" is as difficult to define as it is for subsequent centuries. Legally, the relevant entity was the Holy Roman Empire (q.v.) of the German Nation, which comprised, however, vast lands to both the west and the east of "Germany." Since there was no strong central authority and, in contrast to other European countries, no such strong authority emerged in the course of the 15th and 16th centuries, the defining categories were the various territories and free cities. In the 16th century, the diet (q.v.) of the empire tended to be attended only by the representatives from "German" territories and cities so that in loose approximation one can see its deliberations in the course of the century as reflecting the specific German situation. Generally the term "Germany" is meant to refer to that region in central Europe in which the German language in its various dialects was spoken and thus a measure of cultural cohesiveness prevailed, though even that loose definition does not recognize the reality of Switzerland (q.v.). (See EMPIRE, HOLY ROMAN).

GNESIO-LUTHERANS. The term used for those followers of Martin Luther (q.v.), such as Matthias Flacius (q.v.), Nikolaus Amsdorf (q.v.), Nikolaus Gallus, and Joachim Westphal, who were persuaded that Philip Melanchthon (q.v.) and his followers, such as Justus Menius and Georg Major, had yielded essential Lutheran insights. They were opposed by the Philippists (q.v.), the followers of Melanchthon. The disagreements between these two camps led to several intra-Lutheran controversies, notably the adiaphorist, the synergist, the antinomian, and the crypto-Calvinist controversies. (See also CONCORD, BOOK OF; CONTROVERSIES WITHIN LUTHERANISM.)

GOVERNMENT, ATTITUDES TOWARD. The Protestant Reformation triggered a number of new views of the relationship of the Christian and the political and social order. Intriguingly, Martin Luther (q.v.) reacted against the medieval paradigm in which the church sought to control all of societal life through its precepts and mandates by arguing that human government was an "order of creation," in other words it was not specifically Christian. And even though Luther found the guidelines for good government—unlike his contemporary Machiavelli—spelled out in the Bible (q.v.), especially the Old Testament, he always insisted that that there was nothing distinctively Christian about government, no distinctive Christian manner of governing. Since government had been ordained by God, it was the Christian's duty to support it; even the tyrant had his office from God. John Calvin's (q.v.) views were more appreciative of the role government could play in consort with the church and the establishment of a true biblical social order. Accordingly, in Calvin's Geneva (q.v.) and wherever else Calvin's religion was established, church and state worked hand in glove—for example, in the consistory—to proclaim the greater glory of God both in the sacred and the profane realm.

The Anabaptists (q.v.), part of the Radical Reformation (q.v.), dissented from such mainstream notions categorically. Taking their cue from Jesus' Sermon on the Mount, they concluded that the Christian had to be aloof from the exercise of governmental offices, not participate in warfare, and not swear oaths. While government was ordained by God, it was also part of the kingdom of this world with which the true followers of Jesus could have nothing in common. The attitude toward governmental authority joined in a major issue: the right to resist and even rebel against governmental authority. None of the reformers was willing to argue in support of such resistance on purely political and secular grounds but in varying ways the mainstream reformers, Luther and Calvin, supported the notion that when government persecuted and suppressed the true Christian believers, it was biblically permissible to resist and oppose.

In Luther's case, the argument was a bit more difficult to sustain, given his basic notion that government and religion had nothing to do with each other. When Luther was apprised of certain facts of German constitutional law with respect to the role of the emperor and his relationship to the territorial rulers, Luther concurred that it was indeed permissible to resist the emperor forcefully. With Luther's objections resolved, the League of Schmalkald (q.v.) came into being. In Calvin's case, the issue joined in France (q.v.), where a succession of kings suppressed and even persecuted the Protestant Christians. Calvin argued for a right to resistance which received considerable impetus, when in 1559 the country was thrown into a constitutional crisis over the question of the regency during the minority of the king. (See also RADICAL REFORMATION; TWO KINGDOMS).

GRACE. Generally, grace may be said to mean God's assistance, support, and favor for humans. In Christian history, the controversy between Pelagius and Augustine proved to be incisively significant so that medieval theological history may be said to have been a series of annotations to Augustine. Pelagius had argued that humans, perverted through their own sin and the negative examples of society, need God's "grace" which comes to them in the form of the law and the teaching and example of Jesus. So instructed, the human will is capable of following and doing the good. In contrast, Augustine denied the freedom of the human will to will the good. The effect of the infusion of grace is to change the human will. In subsequent centuries Augustine's teaching was modified into what much later, namely in the 16th century, began to be called semi-Pelagianism, or better semi-Augustinianism (since Augustinian categories pervade the approach), which held that an individual's turning to the offer of grace is a matter of the human will, as is the use of the means of grace in the entire process of salvation but salvation is dependent on grace.

In the late 15th century, this notion was expressed by Gabriel Biel in the pithy sentence that if humans marshal the good within them, God will not refuse his grace. Martin Luther (q.v.) rejected these medieval attempts of juxtaposing divine grace and human effort. It was, according to Luther, the human characteristic to resist grace. The sole ground for salvation was God's grace. This position was expressed in his tract against Desiderius Erasmus (q.v.), entitled *De servo arbitrio* (Concerning the Freedom of the Will), of 1525: grace is God's favor, which cannot become a human quality. Christ is indeed God's grace for humans. Luther's coworker Philip Melanchthon (q.v.) was intent upon allowing the human will to participate in a consenting fashion in the process of conversion, or at least not participate reluctantly. The divergence between Luther and Melanchthon on this topic proved to be the source of one of the several controversies besetting Lutheran theology after Luther's death in 1546.

The eventual resolution of these internal disagreements, the Lutheran *Formula of Concord* (q.v.), affirmed that sinful humans were incapable of preparing themselves for the reception of divine grace but at the same time rejected the notion of the irresistibility of grace. John Calvin (q.v.) echoed Luther's notion that God's grace is personified in Jesus Christ: humans receive such grace, without any precondition, solely as the result of God's eternal election. In the Radical Reformation (q.v.) certain themes of Melanchthon (a bitter enemy of the radical reformers) found expression in that room was provided for the human will to participate in the reception of grace.

In the thought of Thomas Müntzer (q.v.) this was echoed by mystical notions of the central importance of suffering. The Council of Trent (q.v.) offered the Catholic response to the Protestant restatement of a radical Augustinianism in that it rejected both Pelagianism and the Protestant notion of grace as divine favor. The basic sentiment of the Council was to affirm the freely responsible, though not meritorious, participation of humans in the preparation of the freely desired acceptance of the justifying grace.

GRAVAMINA. The Latin term (tr. burden, imposition) refers to the grievances of the German people. In the second half of the 15th century, grievances of this sort were presented regularly, particularly by cities, and can be taken as evidence of the intense anticlericalism of the time. In 1510 Emperor Maximilian asked Jakob Wimpfeling to compile a list of burdens borne by the German nation. Wimpfeling's catalogue of grievances was published in 1519 and contributed to the excitement of the widening notoriety of the indulgences (q.v.) controversy. Most of the specific grievances were directed against Rome. Luther made these grievances an important part of his *Open Letter to the Christian Nobility* in 1520, and at the diet convening in Worms (q.v.) in 1521 the estates apprised the new emperor of the numerous grievances against Rome, whereupon Charles V (q.v.) asked that a list of such grievances be compiled. The matter was taken up at the diet at Nuremberg the following year. (See also REFORM, IMPERIAL).

GREBEL, CONRAD (c. 1498-1526). Anabaptist (q.v.) leader. Son of an influential Zurich (q.v.) family, where his father served on the city council, Grebel studied at the universities of Vienna and Paris, where he was well exposed to Humanist (q.v.) notions. By 1522 he had become an adherent to the new understanding of the gospel and enthusiastically joined Huldrych Zwingli (q.v.) in his study of the Greek New Testament. He became an impatient advocate of speedy and more extensive ecclesiastical reform in Zurich, and at the two important disputations (q.v.) that took place in January and October 1523 in Zurich, Grebel surfaced as an increasingly adamant opponent of Zwingli's process of reform. After efforts to have Zwingli desist from his gradualist approach had failed, Grebel and his associates discovered in Andreas Bodenstein Carlstadt and Thomas Müntzer (qq.v.) two advocates of reform that appeared to be identical to theirs. Grebel's own vision increasingly, in some ways modeled after that of those two other reformers, envisioned a lay church in which only those who confessed to the faith were present, and then were appropriately baptized. In January 1525 Grebel performed the first adult (or believer's) baptism (q.v.) in the Reformation. Grebel then sought to advance his understanding of the gospel in neighboring communities. He was kept in prison in Zurich, where he died of the plague in May 1526. (See also RADICAL REFORMATION).

GREGORY XIII (1502-1585). Pope. In contrast to his predecessor Pius V (q.v.), Pope Gregory XIII (Ugo Boncampagni) enjoyed an unusually lengthy pontificate (1572-1585) but lacked Pius's rigoristic, even ascetic, demeanor. Gregory was sensitive to political considerations and was responsible for changing the office of papal nuncio, which had increasingly become a mere diplomatic post in European capitals, into an instrument of ecclesiastical reform. Since the stipulation of the Council of Trent (q.v.) to establish seminaries proved to be practically impossible in heavily Protestant areas, Gregory pursued a determined policy of supporting existing seminaries in Rome and establishing new ones. He lavishly supported a seminary for the training of Jesuits (q.v.), which quite appropriately was given his name—Collegium Gregorianum. There were also others, such as the Collegium Germanicum, for ministerial students from Germany.

Gregory's greatest cultural achievement was the reform of the Julian calendar, which had become increasingly out of step with the astronomical calendar. Several of Gregory's predecessors had attempted such a calendar reform but had been unsuccessful. The new calendar was introduced in October 1582 by the elimination of no less than 10 days (October 5 through 14). It speaks for the cultural authority of the papacy at the time that all Catholic countries adopted the new calendar immediately; most Protestant countries refused to join—an indication of the Protestant repudiation of all papal authority—even though leading Protestant astronomers, such as Johannes Kepler, vigorously advocated its introduction. A century later, however, all Protestant countries had adopted the new Gregorian calendar.

GRIBALDI, MATEO (d. 1564). Anti-Trinitarian (q.v.). Gribaldi, about whose youth not much is known, was a legal scholar who taught law at various places in southern France and northern Italy. One of his writings on Roman Law saw numerous editions. He became a Protestant, was in contact with John Calvin (q.v.), and after Michael Servetus's (q.v.) execution, which he witnessed, spoke out on behalf of religious freedom. Calvin saw to Gribaldi's banishment from Geneva (q.v.). A period of restless migrations, imprisonment, and Protestant banishment followed. Gribaldi died of the plague at Farges, near Bern, where his deceased wife owned property. Gribaldi, who also wrote two theological works entitled *Religionis Christianae* (The Christian Religion) and *Confessio fidei* (Confession of Faith), espoused an anti-Trinitarian position. It was tri-theist in nature and suggests that the development from the traditional Trinitarian doctrine to the Unitarian Socinianism late in the century was a lengthy one.

GRINDAL, EDMUND (c. 1519-1583). Archbishop of Canterbury. Born of lowly parentage, Grindal was educated at Cambridge where he rose to become fellow and master. Converted to Protestantism during the reign of Edward VI (q.v.), Grindal came to the attention of Bishop Nicholas and was to become bishop of London when Edward died. During Queen Mary's (q.v.) rule Grindal was on the Continent, mainly in Strasbourg, where he played an active leadership role among the English exiles. Upon the succession of Elizabeth I (q.v.) Grindal became bishop of London, even though as one of the Marian exiles (q.v.) He undoubtedly would have preferred a more Protestant religious settlement. He was elevated to archbishop of York in 1570 and of Canterbury in 1576, having shown himself a supporter of the religious settlement, though even more so a determined opponent of conservative Catholic sentiment. His tenure as archbishop fell into the time of an increasing tension over Puritan (q.v.) challenges to the religious settlement of 1559. When Queen Elizabeth ordered him to suppress the so-called "prophesyings," preaching conferences, Grindal refused to comply. He was suspended from his office. Before a determined queen forced him out of office, Grindal died in 1583. (See also ELIZABETHAN SETTLEMENT; PURITANISM).

GRUMBACH, ARGULA VON (c. 1492-c. 1568). Protestant pamphleteer. Born Reichsfreiin von Stauff, Argula von Grumbach grew up in an important but impoverished Bavarian family. She became lady-in-waiting to the Bavarian duchess, under whose tutelage Argula acquired considerable learning. In 1526 she married a Franconian knight by the name of von Grumbach. It is not known when she came into contact with Martin Luther's (q.v.) ideas, which she promptly embraced but by 1523 she claimed that she had read all of Luther's German writings. She corresponded with Luther, Spalatin, and Andreas Osiander (q.v.). Her first publication as an ardent partisan of the Reformation appeared in 1523 and resulted in great suffering for her and her family. Little is known about her later life other than that she was widowed in 1530 and then remarried. At the age of 70 she was jailed in Straubing for reading publicly from "heretical" books, an indication that she persisted in her Protestant notions to the end of her life. (See also PAMPHLETS).

GUNPOWDER PLOT. The succession of James I as King of England suggested to the clandestine English Catholics the hope of improving their state. By 1604, however, Catholic priests were banished and the laws against Catholics reinforced. This prompted an attempt by several Catholics to blow up the Parliament building while both the House of Commons and the House of Lords were in session, and the king, his eldest son, and the royal council were present as well. The plot was discovered and the leaders were arrested and executed. One of the plotters was Guy Fawkes, and a national holiday named after him intensified English hatred of Catholicism.

GÜNZBURG, EBERLIN VON (c. 1455-1534). Humanist (q.v.), pamphleteer, and reformer, Eberlin had entered the Franciscan order but had come under the influence of Martin Luther (q.v.) with the result that he was asked to leave the monastery in 1520. For a brief period in the early 1520s Eberlin published a score of pamphlets, making him by all odds the most prolific writer at that time. In 1521 he published a series of short pamphlets with the title *Die 15 Bundgenossen* (The 15 Comrades in the Covenant), which laid out a comprehensive scheme for the reform of all of society. Undoubtedly familiar with Thomas More's (q.v.) *Utopia*, Eberlin's 11th tract, entitled *Wolfaria*, described a society not unlike that described by More. In 1525 Günzburg entered the service of George II of Wertheim; his literary activities were eminently historical. (See also PAMPHLETS).

— **H** —

HABSBURG. The house of Habsburg dominated German history from the late Middle Ages until the time of Napoleon in that most of the emperors during that time came from the house of Habsburg. Of Alemanic origins in the Aar, Zurich, Alsace, and Freiburg, the Habsburgs began to play a role in imperial politics in the 13th century, when Rudolf I, count of Habsburg, was elected emperor in 1273. The stifling power of the electors (q.v.) made the office unimportant, however. It was not until Frederick III was elected in 1440 (he ruled until 1493) that the dynastic power of the Habsburgs increased with westward expansion into Burgundy (through the marriage of his son Maximilian to Mary of Burgundy). The marriage of Maximilan's son Philip to Juana of Castile added Spain (q.v.) to the Habsburg domain.

To the east, Ferdinand, the younger brother of Emperor Charles V (q.v.), was elected king of Hungary and Bohemia in 1526 upon the death of his brother-in-law Louis. At that time, the possessions of the Habsburgs had reached their 16th-century zenith. Their staunch Catholic sentiment determined much of the course of the Reformation in central Europe. The increasing power of the territorial rulers, notably the electors, did not allow the Habsburg emperors to assert much power in Germany (q.v.). (See also CHARLES V; EMPIRE, HOLY ROMAN.)

HAEMSTEDE, ADRIAAN CORNELISZOON VAN (c. 1525-1562). Martyrologist. Haemstede, originally a priest, was converted to the Reformation cause around 1555 and became pastor of a Reformed (q.v.) congregation in Antwerp. In 1559 he became pastor of the Dutch church in London, where he had fled to escape the increasing persecution in the Low Countries (q.v.). One year later, however, he was excommunicated. Haemstede's lasting achievement is his martyrology, *Historie der Martelaren*, of 1559, which is particularly insightful for the story of the Dutch Reformation martyrs. (See also MARTYROLOGIES).

HANSEATIC LEAGUE. *Hanses* were leagues of cities formed in the 13th century by merchant guilds of towns for greater efficiency in their trade and the protection of their trade. The Hanseatic League was one of the best known of such *hanses*. It numbered at its height some 90 towns and dominated the trade of northern Germany and the Baltic, aided by trade privileges and improved communication and organization. In the 16th century the Hanseatic League suffered a lengthy series of reverses which related to the increasing power of the rulers but also to the reality that, with the European discoveries, the Atlantic Ocean became a more important route than the Baltic Sea.

HEIDELBERG CATECHISM. Alongside Martin Luther's (q.v.) *Small Catechism* and Peter Canisius's (q.v.) catechism, the Heidelberg Catechism stands as one of the most important catechisms of the 16th century. The catechism resulted from the efforts of Elector Frederick III of the Palatinate in the late 1550s to end the theological disagreements between strict Lutherans (q.v.) and the representatives of the Zwinglian/Calvinist (qq.v.) theology. The initial draft was written by Zacharias Ursinus, which was then discussed and in 1563 put into final form. The catechism had three sections (On Human Misery; On Human Redemption; On Gratitude) which dealt with the teaching of the law, the creed, baptism (q.v.), the Lord's Supper (q.v.), the Ten Commandments and the Lord's Prayer. Theologically, the catechism shows the influence of John Calvin (q.v.), though with an appreciation of Luther throughout. The Synod of Dort (q.v.) declared the catechism to be the confession of the Reformed (q.v.) faith. This theological significance can be best understood by its detailed treatment of the various theological loci of importance in the confessional controversies of the end of the 16th century. (See also CATECHISMS).

HELVETIC CONFESSIONS. Two Swiss (Helvetic) confessions (q.v.) of faith were formulated in the 16th century. The first, the *Confessio Helvetica prior*, in 1536, was to serve a purpose similar to that of the Lutheran Augsburg Confession (q.v.) of 1530, namely to constitute a common statement of the beliefs of the Swiss Reformation churches. The confession paralleled the Augsburg Confession in yet another respect. Mostly the work of Heinrich Bullinger (q.v.), the confession offered a somewhat moderate position on the sacrament (q.v.) of the altar, arguing that it was more than a memorial meal. The second Helvetic confession of 1566, the *Confessio Helvetica posterior*, grew out of a personal statement of faith written by Bullinger as a testimonial. On the crucial issue of the sacrament of the altar, the confession embraced the notion of a spiritual presence of Christ in the elements of bread and wine. This proved to be acceptable to both Zwinglian and Calvinist (qq.v.) perspectives and thus became a major factor in uniting these disparate Swiss Reformation branches. The second Helvetic Confession became the most influential Reformed confession in the 16th century, accepted not only in Switzerland (q.v.) but also the Palatinate, Hungary, France (q.v.), Poland (q.v.), and Scotland (q.v.). (See also CALVINISM).

HENRY II (1519-1559). Second son of Francis I (q.v.) Henry became king in 1547. Early in his youth he and his older brother served as hostages for the ransom of their father who had been taken prisoner in the battle of Pavia (1525), which had ended in a disastrous defeat for the French. This experience lastingly influenced Henry. In 1534 he married Catherine de' Médicis, cousin of Pope Clement VII, in a clear attempt to enhance French-papal relations.

Upon his succession to the throne, Henry quickly undertook significant administrative changes but this accomplishment was overshadowed by his incessant hostility against Charles V (q.v.), whom he opposed and confronted whenever possible (to the extent of rendering aid to German Lutherans). He was incisively defeated in 1557 at Saint-Quentin, which led to the final treaty of Cateau-Cambrésis (q.v.) (1559), ending over half a century of conflict between France and Spain (qq.v.).

The emerging Protestant movement in France, grudgingly tolerated by his father, was suppressed by him at every turn. Henry established the *chambre ardente* ("fire chamber"), a special chamber of the Parlement of Paris to try cases of heresy. Henry had proceeded because he had become convinced that the hierarchy was lax in the pursuit of heretics. Opposition of the hierarchy forced him to abolish the "fire chamber" in 1550. Henry died of an injury received at a wedding tournament, leaving the realm (and an enormous debt) to his 15-year old son Francis II.

HENRY III (1551-1589). French king. Third (and favorite) son of Catherine de'Medicis and Henry II (q.v.), last of the Valois kings, Henry took the title of duke of Anjou and—through the influence of his mother—was elected king of Poland in 1573. Already the following year the death of his brother Charles IX prompted his return to France (q.v.) to assume the French crown. His rule was characterized by civil conflict and his own indolent and corrupt life. In 1588 Henry was responsible for the murder of Henry of Guise and his brother. On August 1, 1589, Henry was assassinated by one Jacques Clément, a monk. On his death bed Henry, who was without an heir, named Henry of Navarre, who took the designation Henry IV (q.v.), as his successor.

HENRY IV (1553-1610). French king. Of the house of Bourbon, the sixth son of St. Louis and Jeanne d'Albret, queen of Navarre, Henry was educated as a Protestant and early on distinguished himself in the third French war of religion (1568-1570). In 1572, on the death of his mother, Henry became king of Navarre and married Margaret de Valois, sister of Charles IX. He escaped assassination at the St. Bartholomew's Day Massacre (q.v.) and was responsible for the treaty of Bergerac in 1577, which provided important concessions to the Protestants. He began the seventh war of religion in France in 1580 and, deprived of his right of succession to the French throne by the treaty of Nemours in 1585, undertook the "war of the three Henrys" the following year. The assassination of Henry III (q.v.), who had recognized Henry as his heir in return for support against the Catholic League, made him king but it took a decade to succeed in controlling all of France (q.v.). A major step in that direction occurred in 1593, when Henry converted to Catholicism, realizing that, given Catholic political and military strength, it was not possible to rule the country as a Protestant. Henry's conversion brought the collapse of much of his opposition. In April 1598 Henry issued the Edict of Nantes (q.v.).

Until Henry's assassination by Ravaillac in 1610, the king was able to maintain law and order in the country, despite the fact that the extremists on both sides were unhappy with the provisions of the Edict of Nantes. Guided by his minister Sully, Henry, in the brief years of his tenure, not only undertook financial reform but also established a standing army, furthered a burst of economic energy and activity, and facilitated the conquest of Canada. Thus he laid the groundwork for the dramatic flowering of France in the course of the 17th century. (See also HUGUENOTS).

HENRY VIII (1491-1547). English king. Born in 1491 as the younger son of Henry VII, Henry succeeded to the English throne in 1509 upon the untimely death of his elder brother Arthur. It was to be of fatal significance for Henry's rule that, together with the crown, he also inherited his brother's wife—Catherine of Aragon (q.v.)—who had been married to Arthur in order to cement the diplomatic proximity between Spain and England (qq.v.). In addition, Henry VII handed down to his son a well-filled royal treasury, a relatively prosperous country, and the absence of any opposition.

Thrust onto the royal throne at barely 18 years of age, Henry quickly sought to establish himself as a powerful and magnificent ruler. His artistic patronage deserves some note, whereas his sundry forays into international diplomacy, including the dramatic meeting with Francis I (q.v.) near Calais on the "Field of the Cloth of Gold," remained without larger significance. Henry benefited from the wise and astute counsel of his chief minister Thomas Wolsey (q.v.), who succeeded in combining his devoted service to Henry with a spectacular enhancement of his own role. When Martin Luther (q.v.) and the Reformation began to be important topics on the European Continent, Henry published a weighty defense of the traditional Catholic understanding of the sacraments, a feat (probably aided by

Thomas More [q.v.]) which caused the pope to bestow the title "defender of the faith" on Henry.

Then, in 1527, came the "king's great matter," the "divorce" (q.v.), since Henry had become convinced that his marriage (q.v.) to Catherine had violated divine law and that the papal dispensation which he and Catherine had received in order to marry was invalid. Henry began to seek a papal annulment of his marriage and at the same time a papal dispensation to marry Anne Boleyn. Henry needed this dispensation since he had had sexual relations with Anne's sister, a fact which meant the existence of the same kind of marital impediment as the one that Henry had sought to have the pope remove in his marriage with Catherine. The matter dragged on for several years. Wolsey was unable to provide what his master wanted and was removed from office.

Beginning in 1531 a series of parliamentary maneuvers sought to blackmail the papacy to grant the annulment. When that failed, a series of parliamentary statutes severed the English church from Rome and allowed Henry to "divorce" Catherine (that is, "annul" the marriage) and marry Anne Boleyn in 1533. In September a daughter, Elizabeth (q.v.), was born. But no son was born to Henry and Anne, and in 1536 Anne was accused of adultery and executed. Henry promptly married Jane Seymour, who in 1537 gave birth to a male heir, Edward (q.v.). Jane died soon thereafter, and Henry married Anne of Cleves, in large measure relying on a flattering portrait by the painter Holbein, in 1540. Detesting her looks and personality, Henry had the marriage annulled. He then married Catherine Howard, who two years later was executed for adultery. Henry's last marriage, in 1543, was to Catherine Parr, who not only survived her third husband Henry but married a fourth.

If the continuing marital story of the king forms one element of his life between 1527 and his death in 1547, his role in the Reformation forms another. The break with Rome over the "divorce" from Catherine of Aragon meant, of course, that England had to steer an anti-Catholic course. This is what happened, even though theologically the country under Henry's leadership veered none too far in the Protestant direction. His own religious beliefs were conservative and idiosyncratic. He fancied himself a theologian, though not always one for whom consistency was important. His strongest beliefs appear to have focused on the real presence in the Mass and the priesthood, including its celibacy. Henry held to a high view not only of the royal office but also of himself. He was unfailingly self-confident. Above all,

Henry triggered a revolution, a peaceful one, which the country did not want, but which he undertook without formidable resistance. (See also CRANMER, THOMAS).

HOFMANN, MELCHIOR (1495?-1543). Anabaptist theologian. This Anabaptist leader was probably born in Swabia, in southwest Germany, though the first documented evidence comes from 1523, when he worked as a furrier in Livonia and agitated formidably in support of Lutheran (q.v.) notions. Soon, however, his ideas went beyond Martin Luther (q.v.)—Hofmann rejected the real presence of Christ in the elements and also affirmed the possibility of direct inspiration by the Holy Spirit. Not surprisingly, he was expelled from Livonia in 1526. He began a peripatetic life that took him to Stockholm, where he first began to preach the end of the world to come in 1533; Lübeck; and eventually Strasbourg, a haven for dissident Protestants. Though he saw himself as a true Lutheran, he found that both Catholics and Lutheran theologians opposed his views. While his views on the Lord's Supper (q.v.) were in line with those of the Strasbourg reformers, his full theology in general was not. Moreover, in 1530, Hofmann, having become familiar with the Anabaptists, converted to their belief.

His influential writings helped change early Anabaptism: never a fully homogeneous movement, the Anabaptist movement had nonetheless held to a simple Biblicism that stayed aloof from the two touchy theological issues of the claim to direct inspiration and the insistence of the imminence of the end of the world. Hofmann eloquently and persuasively changed this. He envisioned Strasbourg as the new Jerusalem and saw the throng of 144,000 elect await the second coming in a matter of a few years. Leaving Strasbourg, Hofmann traveled to Holland and North Germany, where he baptized extensively. Convinced that the end would come in 1533 and observing the massive persecution of Anabaptists, Hofmann announced that no more baptisms should be performed and, in 1533, returned to Strasbourg, actively soliciting his arrest by the authorities so as to fulfill his understanding of the Biblical prophecies. He was convinced that Strasbourg would be the spiritual Jerusalem.

The victory of the Anabaptists in Münster (q.v.) in 1534 seemed to confirm his notion of the imminence of the end in light of the victory of the gospel. The debacle in Münster one year later supported his notions but Hofmann continued to languish in Strasbourg, both obstinately and demurely, until his death in 1543. Hofmann's numerous writings focused on eschatology (q.v.). Influenced by late medieval mysticism, Hofmann put his mark on the Melchiorite Anabaptists who combined his eschatological emphasis with spiritualist notions. (See also ANABAPTISM).

HOOKER, RICHARD (1554-1600). Anglican theologian. Educated at Oxford, where he also taught, Hooker became master of the Temple in London in 1585. A prosperous marriage allowed Hooker to devote himself to his literary pursuits. Hooker is best known for his magisterial *The Laws of Ecclesiastical Policy*, the first four books of which were published in 1593, with book five published in 1597. Hooker had not completed the final three books when he died in 1600; they were published in 1648. Hooker argued the most comprehensive defense of the Anglican Church yet. Using the notion of community as his pivotal point, Hooker insisted that the polity of the Church of England with its stress on hierarchical order was but the rational outgrowth of the right of a community to legislate for itself. Hooker's use of arguments from reason as well as Scripture buttressed his case for the authenticity of the Anglican Church. (See also ANGLICANISM; JOHN JEWEL).

HOOPER, JOHN (d. 1555). English bishop. Hooper studied at Oxford, then acquired Protestant views which prompted him to flee England (q.v.) in 1539 for Zurich (q.v.). Upon the succession of Edward VI (q.v.) Hooper returned to England, where he was nominated bishop of Gloucester. Steeped in the Zurich Reformed (q.v.) tradition, Hooper at first refused to wear the episcopal vestments. At the succession of Mary I (q.v.) he was deprived of the episcopal see and, convicted of heresy, burned at the stake in Gloucester.

HÔPITAL, MICHEL DE L' (1505/6-1573). French statesman and Humanist (q.v.). Hôpital's significance lies in the fact that he was, as chancellor of King Charles IX (q.v.), the most important representative of the faction of the "politiques" during the time of the French wars of religion. (See also POLITIQUES).

HOSIUS, STANISLAV (1505-1579). Polish Catholic theologian and cardinal. Hosius was born in Kraków and originally was a devoted follower of Desiderius Erasmus (q.v.). He studied law in Italy and was appointed bishop in 1551. Created cardinal in 1561, Hosius played a crucial role in the final sessions of the Council of Trent (q.v.). He returned to his native Poland (q.v.) in 1564 but returned to Rome in 1569, where he served both as curial official and also as representative of the Polish king. Hosius was also a prolific and insightful author. His summary statement of the Catholic faith, *Confessio fidei catholicae christiana* (Confession of the Catholic Christian Faith), of 1551, saw numerous editions and became one of the important Catholic polemics against Protestantism.

HOTMAN, FRANÇOIS (1524-1590). French jurist and political theorist. Hotman was born in Paris, attended the universities of Paris and Orleans, and early on converted to Protestantism. In 1548 Hotman settled in Geneva (q.v.), where he served as secretary to John Calvin (q.v.), who became his important mentor. In 1555 he was appointed professor at Strasbourg (q.v.). Alongside his career as legal scholar, Hotman soon came to be a tireless pamphleteer for the French Protestant cause in such publications as *Le Tigre* (Tiger of France) of 1560; *Antitribonian* of 1567; and especially his *Franco-gallia* of 1574. While marked by fundamental Protestant premises, these publications also argued stridently against the tyranny of the Catholic Church and of the leading political representatives of the Catholic cause in France (q.v.), such as the duke of Guise. The Saint Bartholomew's Day Massacre (q.v.) served as a crucial catalyst not only for his publishing a detailed account of the massacre and its most distinguished victim, Admiral Coligny (q.v.) but also for the publication of his views on the right of resistance against a tyrannical king or ruler. Hotman argued the originally elective nature of kingship in France. (See also FRANCE; POLITIQUES).

HUBMAIER, BALTHASAR (c. 1480-1528). Anabaptist (q.v.) theologian. Hubmaier was born in Bavaria and studied at the universities of Freiburg (beginning in 1503) and Ingolstadt (1512), where he received the doctorate in theology in the same year. In 1516 he became cathedral preacher in Regensburg. Here he led a bitter attack against the local Jewish community, as a result of which its synagogue was destroyed and the Jews (q.v.) expelled. In 1521 Hubmaier moved to Waldshut in Austria, where he came to accept Reformation notions by 1523 and received enough popular support to cause the Catholic priests in town to leave. The incipient vicissitudes of the peasant uprising triggered a complicated series of events which prompted his temporary refuge in Schaffhausen, where he published his first treatise, *Von Ketzern und ihren Verbrennern* (About Heretics and Those Who Burn Them), a fervent plea for religious toleration (q.v.).

Upon his return to Waldshut he came into contact with the incipient Zurich (q.v.) Anabaptist movement. On Easter 1525 Hubmaier was baptized. Waldshut became embroiled in the Peasants' War (q.v.), with Hubmaier playing an important role in it. When the uprising was crushed, he sought refuge in Zurich, where he was forced to recant his views on infant baptism (q.v.) and expelled from the city. He moved to Moravia, where for about a year he played an important leadership role among the refugee Anabaptists. He found a printer and issued some 16 treatises, which made him the most prolific Anabaptist writer in the first half of the 16th century. His theology, informed by his thorough theological background, was, in fact, the theology of the Reformation without infant baptism, a theological goal he had sought to achieve ever since he embraced Anabaptist notions in 1525. Thus, his last treatise *Von dem schwert* (About the Sword) accepted the right of Christians to bear arms and occupy government offices. In July 1527 Hubmaier was extradited to Austria under charges of his involvement in the uprising of the peasants. He was burned in March 1528, followed by his wife, who was drowned, three days later.

HUGUENOT. The word refers to the French (Calvinist) Protestants. Its origin lies in the German word "eydgenossen" (meaning "Swiss") and suggests the identification of French Protestants with their Swiss/Genevan cradle. The term was first used in 1560 in a pejorative sense but soon became the general label for French Protestants (See also CALVINISM; FRANCE).

HUMANISM. The term refers to the cultural and educational movement that originated in Italy in the late 14th century and within the next two centuries encompassed all of Europe. In the early 16th century, when the Protestant Reformation had its beginnings, Humanism was a formidable educational and even religious movement in central and northern Europe. Virtually all of the first generation of Protestant reformers had been themselves Humanists. Humanists found their inspiration and model for the study of grammar, rhetoric, poetry, history, and moral philosophy in the authors of antiquity. Such Humanistic studies were deemed superior to the traditional scholastic approach to learning, which emphasized logic and debate since they were persuaded that a text needed eloquence to convince. The objective was to persuade, which in turn meant that the Humanists were concerned about practical, rather than speculative, goals.

The Humanist conviction that the authors of classical antiquity (which included certain of the early Christian writers as well) were perfect models led to an ambitious program of editing and publishing ancient texts. The Humanist contribution to the dissemination of the learning of ancient antiquity in early modern Europe through such text editions was truly phenomenal. The invention of movable type in the middle of the 15th century proved to be a crucial tool for the Humanist agenda. While most of such Humanist sentiment tended to be religious, one part of the larger phenomenon of Humanism has been labeled "Christian Humanism" to denote that some Humanists were explicit in their goal to merge classical, biblical, and patristic themes into a program of religious and moral renewal. These Christian Humanists shared with Humanism in general an indefatigable faith in the power of the persuasiveness of the ancient texts. Thus, the return to the Bible (q.v.) and the early church fathers would revitalize both church and theology.

It is understandable that the Christian Humanists did not hesitate to call for reform of the church, and attack its current usages, well before Martin Luther (q.v.). Thus, the *Letters of Obscure Men* was a biting satirical attack on lifeless scholastic theology. The ideals of Christian Humanism were personified in Desiderius Erasmus (q.v.) of Rotterdam, who called his understanding of Christianity the "philosophy of Christ" and pursued his program of renewal through an endless edition of important texts from early Christianity and the Bible and published a summary theology, *Ratio verae theologiae* (The Understanding of True Theology) (1518) and various commentaries on the gospels (*Annotationes* and *Paraphrases*). Most of the early Protestant reformers (with the notable exception of Luther) were steeped in Humanist thought and method, and Erasmus's influence hovers over a great deal of the Reformation, for which the return to the sources, a fundamental Humanist premise, was the linchpin of endeavor. This is particularly true in England (q.v.), where Erasmian notions were the model for much of Henrician and even early Edwardian reform. All the same, it would be erroneous to posit uniformity among the Humanists, even Christian Humanists. They did not share common theological views, only a common approach and method.

HUTTER, JAKOB (c. 1500-1536). Austrian Anabaptist (q.v.) leader. A hatmaker by trade, Hutter traveled extensively and undoubtedly came in contact with Anabaptist ideas in the Tyrol in the late 1520s. Upon the death of Jakob Blaurock, a member of the original Zurich (q.v.) Anabaptist group, Hutter became the leader of the Tyrolean Anabaptists. Intense persecution of the Anabaptist conventicles by the Austrian authorities brought the decision to consider emigrating to Moravia, where a number of nobles had become Protestant and appeared more tolerant. Subsequently, a succession of small groups of Anabaptist refugees found their way to Moravia, to be promptly beset by internal strife which triggered several sojourns by Hutter to Moravia. Eventually, in 1533, he went to stay and asserted himself as leader of the Moravian Anabaptists The worsening of persecution as result of the Münster (q.v.) debacle brought the wholesale expulsion of Anabaptists from Moravia. Hutter himself returned to the Tyrol, where he was arrested in the fall of 1535. After a trial in Innsbruck, he was executed in February 1536. Hutter's significance lies in his role as consolidator of the Anabaptist conventicles in both the Tyrol and in Moravia. While the notion of a community of goods, that is, the notion that among true Christians all things should be held in common, preceded Hutter's arrival in Moravia, his consolidation and leadership meant that this tenet became the hallmark of the Moravian Anabaptists who soon took on his name. (See also HUTTERITES).

HUTTERITES. The term is derived from Jakob Hutter (q.v.), an early leader of the Anabaptist (q.v.) movement in Austria who augmented the general Anabaptist notions of believer's baptism (q.v.) and a literal obedience of Jesus' commands, such as non-swearing of oaths and refusal to governmental service, with an overpowering sense of community. Accordingly, Hutter's followers, driven out of Austria and South Germany to the more tolerant Moravia, settled in communities called *Bruderhöfe*, in which living in a tightly structured community and a sharing of goods, that is communism (q.v.), prevailed. Even though the Moravian Anabaptists had practiced a communal sharing of possessions before Jakob Hutter appeared on the scene, his charismatic leadership skills effected a consolidation of both theology and practice that outlived Hutter's lifetime.

HYMNALS. Precursors of the hymnals of the 16th century were not so much collections of Latin hymns which were used for monastic choirs as collections of hymns, in manuscript form, which were used by confraternities, male and female. The first hymnals in the customary definition were put together by printers to which prefaces by reformers and theologians were added. Since the congregations sang the texts by heart (or in response to a cantor), the purity of the text was not always retained. The Bohemian Unity of the Brethren published a hymnal with some 90 hymns in 1521; that tradition undoubtedly influenced the developed of Protestant hymnals.

The first Reformation hymnal, entitled *Geistliches Gesangbuechlein* (Spiritual Song Book), was published in Wittenberg in 1524. Martin Luther (q.v.) wrote a preface to the 37 hymns, of which 32 were in German, five in Latin. Numerous other hymnals followed, after 1529 some with musical notation. Luther's final hymnal was published in 1545 with 124 hymns and an extensive preface by the reformer. A hymnal published in Strasbourg in 1538, *Neu gesang psalter* (New Psalter for Singing), included all psalms in versified form (together with a number of hymns "sung at many places"), which anticipated the Calvinist (q.v.) tradition of hymnody based on psalms. Hymnals were also published in all European countries in which the Reformation gained a foothold (for example, in Sweden by Olavus Petri in 1526). In the Calvinist tradition it was Clement Marot who published, in 1532, the first psalms in rhymes. John Calvin (q.v.) himself published 13 psalms of Marot, together with eight hymns of his own, in his *Aulcuns psaulmes et cantiques* (Several Psalms and Hymns) of 1539. In 1562, the entire psalter in verse form suitable for singing was published; 49 psalms were rendered by Marot, 10 by Theodore Beza (q.v.). Translated into no less than 22 different languages, this hymnal became the standard Calvinist/Reformed (q.v.) hymnal. The *Geistliches Liederbuch* (Spiritual Song Book), the earliest Anabaptist (q.v.) hymnal, was published in 1529. The standard Anabaptist hymnal was the *Ausbund,* first published in 1564, though earlier hymnals are known.

Understandably, this Protestant emphasis on congregational singing was paralleled by a Catholic effort to publish hymnals. Catholic hymnals included pre-Reformation materials, new hymns as well as Protestant hymns. Chronologically, these Catholic hymnals appeared somewhat later, the first notable example being the *Neu Gesangbuechlein* (New Hymnal) published by Michael Vehe at Leipzig in 1537 with some 52 hymns. (See also CHURCH MUSIC).

— I —

ICONOCLASM. The public destruction and rejection of pictorial representations of figures in the story of salvation. Despite the prohibition of images found in the Hebrew Bible (Exodus 20; Deuteronomy 4) the medieval church was characterized by an abundance of artistic portrayals and sculptures, stained glass windows, and paintings, all of which had the approval of the church. In the Reformation the question of images quickly moved to the fore. Martin Luther (q.v.) was much in favor of images, since he saw in them pedagogical tools for spreading the gospel. His colleague Andreas Carlstadt (q.v.), however, was the first to denounce images in a strict reading of the biblical mandates. This theme was echoed by Huldrych Zwingli and the entire Zwinglian/Calvinist (qq.v.) tradition. This theological perspective meant that, wherever the Reformation was introduced in the context of Zwinglian theology, images, statutes, and paintings were removed from the churches, sometimes quietly and without turbulence, at other times in the form of popular riots. The *Heidelberg Catechism* (q.v.) explicitly took issue with the notion that pictures are the books of the laity (q.v.) and stated that God wished his people to be instructed not by silent ideals but by the living word. This tradition found its way into English Puritanism (q.v.) .

IGNATIUS OF LOYOLA (1491-1556). Don Inigo Lopez de Recalde of Loyola was an officer in the town of Pamplona in 1521 when a French attack seriously wounded him. During a lengthy and painful convalescence, realizing that his military career was over, he became attracted to a kind of religious heroism and experienced a spiritual conversion. A vigil at Montserrat was to signify the end of his former life and his new dedication to the Virgin Mary, in whose service he planned to travel to the Holy Land to convert the infidels. The plague forced a layover at Manresa lasting for half a year during which time he conceptualized the *Spiritual Exercises,* by all odds the most influential devotional piece of writing in the Catholic tradition. A brief visit to the Holy Land (March 1523 to January 1524) convinced him that he lacked the learning and education necessary to realize his objectives successfully.

He began formal studies in theology that lasted from 1526 to 1535, first in Salamanca and from 1528 in Paris. He gathered a small group of like-minded followers who in August 1534 vowed to work in the

Holy Land for the glory of the church and their fellow human beings; if that should prove to be impossible, they would offer themselves to the pope to serve where he assigned them. Military conflict in the Eastern Mediterranean made a voyage to the Holy Land impossible. The small group devoted itself to deeds of Christian mercy.

The new organization, known formally as the Society of Jesus (q.v.), (Jesuits), was formally approved by the pope in September 1540 despite vehement opposition from within the church and the existing monastic orders, especially the newly founded Theatines (q.v.), whose goals and objectives appeared identical to those of Ignatius and his followers. In addition to the customary three monastic vows of poverty, celibacy, and obedience (to the superior) came the vow of a special submission to the instructions of the pope. The strategy employed by Jesuits was, alongside preaching and charitable works, the use of the *Spiritual Exercises* as a means for devotional guidance. Soon the Society of Jesus spread, despite internal opposition from Catholic ranks, in Spain, Italy, and Portugal but also in an important way overseas. Francis Xavier traveled indefatigably to the Far East, visiting India and Japan, and planned to go to China. Ignatius himself died on July 31, 1556. (See also SOCIETY OF JESUS).

IMPERIAL FREE CITIES. The term refers to German cities which were subject not to the territorial ruler in whose territory they were located but were subject directly to the emperor. The empire, officially the Holy Roman Empire (q.v.) of the German Nation, was thus comprised of both ecclesiastical and secular territories and of cities which were subject only to the emperor. These imperial free cities differed in size and rank, the most important ones being Strasbourg, Nuremberg, Augsburg, and Frankfurt. Most of them were in southern Germany. Their number differed but was roughly 80 in the early years of the 16th century. At that time, many of these cities, the typical population of which was probably around 10,000, were characterized by external as well as internal tensions. The external tensions had to with conflicts with the neighboring territorial rulers, who were intent on curtailing the territories of the cities as much as possible. Internal tensions had to with a reordering of governance. Questions and criticism about the precise parameters of the role of the church in civic affairs added their own complexity to the pre-Reformation scene.

Virtually all of these cities turned Protestant, though some not permanently, a fact which has prompted scholars to offer not only the observation that the Reformation was an "urban event" but also to find common characteristics. The suggestion has been made that the Reformation message could be interpreted, mainly on account of Martin Luther's (q.v.) postulate of the priesthood of all believers, as expressive of a communal ideal, both sacred and secular, where traditional differentiations, such as between clergy and laity (q.v.), were removed. Also, attention has been called to the presence of social tensions in virtually all cities, with the notion that the proclamation of the Reformation merged with the effort to resolve these tensions. It must be noted that the cities obviously were characterized by greater literacy; that communication of ideas was easier, since more direct; and that charismatic leadership figures were bound to have an impact on their communities.

INDEX OF PROHIBITED BOOKS. In the final period of the Council of Trent (q.v.) a list of prohibited, that is heretical, books was compiled by the council members. The dramatic proliferation of the printing (q.v.) press and the number of published books meant that a guide to this veritable flood of publications was considered necessary, both to monitor actual publications and to identify those which were considered heretical. It stipulated that the books on this index were not to be read by the faithful. The famous index was thus a Catholic initiative, even though toward the end of the 16th century Lutheran (q.v.) authorities were so concerned about the dangers of Calvinism (q.v.) that a Lutheran index was compiled at the time.

INDULGENCES. An indulgence, according to Catholic teaching, is the remission (complete or partial) by the church of temporal punishment (opposed to the eternal punishment the sinner suffers in hell) for sins that have been confessed and forgiven in response to the fulfillment of certain conditions. This is made possible through the treasure of merit which has been acquired by Jesus, Mary, and the saints. The conditions to be met in order to qualify for an indulgence could be the reciting of the Rosary or the Lord's Prayer, going on a pilgrimage, or contributing to a worthy cause. In the later Middle Ages this practice, which required the truly penitent to be contrite over his or her sin, fell into abuse and misunderstanding. Increasingly, indulgences were thought to effect, through a payment of money, forgiveness of sins.

INDULGENCES CONTROVERSY. This controversy may be said to have constituted the beginning of the Reformation in that it was the sale of indulgences (q.v.) by Johann Tetzel (q.v.), a Dominican friar, which triggered Martin Luther's (q.v.) Ninety-five Theses. These were written in reaction to Tetzel's preaching. Since there was no normative doctrine of indulgences, Luther's exploration of what should be proper biblical teaching was not only in keeping with the role of university faculty at the time but also could be seen as an important step in helping clarify the topic. Tetzel's indulgences sale, in turn, was related to a jubilee indulgence announced by Pope Leo X, with the proceeds meant to allow the construction of a new basilica of St. Peter in Rome. Archbishop Albert of Brandenburg had authorized the sale in his territories in return for having received, with papal dispensation, the prestigious archbishopric of Mainz with which he also became one of the seven German electors (q.v.). The doctrine of indulgences had not as yet been defined by the church but evidently Tetzel's preaching, eloquent as it was, suggested a very simple manner of attaining forgiveness of sins in return for a purchase of an indulgence.

The indulgences controversy broke out when Luther drafted a set of Ninety-five Theses in late October 1517 that were meant to demonstrate the controversial aspects of that teaching and practice. Having been sent both to Albert and also to several friends, they quickly triggered two developments. One was the commencement of formal proceedings in Rome to ascertain Luther's orthodoxy. Secondly, and every bit as important, a theological controversy erupted in which defenders of the practice, or at least of its theological presuppositions, were opposed by Luther and his followers. While conducted in Latin, and thus confined to theologians, the controversy quickly began to have a ripple effect, drawing wider circles of people into its orbit. Luther contributed to this popularization by publishing a large number of German-language pamphlets (q.v.) which were repeatedly reprinted and were the major cause for his increasing popularity.

INQUISITION. This institution (from the Latin "to inquire") had its origins in the Middle Ages and was intended as an ecclesiastical body monitoring the rightness of belief of the faithful. Before the Reformation a variety of regional inquisitions had begun to be formed and had made their mark. The Spanish Inquisition, or Holy Office, was established by Ferdinand and Isabella for the purpose of dealing with the Jews (q.v.), specifically the behavior of those who had formally converted to Catholicism. Portugal established a similar Holy Office in the 1530s. The coming of Protestant notions to Spain (q.v.) at the same time gave the Spanish Inquisition a new field of endeavor, even though the Protestant threat evidently was never thought to be as serious as that of the Judaizers, that is, of those Spanish Jews who had converted to Christianity but were supect of having retained their Jewish beliefs and practices. The charge to the Inquisition was to root out all heresy. The Spanish Inquisition was headed by a grand inquisitor, nominated by the king and approved by the pope. A high council, or *consejo supremo*, was chaired by the grand inquisitor and consisted of five members and additional advisors, generally members of the Dominican order. In important cases, this council served as the court which tried them.

The Roman Inquisition was established in 1542 for the same purpose, namely to eradicate heresy in Italy. It was presided over by a committee chaired by the pope and consisting of six cardinals. Both inquisitions conducted their proceedings in secret. The accused were not able to confront their accusers, though they were given legal counsel. Apart from a few dramatic miscarriages of justice, the proceedings took place with grave determination but with meticulous care. Like 16th-century justice in general, the Inquisition was confident that the use of torture would reveal the truth.

INSTITUTES OF THE CHRISTIAN RELIGION. The first edition of what is probably the most famous Protestant theological writing in the 16th century was published in 1536, when its author, John Calvin (q.v.), was barely 26 years old. Calvin meant his book to be not more than a catechism (q.v.) offering a systematic summary of the new Protestant faith. The first edition was fairly modest in size. Calvin continued to work on the *Institutes* until the final, third, edition, significantly enlarged, was published in 1559. The reality of a systematic theology from Calvin's pen has prompted the conclusion that all of Calvin's thought can be found in the *Institutes*. This is certainly correct, say in comparison with Martin Luther (q.v.) from whose pen no similar treatment exists. By the same token, however, Calvin's extensive biblical commentaries are enormously important for the full understanding of his thought.

The 1536 edition of the *Institutes* covered six chapters. Four of these dealt with the Law, the Creed, the Lord's Prayer, and the sacraments (baptism and the Lord's Supper [qq.v.]). The remaining two chapters were controversial in nature, dealing with the five Catholic sacraments, while the last chapter on "Christian Liberty" dealt with issues of the relationship between the church and society. Calvin constantly revised and enlarged the *Institutes,* which appeared in several French and Latin editions during his own lifetime. The definitive edition, of 1559, was over five times the size of the original edition. It was divided into four "books," which in a general way follow the structure of the Apostles' Creed, dealing with the Father, the Son, the Holy Spirit, and the church. (See also CALVINISM).

INTERIM. After his victory over the League of Schmalkald (q.v.) in 1547, Emperor Charles V (q.v.) saw himself in a position to accomplish two major policy goals as emperor—to return the empire (q.v.) to ecclesiastical unity and to reform the administrative structure of the empire so as to give more power to the emperor. A new diet, to be convened in Augsburg in November 1547, was to realize both objectives. The diet, which was in session until the end of June 1548, heard the emperor's proposal for creating an imperial league (*Reichsbund*) to deal with financial and military matters, which were of general concern and import, with a significant role provided for the emperor. Understandably, the estates were not exuberant about the emperor's proposal but at first did not openly confront Charles. Rather, they presented numerous counterproposals with the result that no action was taken on Charles's proposal. As regards the religious controversy, Charles V had also presided over the diet in Augsburg (q.v.), back in 1530, when the issue had been the orthodoxy of the Protestants. That topic was no longer on the agenda.

The emperor's victory in the War of Schmalkald (q.v.) seemed to give him the power to impose his will on the defeated Protestants. Charles wisely thought that an interim arrangement would best achieve his real goal of forcing the Protestants back into the Catholic Church. The interim religious solution, worked out by a committee of moderate theologians, offered some theological concessions to the Protestants. The Augsburg Interim affirmed, in its 26 articles, traditional Catholic doctrine (such as the seven sacraments and transubstantiation), though it allowed Communion under both kinds and a married clergy. The emperor had originally intended to have this interim resolution be normative for both Catholics and Protestants; the adamant resistance of the Catholics meant, however, that in the end the recess of the diet declared the Interim applicable only to Protestants.

As matters turned out, Charles's well-meant compromise proved counterproductive. Catholics were convinced that Charles had offered too many concessions, while the Protestants felt that not enough note had been taken of their positions. Legally, the emperor's solution was embodied in an imperial law. Charles failed in his effort, and the reasons were several. For one, he had underestimated the dynamic resistance of the Protestants. Demonstrably, the Protestant clergy had shown themselves superior to Catholic priests in the exercise of the ministerial office, and when the Lutheran clergy were expelled from their positions, there simply were no well-trained Catholic priests to take their place. In North Germany, the city of Magdeburg defied the emperor outright; efforts to subdue the city were unsuccessful, which only strengthened the resistance against the Interim in Protestant quarters.

Above all, there was the deep conflict between emperor and pope. Each distrusted the other. The emperor was annoyed because Pope Paul III (q.v.) did not support his strategy to resolve the religious controversy. Charles V wanted the ecumenical council which had just convened in the North Italian town of Trent to deal with issues of church reform first and with theological points of controversy later. Conversely, the pope was dismayed because Charles seemed to torpedo—with his unilateral efforts to resolve the religious controversy in Germany (q.v.)—the strategy that was being pursued by the Council at Trent (q.v.). Once again, the Catholic camp lacked unanimity, prompting Paul to dissolve his alliance with Charles and withdraw the papal troops which had been an important contingent in the emperor's military coalition against the League of Schmalkald. The discussions at Trent, particularly over the issue of justification, proved to be a thorn in the emperor's flesh. The council deliberated for seven months, finally in December agreeing on a statement which, while a winsome compromise of the various Catholic views and perspectives, seemed to be categorically anti-Protestant. Charles was convinced that the Protestants would never accept decrees of the council promulgated without their involvement and participation.

Then, in March 1547, the council fathers decided to move from Trent to Bologna—from an imperial to a papal territory—which not only meant that any Protestant presence at the council was most unlikely but also that the emperor's strategy of using the council to placate the German Protestants had become outrightly impossible. At the same time, Charles lodged a formal protest with the pope demanding the return of the council to Trent. The Interim was widely ignored (the Catholic territories and cities had been, for obvious reasons, exempted from its provisions): in South Germany it was more or less observed, while North German Protestant territories vehemently resisted its introduction. The conspiracy of territorial rulers to oppose the emperor's plans for imperial reform weakened the emperor's position dramatically and by 1552 new negotiations were underway to provide legal recognition for Protestants. This rendered the Interim invalid.

— J —

JEANNE OF NAVARRE (Jeanne d'Albret, 1528-1572). Queen of Navarre. Daughter of Henry d'Albret and Margaret d'Angoulême (sister of King Francis I [q.v.]), Jeanne was to be betrothed to the duke of Cleves at the insistence of Francis I for political reasons in 1540 but her adamant (and courageous) opposition (together with a changed international situation) brought the matter to naught. Jeanne married Antoine of Bourbon in 1548 who, despite some public vacillation, stayed a loyal Catholic. Jeanne, in turn, publicly acknowledged her Protestant conviction in December 1560. She established Protestantism in Béarn, prompting her excommunication by the pope, whereupon intriguingly the French crown came to her support, against papal interference with the Gallican liberties of the church. Jeanne's conversion triggered a rebellion of her Catholic subjects who, during the Third War of Religion (1569-1570), were supported by the king. Jeanne died of tuberculosis in 1572, a few weeks before the wedding of her son Henry (whom she desperately wished to see on the French throne) and Marguerite of Valois, daughter of Henry II and Catherine de' Médicis, and the Saint Bartholomew's Day Massacre (q.v.). She was thus spared what might have been her greatest disappointment. Jeanne was a devout Christian who also sought to express her faith in literary form.

JESUITS. Formally known as the Society of Jesus (Societas Jesu). (See also IGNATIUS OF LOYOLA; SOCIETY OF JESUS).

JEWEL, JOHN (1522-1571). English theologian and bishop.

Educated at Oxford, where he was exposed to English Humanism (q.v.) and Reformation thought. During Mary's rule Jewel served, much to his later dismay, as notary at the trial of Thomas Cranmer (q.v.) and Nicholas Ridley but then emigrated to the Continent. With Elizabeth I's (q.v.) succession Jewel was appointed bishop of Salisbury. Most of his energies were devoted from then on to his diocese, though not without his having preached, in November 1559, an important sermon in which he turned the customary anti-Catholic polemic on its head: he challenged the Catholics to prove that their teachings and practices had in fact been known by the church during the first six centuries. Out of this sermon grew his famous *Apologia Ecclesiae Anglicanae* (Apology for the English Church), published in 1562, in which his patristic learning found persuasive expression for the legitimacy of the emerging Anglican (q.v.) tradition.

JEWS. The role of the Jews in late medieval Europe differed both in different countries and over time. The numerous pogroms at the time of the crusades, which marked in a real sense the beginning of European anti-Semitism (q.v.), had given way to various manners of royal protection, generally through the payment of subsidies. The failure of the Holy Roman Empire (q.v.) to develop a meaningful central political authority meant, as regards the life of the Jews in Germany, that one cannot speak of a German history but must differentiate between specific territories and cities.

By the early 16th century the European-wide situation was characterized by the fact that most European countries, notably Spain (q.v.), as is so well known, had expelled the Jews. This was also true in Germany, where most territories expelled the Jews in the second half of the 15th century, as did many of the imperial cities. Thuringia expelled the Jews in 1401, Austria in 1421, Bavaria in 1442, Brandenburg in 1510, to name just a few instances. Of the cities, Cologne expelled its Jews in 1424, Zurich in 1436, Constance in 1440, Nuremberg in 1499, and Regensburg in 1519. Major areas of Germany were thus closed to Jews; only a few free imperial cities continued in their toleration—notably Frankfurt, Worms, and Prague. However, efforts to expel them from the entire empire failed. This wave of expulsion triggered an eastward migration of Jews to Poland, even as it forced other Jews to live under destitute conditions in rural areas in Germany.

Once the Reformation controversy had erupted, Jews—never really a pivotal part of the theological discourse—moved further to the margin. There was a pogrom in Ingolstadt in 1519 in which the future Anabaptist (q.v.) theologian Balthasar Hubmaier (q.v.) participated, and Martin Luther (q.v.) wrote a pamphlet in 1523 entitled *That Our Lord Jesus Christ was born a Jew*, a fairly gracious effort on the reformer's part to persuade the Jews—now that the true gospel had been restored—to convert to Christianity. A few years before his death, however, a more vitriolic tract issued from Luther's pen—*Concerning the Jews and their Lies*—in which the two strands of anti-Judaic polemic noted above were rather stridently fused. Luther fiercely argued the theological inadequacy of the Jewish religion but at the same time reiterated the traditional moral strictures and echoed the ruthless measures to be taken against them: burning their synagogues, taking their books, forcing them to do manual labor, etc. Luther recommended as the ideal solution the expulsion of the Jews. The reformer Martin Bucer (q.v.), in a theological brief for Landgrave Philip of Hesse (q.v.), had been more open to the possibility of a Jewish presence and had argued for toleration (q.v.) albeit under severe restrictions.

It has been pointed out that Luther stopped short of actually insisting on expulsion, though it seems clear that this was Luther's hope. This polemic was also echoed by Catholic theologians, such as Johann Eck (q.v.), as well as by other Protestant theologians. In short, no significant change in Christian attitudes toward Jews occurred in the Reformation and the 16th century.

The limitations placed on Jewish life were numerous and burdensome. Nowhere were Jews able to be citizens, a double bind situation, since this impossibility was juxtaposed with the charge that Jews did not contribute to the commonweal. Jews were not allowed to own real estate nor were they allowed to engage in commerce. The late 15th century saw the establishment of separate living quarters for Jews—the ominous term "ghetto" made its appearance—which segregated the Jews in one part of town, with gates that were locked in the evening and strict regulations about curfew hours, etc. Jews could engage in financial ventures. Since Christians were not allowed to charge interest for loans—a stipulation which was, however, mildly circumvented, Jews had no real competition in this regard but promptly found themselves ubiquitously chided for being usurers. The political protection they bought with subsidies generally avoided outright persecution and pogroms. Still, the periods immediately preceding and following the Reformation were not completely devoid of violence.

Thirty-six Jews were executed in Berlin in 1510 for allegedly desecrating the host, a charge that was fairly common in the medieval period. Jews labored not only under the theological indictment that they had failed to recognize Jesus as the Messiah but also under various moral strictures (such as usury).

In addition, the impact of the Ottoman onslaught at the southeastern border of the empire gave rise to the allegation that Jews maintained secret contacts with the Turks. At the diet at Speyer in 1540, a charter of privileges, the most favorable granted to Jews to date, sought to put an end to expulsions in the empire, forbade blood libels, eased the obligation to wear a distinctive badge on the outer garment, and permitted charging higher rates of interest than was customary among Christians. Even though the provisions of this charter were not effectively implemented, they constituted an important milestone in the history of the Jews in Germany.

The provisions of the Peace of Augsburg (q.v.), with their potentially adverse impact on Jews, seem to have had no effects on them. While some expulsions did continue to take place, such as in Bohemia, no Protestant territory expelled Jews in the 16th century, with the exception of electoral Saxony, and there only briefly. The overall climate slowly began to change. Cities and territories promulgated "*Judenordnungen*," or "orders pertaining to Jews," that offered a semblance of legal protection. The fundamental underlying assumption, however, that society had to be uniformly Christian was not challenged, nor was the corollary notion that the presence of Jews in such a Christian setting constituted the acceptance of blasphemy. (See also INQUISITION).

JOSEL OF ROSHEIM (c. 1478-1554). Jewish leader and spokesperson for Jews in the empire (q.v.). Josef ben Gershon (usually called Joselman or Josel of Rosheim) was born in Hagenau in Alsace. His father, personal physician to Emperor Maximilian I, had taught Hebrew to Johannes Reuchlin (q.v.), the eminent Christian Hebraist of the age. Josel became a rabbi, and at the age of 31 (1509) he was made the spokesman for the Jews (q.v.) in his district in Alsace, where he first demonstrated both his negotiating and interpersonal skills. Whenever, from that time onward, Jews were threatened with expulsion or persecution in South Germany, Josel was actively involved as negotiator on their behalf. During the German Peasants' War (q.v.) Josel showed himself equally adept and successful in negotiating with the peasants on behalf of some cities and his co-religionists. Josel succeeded in having King Ferdinand undo an expulsion order for Jews in Alsace and deflect the charges made near Bratislava that Jews had ritually murdered a Christian infant.

These successes elevated Josel to the role of spokesman for the Jews in Germany (q.v.). At the diet at Augsburg (q.v.) in 1530, Josel was a participant in a public debate with one Antonius Margaritha, a converted Jew who had written a devastating book about Jews, and succeeded in obtaining letters of protection and charters of rights from Emperor Charles V (q.v.) that aspired to a uniform legal situation for all Jews in Germany. The resistance of the territorial estates made the emperor's concurrence invalid and practically worthless. In 1544, however, Josel succeeded. A charter of privileges promulgated at the diet in Speyer that year assured Jews of safe conduct, forbade expulsions and blood libels, gave them legal standing before imperial courts, and permitted them to charge higher interest rates than did the Christians. This latter provision was in recognition of the extensive economic restrictions placed upon Jews.

JULIUS III (1487-1555). Pope. Born Giovanni Maria Ciocchi del Monte, he studied law at Perugia and Sienna and in 1542 was entrusted with the preparatory work for the planned Council at Trent (q.v.). The following year he was made cardinal, and when the council convened in Trent in December 1545, he served as the first presiding officer. The continuing tensions between Emperor Charles V and Francis I (q.v.) forced Julius to call a recess for the council, which disheartened him and also lessened his determination to undertake reform in the church. He did support the establishment of the Collegium Germanicum in Rome in 1552 for the training of German priests and sought ways to restore monastic discipline.

— K —

KAPPEL, BATTLE AND WAR OF (1531). The introduction of the Reformation in Zurich (q.v.) and elsewhere in Switzerland (q.v.) created enormous tensions with the Catholic cantons in which long-standing problems came to the fore again. Both Zurich and the Catholic cantons concluded political alliances to strengthen their own cause. In June 1529 conflict broke out between the Protestant and the Catholic cantons in which fighting was averted when Zurich's ally Bern indicated that it would support Zurich only if it had been attacked by the Catholics. Each side was suspicious that the other was about to attack and use military means to resolve the conflict. Huldrych Zwingli (q.v.), the Zurich reformer, unsuccessfully pursued plans of a grandiose anti-Habsburg alliance since Habsburg (q.v.) was the strong protector of the Catholic cantons.

In January 1531 the Catholic cantons went on record that they could not co-exist with the Protestant cantons. In response, Zwingli sought to get Zurich to declare war on the Catholics. But only an economic blockade was agreed upon. The reaction of the Catholic cantons was to invade Zurich territory. The battle at Kappel took place on October 11, 1531, when the Catholics inflicted a disastrous defeat on the Protestants. The (second) peace of Kappel, of November 1531 essentially affirmed the stalemate that existed in the Swiss Confederation with respect to the religious issue. Neither side had proved politically strong enough to impose its will on the other, and the old and new faiths were compelled to coexistence. Zwingli, who had accompanied the Zurich forces into the battle as a chaplain, died on the battlefield. Thus, the defeat of Zurich also deprived the city of its religious leader. (See also SWITZERLAND).

KNOX, JOHN (1513-1572). Scottish reformer. Born in Haddington, in East Lothian, Scotland (q.v.), educated at the University of Saint Andrews, Knox was a lawyer and priest who, undoubtedly under the influence of the first Scottish reformer, George Wishart, was converted to Protestantism. When Wishart was burned for heresy in 1546, a group of his supporters, who were adamantly pro-English, murdered Cardinal Beaton, whom they held responsible for Wishart's death, hanging the cardinal's body over the castle wall. Knox preached a sermon to the assassins on Easter 1547 in the castle, and when the French came to the aid of the anti-English party and occupied the castle a few weeks later, Knox was sent to the galleys for two years. On his release, he went to England (q.v.), where he came to play an important role in the latter stages of reform under Edward VI (q.v.), including influential changes in the 1552 edition of the *Book of Common Prayer* (q.v.). The succession of Mary Tudor (q.v.) made him one of the Marian Exiles (q.v.) who bombarded England with vehement Protestant diatribes. Unable to return to England upon Mary's death, Knox found his way to Scotland, where he rallied the adamant Protestants, who realized their initial goals of reforming Scotland in the Reformation Parliament of the summer of 1560. His fiery and intense proclamation of the Calvinist (q.v.) gospel continued unabated, and he was a contributor to *The First Book of Discipline*.

— L —

LAITY. A major distinctive feature of the Protestant Reformation was the emphasis on the laity. Against the Catholic distinction of an indelible priesthood as a sacramentally ordained order, the Protestant reformers argued for what they called the priesthood of all believers. The traditional distinction between clergy and laity was repudiated by the reformers in favor of a communal definition of the church, where all were "priests" and where certain members were called to serve the function of proclaiming the gospel and administering the sacraments (q.v.). This theological affirmation resonated in the practical course of the Reformation in that the proclamation of the reformers deliberately addressed itself to the common people, the laity. A large number of the *Flugschriften* (pamphlets [q.v.]) were addressed explicitly to the laity and made laymen, peasants, artisans, unlearned though they were, the arbiters of profound theological disputes.

This emphasis on the laity led to the notion of having the minister called by the congregation rather than appointed by the bishop. While it did not always work out this way in practice, and governmental authorities quickly assumed control over congregational affairs, with the Protestant pastor in this regard not too distinguishable from the Catholic priest, the notion of important lay participation in ecclesiastical affairs was always emphatically affirmed. In the Calvinist-Reformed (q.v.) tradition, the office of the elders (presbyters) vouchsafed the continuing and strong influence of the laity on congregational affairs. In the Anabaptist (q.v.) wing of the Reformation the entire 16th century was characterized by the lack of a formally trained clergy; rather, the ministers of the Anabaptist congregations were chosen (in the Hutterite [q.v.] and often in the Anabaptist congregations by lot) from within the congregations.

LATIMER, HUGH (c. 1485-1555). English reformer and polemicist. Latimer studied at Cambridge, where he received his master's degree in 1514. He was ordained to the priesthood at that time and remained a loyal Catholic until the mid-1520s. His conversion to Lutheranism (q.v.) caused problems but his eager support of Henry VIII's (q.v.)

position in the "divorce" (q.v.) brought him the king's favor. Promoted to bishop of Worcester in 1535, he soon thereafter was forced to resign when his Protestant sentiment was out of step with Henry's disposition to have England (q.v.) steer a moderate religious course. Latimer's eloquence as preacher, which emphasized the social and moral dimensions of the true Christian faith, made him an important figure during the Edwardian Reformation. He was arrested soon after the succession of Mary Tudor and burned at the stake in 1555.

LEIPZIG DEBATE. The major theological debate in the early Reformation was held at Leipzig from June 27 to July 16, 1519. The occasion itself was to resolve in an actual debate the months of theological controversy that had been going on, as a result of Martin Luther's Ninety-five Theses, between Johann Eck and Andreas Carlstadt (qq.v.) on the topics of the authority of Scripture and free will. Duke George of Saxony agreed to serve as host of the debate, which began with a week of exchanges between Eck and Carlstadt. Eventually Luther was drawn into the debate. Skillfully drawn out by Eck, Luther observed that the pope exercised his authority by human and not divine right and that even church council could be in error. This statement marked a major milestone in the identification of the Bible (q.v.) as the sole norm of Christian belief. The universities of Erfurt and Paris were asked to render their judgment on who had won the debate but neither came forth with a judgment.

LEO X (1475-1521). Pope. Giovanni de' Medici, the future Pope Leo X, was born the second son of Lorenzo the Magnificent, ruler of the Florentine Republic. As the second son, he was destined for an ecclesiastical career. In 1492 he was elevated to the College of Cardinals. Exiled from Florence in 1494, he traveled in northern Europe for six years, returning to Italy and Rome in 1500. Assuming increasingly important ecclesiastical offices, Giovanni was elected pope upon the death of Pope Julius II in 1513, and he was promptly ordained to the priesthood. Unlike his predecessor, who had engaged in virtually continuous political and military ventures, Pope Leo X was irenic and preoccupied with matters of cultural import. With lavish expenditures Leo X set out to turn Rome into the cultural center of Europe. The basilica of St. Peter's and the Vatican Library are two enduring monuments to his efforts.

As far as ecclesiastical affairs were concerned, the Fifth Lateran Council overshadowed the first five years of Leo's rule. Convened to attend to pressing matters of church reform, the council received little, if any direction and impetus from him. Leo seemed more interested in appointing family members to important church posts. He was also intent on making the Papal States predominant in Italian affairs. This meant that, upon the death of Emperor Maximilian I, Leo was unwilling to support either of the two major candidates, Charles (q.v.) of Spain and Francis (q.v.) of France and settled on Elector Frederick of Saxony instead. By that time (1519) the indulgences controversy (q.v.) and Martin Luther (q.v.) had begun to gain notoriety. Leo did not take the matter seriously but was persuaded that swift and categorical action, ending in Luther's excommunication, was the best strategy to maintain concord in the church.

LITERACY. Gutenberg's invention of movable type around 1450 began a revolution in book publishing in Europe which was accompanied by an increased emphasis on education. Books are only useful to readers. While the Catholic Church had dealt with the formidable problem of communicating the Christian gospel to a populace essentially illiterate through the avenues of various non-verbal means of communication (ornamentation of churches, the body language of the Mass, etc.), the new ease of book printing (q.v.), together with the revival of ancient learning found in Italian Humanism (q.v.), made literacy an important goal. Quantitative data about the extent of literacy in early 16th century Europe are impossible to come by. Estimates are that some 90 percent of the people were indeed illiterate. However, in the course of the 16th century major strides were made, not only because of the Protestant emphasis on the priesthood of all believers but also because of the universal emphasis on schools and education triggered by Humanism. (See also PRINTING).

LITERATURE. There can be little doubt that the Reformation of the 16th century was the foremost literary stimulus throughout Europe. Gutenberg's invention of movable type had prepared the way in that throughout Europe there was an increasing proliferation of printed materials. Literature became the pivotal vehicle for intellectual discourse, with the Reformation playing a major role. Since an increasing number of publications were in the various vernaculars (it was one thing to be able to read, another to read Latin), a parallel consequence was the emergence of discourse in the national languages. The cities played a central role, since literacy was most widespread there.

All European countries and all genres of literature were influenced by the Reformation. Foremost, of course, were the writings of individual reformers and Humanists (q.v.), such as Martin Luther, John Calvin, Desiderius Erasmus, and Thomas More (qq.v.). Their literary output was phenomenal. A second category of literature was the pamphlet (q.v.), generally written in the vernacular, often anonymously or from the pens of little-known and even unknown authors. While most of the pamphlets were in straightforward prose, some used other literary devices, such as dialogues or verse. While not equal in output to Protestant publications, nonetheless Catholic authors published prolifically. The use of hymns (q.v.) in the 16th century must also be mentioned. The common people delighted in singing, evidenced by the numerous new compositions and verses alongside translations of late medieval hymns. A popular literary form was the fable, which allowed the author to combine a distinct moral with an interesting narrative. Later in the century, in Germany, a whole genre of literature used the term "devil" to write about certain vices (such as the gambling devil, the drinking devil). The 16th century also saw an increased production of drama and prose works.

LORD'S SUPPER. Disagreement over the meaning and significance of the Lord's Supper (also called Communion or the Eucharist [q.v.]) proved to be the major issue dividing the Protestants. Apart from Martin Luther's (q.v.) repudiation of the Catholic sacramental system in his tract *The Babylonian Captivity of the Church*, 1520, the opening salvo was fired by a Dutch physician, Cornelis Hoen, who in a letter to the Zurich reformer Huldrych Zwingli (q.v.) suggested in 1523 that the words of institution ("this is my body . . . this is my blood") were to be interpreted symbolically to mean "this symbolizes my body." This triggered a vehement controversy between Zwingli and Luther, with Luther adamantly opposing Hoen's interpretation. Before long it became evident that this issue was the major theological topic dividing the Protestant reformers (See also MARBURG COLLOQUY; WITTENBERG CONCORD).

LOW COUNTRIES, THE. In the 16th century the Low Countries, or the Netherlands, were a group of 17 territories that had been amassed by the dukes of Burgundy and had become Habsburg (q.v.) possessions with the death of Philip the Fair in the latter part of the 15th century. Even though these provinces had a single ruler, there was little that tied them together. The northern provinces spoke Dutch (the low Saxon German dialect), the central provinces spoke the low Franconian dialect, while the southern provinces spoke French. There were real economic differences between the provinces as well. The north was agricultural and poor; the south was wealthy. While there was an Estates General, occasionally convened by the ruler to levy taxes, the real power lay in the parliaments of the individual provinces.

Charles V (q.v.) had been the ruler of the provinces ever since his succession to the Habsburg hereditary lands but in 1555 he transferred power to his son Philip II (q.v.). Philip, who had been brought up in Spain, did not know any of the languages spoken in the provinces. Moreover, Philip left the Netherlands in 1559 never to return. Philip's rule was overshadowed by the revolt of the Netherlands, which began in the mid-1560s. Political and religious motives converged in the opposition against Philip. By the middle of the century, Protestantism (q.v.) had made considerable headway in the northern provinces, and Philip's grim determination to eradicate heresy was bound to evoke opposition. But even Catholics resented Philip's encroachment of ancient "liberties" expressed by his heavy taxation and evident effort to centralize government.

Cardinal Granvelle, Philip's representative, excluded the higher nobility from participation in governmental affairs. In addition, Philip adamantly sought to suppress the Protestant heretics with a severity that struck people as too ruthless. Opposition against Granvelle succeeded in getting him dismissed from his post in 1564, after Spanish troops had been removed from the Netherlands three years earlier. Margaret of Parma, (illegitimate) daughter of Charles V, acted as regent on Philip's behalf until 1567. When a petition (the "request") signed by a large number of the lesser nobility was presented to Margaret in 1566, Philip responded by dispatching the Duke of Alva to the Netherlands to make sure that things did not get out of hand. Violence broke out but Alva succeeded in suppressing all resistance.

By 1572, however, William of Orange had emerged as Alva's great antagonist when a serious revolt occurred in Holland and Zeeland, where the Calvinist (q.v.) rebels succeeded. As at other places in Europe, the Dutch situation received its momentum from the convergence of religious and political motivation. Four years later revolt broke out in the southern provinces of Brabant, Flanders, and Hainault. Unrest and revolts continued. In 1578 the Duke of Parma arrived in the Low Countries. Three years later the rebels declared Philip deposed but Parma succeeded in reconquering all the territory south of the Meuse River by 1585. But then his efforts stalled. In 1609 a Twelve Year Truce was concluded which entailed the provisional acceptance of the independence of the new Dutch Republic. At the end of the truce, hostilities were resumed, only to be ended with the definitive recognition of Dutch independence at the Peace of Westphalia signed at Münster in 1648.

LUTHER, MARTIN (1483-1546). Reformer. Martin Luther was born on February 10, 1483, in Eisleben, in central Germany (q.v.). His father Hans Luder had attained a modest prosperity in the mining business, and he saw to it that his son undertook university studies. This took place at the University of Erfurt, where Martin matriculated in 1501, obtained his bachelor's degree in 1502, and received his master of arts degree in 1505. In accord with the wishes of his father Martin began the study of law that summer but just a few weeks later he abandoned his legal pursuits and entered the monastery of the Augustinian Eremites in Erfurt. Martin's own statement, many years later, was that in a terrifying thunderstorm he had vowed to become a monk. Undoubtedly, Luther had this experience but it is important to note that, inasmuch as he could have ignored the implementation of the vow, quite in keeping with normative theological teaching, there must have been a deeper reason for his joining the monastery.

Most commentators are of the opinion that Luther must have been experiencing a deep spiritual restlessness for which the monastic profession seemed the appropriate solution. Luther was ordained to the priesthood in 1506, and he then began the study of theology, at the behest of his monastic superior, Johann von Staupitz. Ordinarily, this would have proved to be an arduous and fairly lengthy undertaking but a series of monastic transfers from Erfurt to Wittenberg, where a new university had been established less than a decade earlier, and back to Erfurt, then back to Wittenberg, allowed Luther to take advantage of the lenient degree requirements at the new university. Luther received his doctorate in theology in 1512 and with it the professorship in biblical studies at the University at Wittenberg (q.v.). The next half decade of his life were not untypical of a talented young theologian.

Luther acquired increasing administrative responsibilities in his monastic order and, by 1517, published his first book.

That same year, however, he also penned a set of Ninety-five Theses on the topic of indulgences (q.v.), triggered by the indulgences preaching of one Johann Tetzel (q.v.), which began to catapult him into the public limelight. For a long time, Luther scholars were convinced that by the time the controversy over the Ninety-five Theses erupted Luther had moved theologically away from medieval theology. Luther himself related that it was an existential theological reorientation which caused him to reject the notion that grace and works justified a human being. This "evangelical discovery" convinced him that justification before God takes place *sola gratia*, alone through grace (q.v.). Luther claimed that he had discovered this in Paul's Letter to the Romans. Nowadays, the scholarly consensus holds that Luther came to this experiential insight later in the context of the indulgences controversy.

It is clear, all the same, that this experience proved fundamental; Luther began to formulate his entire theological thinking anew. This meant that in the controversy the focus quickly shifted away from indulgences and fixed on such topics as the church, the locus of authority, and eventually the sacraments (q.v.). Luther increasingly used his pen to propagate his views, and he did so with a literary flair and a cogency of style which, quite apart from the merits of the content, was bound to sway the readers. By sounding a note of devotional seriousness, mixed with theological innovation and anticlerical criticism, Luther soon found himself the head of a movement of reform. In the summer of 1520 the papal bull *Exsurge domine* served Luther notice that he would be excommunicated unless he recanted. With the flair that was to be characteristic of him, Luther had his students build a bonfire on the last day of grace proffered him by the papal bull and then threw a copy into the fire.

In January 1521 Luther was excommunicated. After intense bickering among the German estates, Luther was given the opportunity to appear in April before the German diet (q.v.) which had convened in Worms, though it was unclear for what exact purpose. Luther was asked if he was prepared to recant his views, which he declined. Even though he had been offered safe conduct for his journey to Worms, the precedent of Jan Hus hardly inspired confidence: Hus had, just about 100 years earlier, also been given safe conduct to travel to the Council of Constance but had been detained and eventually burned at the stake. Luther's territorial ruler, Elector Frederick of Saxony (q.v.), had him spirited away to a hiding place on the Wartburg. There Luther spent the better part of a year, in the mind of many he had been silenced by emperor and pope. Up to that time, the story of Luther and the story of the incipient Reformation intertwine. From 1521 onward, the stories diverge, and the story of Luther is no longer the story of the Reformation.

To his dismay Luther found that not all of his followers who took the Bible (q.v.) to be the final authority concurred with him in its interpretation, and the decade of the 1520s is filled with his controversies with Andreas Carlstadt, Thomas Müntzer, and Huldrych Zwingli (qq.v.). The uprising of German peasants and others in 1524-25, who claimed him as their mentor in their pursuit of socio-economic reform goals based on the principles of the gospel, was fiercely repudiated by him in a way some contemporaries (and commentators) felt cost Luther a great deal of support among the common people. In the height of the turbulence of the Peasants' War (q.v.) Luther married Catherine von Bora (q.v.), a former nun.

Luther indefatigably provided theological insight and sentiment for the emerging churches that eventually were to bear his name. An early preoccupation was with a German translation of the Bible (a translation of the New Testament, the result of his stay on the Wartburg) which appeared in 1522. Also important were his academic lectures at Wittenberg and matters of practical churchmanship, that is, the rebuilding of the liturgical life of congregations now divorced from Rome. The latter resulted in his catechisms, hymns (qq.v.), and postils (sermon books)—the list is lengthy and encompasses not only theology in the narrow sense but music, literature, and the arts. By the same token, the final years of his life (he died in his place of birth Eisleben in February 1546) were marked by an increasing intensity, vehemence, and bitterness of tone which resulted in fierce diatribes against all who disagreed with him—the papacy, the Jews, the Anabaptists (qq.v.). It may be, as has been suggested, that physical infirmity caused these explosions of bad temper. But, then, Luther never had been able to be very diplomatic and political.

During the period of Orthodoxy (q.v.) in the 17th century, Luther acquired virtually canonical status among Lutherans as the foremost exponent of the true gospel. While Luther appropriated a great deal from the theological tradition, and in some ways shows himself not quite so original as Protestant historiography has made him out to be, he still reconceptualized theology. His theological point of departure was the relationship between human righteousness and divine justice, the doctrine of justification. Luther saw this relationship in terms of what is called the "theology of the cross." This was Luther's notion that God always works in history in a veiled way, where external appearance is not reality. Luther saw this exemplified in Jesus on the cross, externally the execution of a criminal, in reality however the redemption of humankind. This principle of distinguishing fundamentally between appearance and reality allowed Luther a wide range of applications with regard to the church, the sacraments, etc. Luther's stature and role in Reformation events have been seen differently, with a fundamental divergence in the traditional perspective of Protestant and Catholic scholars. In the 20th century this divergence has lessened dramatically.

LUTHERAN. The initial self-designation by Martin Luther (q.v.) and his followers during the indulgences controversy (q.v.) and thereafter was "evangelicals," signifying that they were committed to the gospel. Catholics in turn used the term "Martinians" or "Lutherans" as a sectarian and sarcastic designation. Subsequently, Lutherans used the simple term "our church" when in need of a self-designation. Other terms used were "subscribers to the Augsburg Confession (q.v.) and other adherents" or, after 1529, the "protesting" (or, Protestant [q.v.]) churches. Toward the end of the 16th century, when both Lutherans and Calvinists (q.v.) sought to express their theological distinctiveness and disagreements ever more succinctly, the designations "Lutheran Church" and "Reformed Church" became standard. "Lutheran" began to be officially used in 1585 and by the time of the Thirty Years War (1618-1648) it had become standard nomenclature, a development aided by the increasing veneration of the person of Luther.

LUTHERANISM. The term refers the new churches in the 16th century that saw Martin Luther (q.v.) as the authentic interpreter of the Bible (q.v.). These new churches stood in contrast to the Catholic Church, the Anglican church (q.v.); the churches influenced by Huldrych Zwingli (q.v.) and, subsequently, John Calvin (q.v.); and the various Anabaptist (q.v.) conventicles. Initially, such Lutheranism expressed itself in individual congregations in cities and territories that declared to follow Luther's teachings. Beginning in the mid-1520s city councils and territorial rulers began to "reform" all the churches within their jurisdiction. This meant the beginning of a striving for doctrinal and liturgical uniformity which was enhanced by Philip Melanchthon's Augsburg Confession (qq.v.) of 1530.

The distinctive mark of the emerging Lutheran church orders (q.v.) was, on the one hand, the repudiation of the Catholic mass and, on the other, the repudiation of the Zwinglian notion of only a spiritual presence in the elements of Communion (q.v.). The various theological controversies (q.v.) which beset Lutherans before and especially after Luther's death and which ended with the endorsement of the Formula of Concord and the *Book of Concord* (qq.v.) clarified the self-definition of Lutheranism. Only German Lutheranism, however, accepted the *Book of Concord* as the defining document. Elsewhere in Europe, where Lutheranism became an important ecclesiastical force (foremostly Scandinavia), the Augsburg Confession was accepted as the doctrinal embodiment of Lutheranism. Lutheranism made a modest impact also in Hungary and Poland.

The theological characteristics of Lutheranism include the general Protestant (q.v.) affirmations of the priority of Scripture and of grace (q.v.), together with the affirmation of the priesthood of all believers. In terms of its polity, Lutheranism has been flexible. It has had both bishops standing in the apostolic succession (Sweden [q.v.]) and superintendents in lieu of bishops.

— M —

MARBURG COLLOQUY (1529). The Marburg Colloquy was held from September 30 to October 4, 1529, at the initiative of Landgrave Philip of Hesse (q.v.) in order to explore the possibility of agreement between Huldrych Zwingli and Martin Luther (qq.v.) concerning the Lord's Supper (q.v.). The important participants were Zwingli and Johann Oecolampadius (q.v.), representing the Swiss-South German theology, and Luther and Philip Melanchthon (q.v.), representing the Wittenberg theology. The Wittenberg theologians had, in preparation for the colloquy, drafted a comprehensive statement of faith, which subsequently became known as the Schwabach Articles. Luther wanted to discuss these articles at Marburg, since he was convinced that the divergent views of the Lord's Supper were only an indication of deeper disagreements. Zwingli and the South German theologians were concerned about the issue at hand, namely the Lord's Supper, about which such a bitter controversy had raged between the two sides ever since 1525. Their insistence was successful, and the discussion focused on the Lord's Supper.

The incisive aspect of the controversy between the two sides was over the interpretation of Jesus' words of institution ("This is my body . . . this is my blood") and the consequences to be drawn from the interpretation. Zwingli interpreted Jesus' words metaphorically to denote a kind of spiritual presence of Christ in the elements of bread and wine, while Luther insisted on a literal reading to denote a true presence. No agreement proved possible, even though the agreement reached at Marburg in 1529, signed by all present, denoted agreement in its 15 articles—"even though we found ourselves unable to agree at this time if the true body and blood of Christ is physically present in wine and bread," Behind the specific disagreement stood a fundamental disagreement concerning the means of grace (q.v.). According to Zwingli, the spiritual could not be in the bodily, physical. There also was, however, a political context to the deliberations at Marburg. When Landgrave Philip convened the colloquy it was clear that the emperor's return to Germany, from where he had been absent for almost a decade, would by necessity mean addressing the unresolved religious controversy.

For the Protestants (q.v.), as they began to be called after their "protest" at the diet of Speyer (q.v.) in 1529, this raised the possibility that the emperor might use force to subdue them. Two perspectives seemed possible: that the religious controversy might be resolved, because the disagreement was not over fundamentals. The other perspective assumed that no conciliation was possible and that the future of the Protestant cause lay in its military strength. Luther and Melanchthon, in a way representing the Saxon policies, held to the first of these notions, while Landgrave Philip held to the second. The Marburg colloquy must thus also be seen as part of the broader political strategy with which to deal with the complex question of how to secure the future of the Protestant cause. (See also EUCHARIST).

MARIAN EXILES. The succession of Mary Tudor (q.v.) to the English throne in 1553 meant the beginning of a determined policy of re-Catholizing England (q.v.). Persecution of Protestants (q.v.) soon followed, prompting the adamant among the Protestant reformers in England to leave for the Continent. Many of these emigrants found on the Continent, as for example in Geneva (q.v.) or Frankfurt, the kind of reformed church which they had yearned for in England. Upon Mary's death in 1558, these exiles returned to England and formed the group of those pressing for extensive religious change.

MARPECK, PILGRAM (d. 1556). Anabaptist (q.v.) theologian. Marpeck was born in the Tyrol in the last decade of the 15th century and became in the 1520s a prosperous mining engineer in Rattenberg in the Tyrol. He himself reported later that he came to accept the Lutheran (q.v.) interpretation of the gospel and, probably in 1528, accepted Anabaptist beliefs. His Anabaptist conviction, of course, made his continued presence in Rattenberg impossible, and he fled the city, his property being confiscated. Eventually he found his way to Strasbourg, a city gaining a reputation for its tolerant hospitality to dissenting opinion.

Marpeck quickly rose to be a leader in the Anabaptist congregation there. While he put his mining expertise in the service of the city, he also took on the role of advocating Anabaptist tenets. In 1531 he challenged the Strasbourg clergy to a theological debate, an indication that in the years since his flight from Rattenberg he had acquired extensive biblical competence and self-assurance. After further debates with Strasbourg clergy, such as Martin Bucer (q.v.), Marpeck was expelled from the city. His whereabouts for the next years are unknown. In the early 1540s, however, he engaged in a debate with Caspar von Schwenckfeld (q.v.). Out of this grew several major theological treatises that afford us the best summary of the mainstream Swiss-South German Anabaptist beliefs at midcentury. From 1544 until 1556, Marpeck appeared on the tax rolls of Augsburg, where he was employed, once again, as an engineer whose Anabaptist convictions proved a thorn in the flesh of the authorities. Marpeck was author of several Anabaptist tracts but most of these remained unknown until earlier this century; only then could his theological significance for mid-16th-century Anabaptism be properly assessed.

MARRIAGE. In the medieval church marriage was considered a sacrament (q.v.), thus a vehicle of divine grace. By the same token, celibacy was considered (obviously, only for some) to be a morally superior state lived by priests, monks, and nuns. The Protestant (q.v.) reformers rejected both notions, removing marriage from their list of sacraments and also rejecting the concept of celibacy as a spiritually superior state. For Martin Luther (q.v.) marriage was one of the "orders of creation," created by God for all humans both for the propagation of the human race and as a remedy for sexual concupiscence. Marriage was an orderly way to deal with that. All reformers, in affirming the permanence of marriage, allowed for divorce (q.v.) only under restricted circumstance (for Luther, for example, in case of impotence), and they drew a distinction between divorce and remarriage. (See also WEDDINGS).

MARTYROLOGIES. The compilation of the lives and sufferings of Christian martyrs long preceded the age of the Reformation but received new stimulus in the course of the 16th century. A large number of martyrologies, or martyr books, were published, generally around the middle of the 16th century. Jean Crespin's *Le livre de martyrs* appeared in 1554; a martyr book by Ludwig Rabe had appeared two years earlier. Adriaaen van Haemstede (q.v.) published his *De Gheschiedenisse ende den doodt der vromer Martelaren* (The Histories and Death of Pious Martyrs) in 1559 and included accounts of Anabaptist martyrs. The first Anabaptist martyrology was *Het Offer des Heeren* (The Sacrifice of the Lord), also published in 1562. It became the source for the most important Anabaptist martyr book, *The Martyrs' Mirror*, compiled by Tieleman van Braght and published in 1660. Undoubtedly the most famous of 16th-century martyrologies was John Foxe's (q.v.) *Acts and Monuments*, which became an crucial element in English anti-Catholic sentiment in the 16th and 17th centuries by its special emphasis on the persecution of Protestants in England under Queen Mary (qq.v.).

The factual accuracy of the accounts found in these martyrologies has been much discussed in scholarship. However, it is clear that these books were meant to be less books of history than books of edification and inspiration. As such they played an important role in consolidating the emerging Protestant (and Catholic) traditions and were important in the process of confessionalization (q.v.).

MARY I (MARY TUDOR) (1516-1558). Queen of England (q.v.) and Ireland. Mary was the third but only surviving child of the marriage between Henry VIII and Catherine of Aragon (qq.v.). Taken from her mother upon the dissolution of her parents' marriage in 1532, Mary was declared to be illegitimate by act of Parliament the following year. She sided with her mother and was ill treated by her father but upon Anne Boleyn's (q.v.) execution was reconciled with him upon acknowledging her illegitimacy and the king's ecclesiastical supremacy. In 1544 she was declared to stand in the line of succession after the king's legitimate children. Mary became queen in July 1553 upon the death of her half brother Edward.

As daughter of Catherine of Aragon and a faithful Catholic herself who had refused to give up Mass during Edward's (q.v.) reign, Mary was destined to restore Catholicism. Parliament declared her legitimacy and rescinded all the ecclesiastical changes that had occurred during both her half brother's and her father's reign. Mary was determined to stamp out all vestiges of Protestantism (q.v.) in England and began a policy of suppression and persecution. Some 300 Protestants were put to death during her reign. In July 1554 Mary married Philip of Spain (q.v.), whose stay in England was, however, of brief duration.

Mary was determined in her brutal anti-Protestant policies, a fact that has tainted her historical image. Personally, she was a deeply religious person, devoted to her husband Philip. She also took determined stands against papal policies, particularly when she thought those to jeopardize her relationship with her chief advisor Reginald Pole.

MELANCHTHON, PHILIP (1497-1560). German reformer and theologian. Born in Bretten near Karlsruhe in southwest Germany on February 14, 1497, as Philip Schwarzerdt later graeicized (in Humanist (q.v.) fashion, into Melanchthon. After university studies in Heidelberg and Tübingen, where he also taught, Melanchthon was appointed professor of Greek at the University of Wittenberg (q.v.) in 1518. His inaugural lecture on the reform of university studies was marked by the Humanist ideal to find access to the meaning of Scripture through its language. Soon Melanchthon came under the influence of Martin Luther's (q.v.) new theology, and the two colleagues became not only personal friends but also shared the program of theological reform. Melanchthon was never ordained nor did he receive the theological doctorate; his function, between 1518 and his death in 1560, was that of a teacher of theology at Wittenberg and also, certainly after 1530, as spokesperson for the Lutheran cause in Germany (q.v.).

In 1521 Melanchthon published his *Loci communes rerum theologicarum* (The Common Terms of Theological Topics), which provided, though restricted to the topics of soteriology and ethics, the first systematic summary of the new understanding of the Christian faith. The *Loci* discussed such topics as sin, law, grace (q.v.), and gospel which are taken to be fundamental for the understanding of the entire Bible (q.v.). Melanchthon's theology never obscured his indebtedness to Humanistic ideas and ideals, though scholarship continues to be divided as to the import of this juxtaposition of Humanism (q.v.) and the Reformation: did Melanchthon deviate from Luther's understanding or offer a creative synthesis of Humanistic and biblical ideals without surrendering Luther's deepest insights? The issue here was that Melanchthon embraced the categories of reason and tradition, insisting that humans can not only recognize the natural law but in fact fulfill it, even though such fulfillment does nothing in the sight of God.

Regardless of how his relationship to Luther's theology must be seen, it is clear that Melanchthon was responsible for putting ideas that allowed the Lutheran Reformation to work in harmony with the educational ideals of the time. In the 1530s and 1540s Melanchthon emerged as the major spokesperson for the Lutheran Reformation, as for example at Augsburg in 1530, where he was responsible for the Augsburg Confession (q.v.). More so than other Lutheran theologians, Melanchthon was concerned about Christian unity and went to great lengths in supporting theological compromise formulae that would have brought about a restoration of unity in the church. This evoked both support and opposition, especially after Luther's death, when Melanchthon emerged as the theological heir to Luther. Most of the theological controversies besetting Lutheranism (q.v.) in the second half of the 16th century somehow or other related to Melanchthon, as is evidenced by the emergence of the "Philippist" (q.v.) party, which was bitterly opposed by the Gnesio-Lutherans (q.v.). Still, there can be little doubt but that Melanchthon was largely responsible for the future development of Lutheranism with respect to its theology, creed, education, and cultural ethos. (See also *CONCORD, BOOK OF*; CONCORD, FORMULA OF).

MENNO SIMONS (c. 1496-1561). Anabaptist (q.v.) theologian and church leader. Undoubtedly the most important Anabaptist leader in the 16th century, Menno Simons was born in Witmarsum, Friesland. He became a priest at age 28, having received some formal training in theology. Doubts over the real presence of Christ in the elements of the Eucharist (q.v.) began to haunt him almost at once. Subsequently, Menno became aware of Anabaptist teachings, particularly with regard to believers' baptism (q.v.). The Anabaptist debacle in Münster (q.v.) in 1534-35 made an enormous impression on him in that he was convinced that his voice must be heard unless such false abomination should occur again among Anabaptist conventicles.

This "conversion" experience prompted him to begin to preach publicly Anabaptist notions, which in turn forced him, in January 1536, to flee his home community. He began an itinerant ministry which was to remain characteristic for the remainder of his life, making it impossible, since he was a hunted heretic, to trace his travels and whereabouts until his death in January 1561. Immediately after embracing Anabaptist tenets, Menno turned to the pen. Beginning in 1536, he published a steady stream of devotional and theological tracts, notably his most important writing *Dat Fundament des Christelycken leers* (The Foundation of Christian Teaching*)*, which was first published in 1540.

Menno Simon*s'* significance lies in his work as consolidator of the confounded and disheartened Anabaptists in northwest Germany and Holland after the catastrophe in Münster. Menno succeeded in convincing the Anabaptists that the intense eschatological and chiliastic emphasis of the Münsterites had been in error, and he re-directed the Anabaptists in the North to the biblicistic notions of the Swiss-South German Anabaptists of the 1520s. No longer was a feverish anticipation of the end to be the hallmark of the Anabaptists; rather, it was their quiet determination to live godly lives. By the time of Menno's death, the Anabaptists in North Germany and Holland were beginning to be called "Mennists," or Mennonites (q.v.), an indication of Menno's theological and organizational contribution.

However, the consolidation he had achieved was severely threatened by internal Mennonite controversies over church discipline. Menno's own rigid position, that the purity of the church, and therefore church discipline, must supersede all human bonds, such as marriage (q.v.), was bitterly contested by other Mennonite theologians but expresses the intense theological debates that characterized the Mennonite tradition in North Germany and Holland in the second half of the 16th century.

MENNONITES. The term "Mennonite" is derived from Menno Simons (q.v.), the Dutch priest and convert to Anabaptism (q.v.), who played a major role in the consolidation of the Anabaptist movement in North Germany and the Netherlands following the debacle at Münster (q.v.) in 1535. The usage of the term testifies to Menno's important role. The term was increasingly used in the second half of the 16th century to refer to the North German-Dutch Anabaptists, later to Anabaptists in general. As the terms "Lutheran" and "Calvinist," the term "Mennonite" was coined by outsiders. Again, much like the Lutherans and Calvinists, the Mennonites eschewed an appellation that tied them to a human figure. In Holland the term Doopsgezinden (Baptism-Minded) became the standard appelation.

MONASTICISM. From its origins in the fourth century, monasticism played an enormously important role in Christianity. Not only did the monastic profession allow for a more dedicated pursuit of spiritual goals, the cultural and societal contributions of medieval monasticism were far-reaching and enormous. The medieval period was marked not only by a proliferation of monastic orders but also by repeated reform efforts that in various ways sought to return a specific order, or all of monasticism, to the vision of the original founder. By the late Middle Ages monasticism had lost a great deal of its luster. Monasteries and convents had frequently acquired enormous wealth but the monastic life increasingly failed to be attractive. Monks and nuns were viewed as all-too-worldly, and biting criticism of their demeanor was widespread in early 16th-century Europe.

Undoubtedly this criticism was part of the extensive anticlericalism (q.v.) on the eve of the Reformation. On the other hand, there can be no doubt but that, despite such criticism of worldliness and also sexual shortcomings, the monastery still was seen as the place to live a committed and devoted Christian life. None other than Martin Luther (q.v.) serves as an illustration here, since he demonstrably entered the monastery to live a spiritually committed life. After Luther had reformulated his understanding of the Christian faith, however, his attack on monasticism was sharp and categorical, both for its notion of spirituality far removed from the rigors of the daily round of ordinary folks and for its insistence on the ideal of celibacy, which Luther thought to be impossible to keep. Consequently, monasteries and convents were dissolved wherever the Reformation was introduced. This was notably the case in England (q.v.), where the dissolution of the monasteries in 1536 and 1539 meant the transfer of about a tenth of the national wealth to new owners.

Sixteenth-century Catholicism, on the other hand, reaffirmed its commitment to the monastic life. Indeed, it bespeaks the continuing vitality of the Catholic Church that in the course of the century a number of new monastic orders came into being, most famously, of course, the Society of Jesus (Jesuits) (q.v.) but in addition the Theatines (1524) (q.v.), Capuchins (1528) (q.v.), Barnabites (1533) (q.v.), Angelines (1535), and Ursulines (1535). The Council of Trent (q.v.) vigorously affirmed the pivotal centrality of monasticism for the Catholic Church.

MORE, THOMAS (1478-1535). English Humanist. Influenced by the English Humanists William Grocyn and Thomas Linacre, Thomas More devoted his early literary efforts to political and social topics. Originally intending for a monastic life, More became a government official who rose slowly through the ranks, though without having a distinguished career. His friendship with Desiderius Erasmus (q.v.) stemmed from Erasmus's Oxford stay in 1499. In 1516 More published his most famous work, *Utopia,* which gained him a Europe-wide reputation. In the book he winsomely described an ideal island community in which political, economic, and social equality prevailed, where those in political authority were elected, and limited labor made possible intellectual pursuits. No religious uniformity was enforced. When the Reformation controversy reached England (q.v.) More took an adamant stance against it, also writing intensively and extensively against Martin Luther (q.v.). The otherwise polite Humanist wrote with surprising invectives.

In 1529 Henry VIII (q.v.) appointed him Thomas Wolsey's (q.v.) successor as lord chancellor, even though More's position on the "divorce" (q.v.) was well known. As lord chancellor he stayed aloof form the king's varied attempts to secure an annulment of his marriage to Catherine of Aragon (q.v.) but vigorously persecuted all manifestations of the Lutheran heresy in England. When the king made it clear that he was determined to achieve his goal of dissolving the marriage even if it meant a break with Rome and the papacy, More resigned the lord chancellorship in 1532. He became, together with John Fisher, the symbol of the Catholic resistance.

While ostensibly now in retirement, More failed to stay completely aloof from the political events. Refusing to swear the oath to the Act of Succession (q.v.), which would have entailed recognition that Catherine's daughter Mary was illegitimate, More was sent to the Tower of London. The severe Treason Act made the overt denial of the king's supreme "headship" of the church a matter of high treason, punishable by death. More was indicted on charges that he had indeed explicitly denied the king's title, and a vindictive king saw to it that

More was convicted. Together with John Fisher (q.v.) More was executed in the summer of 1535. More has left a legacy as one of the eminent Humanists of the early 16th century and as a martyr to his faith. He was canonized in 1935.

MÜNSTER. Münster, a town in Westphalia, in northwest Germany, was under the jurisdiction of the bishop of Münster. It experienced the thrust of the Reformation much like other cities in the Holy Roman Empire (q.v.), even though in Münster the internal tensions (between bishop and city council, on the one hand, and between city council and guilds, on the other) were particularly pronounced. The key figure was Bernd Rothmann (q.v.), the forceful and insightful preacher at the St. Lamberti Church in the city, a church not more than a stone's throw from the episcopal cathedral. Rothmann's eloquent propagation of the Reformation gospel led to the formal introduction of the Reformation in the city. The subsequent course of events in Münster was decisively influenced by Rothmann's own further theological development. Rather than continuing to affirm the Lutheran or the Zwinglian (qq.v.) interpretation of the Christian faith, Rothmann accepted notions of Melchior Hofmann and his brand of Anabaptism (qq.v.). This meant that in Münster (even as a decade earlier in Zurich [q.v.]) three ecclesiastical factions vied for acceptance: a Catholic minority, the mainstream reformers (Lutherans), and the Rothmann brand of Anabaptism.

Rothmann's conversion to Anabaptism triggered an influx of persecuted Anabaptists from northwest Germany and Holland into the city. Elections to the city council early in 1534 brought an Anabaptist majority. This led to a mass emigration of conservative Münsterites from the city which in turn consolidated, together with the continuing influx of Anabaptist refugees, the Anabaptist character of Münster. Soon the leadership in the course of religious affairs moved from Rothmann to Jan Matthijs, a lay preacher, with a charismatic hold on his followers. The bishop of Münster promptly undertook, with the support of Philip of Hesse (q.v.), to besiege the city. When Jan Matthijs was killed in a skirmish, his place was taken by another refugee from Holland, Jan van Leyden, who proceeded to turn Münster into the New Jerusalem. Rothmann, whose role was that of a theologian, provided the proper scriptural support for the changes that were now undertaken—the establishment of a royal court, with Jan as king, together with the introduction of communism (q.v.) and polygamy.

These changes have been seen as proof positive for the moral depravity of the Münsterite kingdom, though it is better to see them as having been occasioned both by the economic necessities of an ever more formidable siege and a literalist reading of the Bible (q.v.). In June 1535 Münster was taken by the besieging forces. Catholicism was reintroduced. One consequence of the Münster debacle was that persecution of Anabaptists everywhere intensified. The Anabaptists, in turn, eschewed the intense chiliasm that had been the hallmark of the Münsterite kingdom.

MÜNTZER, THOMAS (1491?-1525). Protestant theologian and reformer. Müntzer was one of the many clerics who, in the course of the indulgences controversy (q.v.), came under the influence of Martin Luther's (q.v.) new theology and became ardent advocates of the message of reform. At Luther's recommendation, Müntzer received an appointment as priest in Zwickau in 1519. His ardent proclamation of the new gospel quickly led to conflict with both the Zwickau city council and the conservative clergy in town, prompting him to leave the city. He moved to Prague, undoubtedly assuming that his preaching would find a positive reception in an area so lengthily and emphatically influenced by the Hussite (q.v.) movement. Müntzer's "Prague Manifesto," published at that time as an appeal to the people there to embrace his understanding of the gospel, was the first publication from his pen. Since he did not get the kind of response he had hoped for, he left Prague soon thereafter and was lost sight of until he surfaced in the small Saxon town of Allstedt in the summer of 1523.

At Allstedt his theological perspective found expression on the printed page. A long series of pamphlets (q.v.) flowed from his pen. One of the first publications was a rendering of the Mass in the German vernacular, the first effort of this kind, and then followed several publications which outlined Müntzer's understanding of the gospel in sharp contrast to that of Martin Luther (q.v.), whom he attacked with biting humor and pointed theological polemic. In the summer of 1524 Müntzer was given the opportunity to preach to the Saxon rulers, which he did with a lengthy, somewhat esoteric sermon on Daniel's dream but far from being swayed by him, the rulers saw to it that he was expelled from Saxony. Once more, Müntzer disappeared from sight, undoubtedly traveling southward to South Germany and Switzerland (q.v.), until in the spring of the following year he appeared in consort with the rebellious peasants in central Germany.

A new literary flourish followed until, in May of that year, Müntzer was taken prisoner by the authorities after the peasants had lost the decisive battle of the German Peasants' War (q.v.) in central Germany near Frankenhausen. He was interrogated and beheaded as a rebel. Luther called him the "archdevil of Allstedt," which indicated his judgment. That harsh sentiment on the part of Luther is understandable, since Thomas Müntzer had argued all too eloquently that Luther's vision of the Christian faith was fatally in error. Luther, according to Müntzer, had defined faith too nicely and too easily, rather than insisting that faith was always accompanied by a profound agony of spirit. Accordingly, Müntzer questioned the baptism (q.v.) of infants, as was general custom in Christendom. He thus can be seen as the mentor of the subsequent Anabaptist (q.v.) movement. Marxist historians have long argued Müntzer's role as a theological revolutionary because of his involvement in the German Peasants' War but probably that involvement was nowhere near as intense as they have sought to make it. (See also, COMMUNISM; EARLY BOURGEOIS REVOLUTION).

— N —

NANTES, EDICT OF. With the assassination of Henry III (q.v.) by a Dominican monk in 1589, Henry IV (q.v.), a Protestant, became French king. Given the strong Catholic sentiment in the country, not to mention forcefully advocated Jesuit (q.v.) notions of tyrannicide, it was obvious that France (q.v.) could not be restored to peace and tranquillity with a Protestant king. In 1593 Henry converted to Catholicism. The Peace of Vervins ended both the French civil war and the war with Spain (q.v.) in 1598. Immediately thereafter, the Edict of Nantes (April 13) was promulgated under the influence of the increasingly powerful faction of the "politiques" (q.v.).

The edict declared Catholicism to be the religion of the realm; all French people had to submit to Catholic marriage laws and observe Catholic holidays; all had to pay the tithe; Catholic rites could be celebrated anywhere. Protestants, however, received freedom of religion and the right to conduct their religious services in all places where such services were held in 1597. Protestants, moreover, could serve in all governmental offices. Protestants also were perrmitted to hold 200 fortified places throughout the country. Also, half of the judges in several parlements could be Protestants. Neither the adamant Catholics nor the adamant Huguenots (q.v.) were pleased with the edict but Henry IV succeeded, with the help of his Protestant minister Sully, in using the edict to restore peace and order to France. The edict was revoked in 1685. By that time, however, it had served its crucial purpose of guaranteeing to French Protestants civil rights and allowing the existence of Protestantism (q.v.) in the land without declaring it to be a legal heresy.

NUREMBERG, PEACE OF. The formation of the League of Schmalkald (q.v.) early in 1531, together with the Turkish onslaught in the east, made it impossible for Emperor Charles V (q.v.) to carry out the recess of the 1530 Augsburg (q.v.) diet. In return for Protestant support against the Turks, Charles agreed to the Peace of Nuremberg (July 23, 1532), which granted the Protestants cessation of all proceedings before the imperial cameral (supreme) court and guaranteed that no force would be used against the Protestants until the convening of a general council or the next diet (q.v.), whichever would occur first. Charles proceeded to Vienna to command the imperial troops against the Turks but by the time of his arrival the Turks had already been repelled. Since the convening of a general council was an integral part of the provisions of the Peace of Nuremberg, Charles met with Pope Clement VII (q.v.), who evasively agreed to convene a council. In retrospect, it is clear that the pope had no intention of convening a council, but his assurance prompted Charles to conclude that the council would settle the religious controversy in Germany (q.v.). Accordingly, Charles did not return to Germany but continued on to Spain (q.v.), not to return to Germany for about a decade.

—O—

OECOLAMPADIUS, JOHANN (1482-1531). Swiss reformer. Born in Weinsberg, Oecolampadius studied at Heidelberg and Bologna, then became (1506-8) tutor for a noble family in Mainz. He was ordained in 1510 and appointed priest in Weinsberg. Between 1513 and 1514 Oecolampadius studied Greek and Hebrew in Tübingen and Stuttgart (with Johannes Reuchlin). In 1515 he moved to Basel and aided Desiderius Erasmus (q.v.) with his edition of the Greek New Testament. Three years later he received his doctorate in theology at Basel and became cathedral preacher in Augsburg. The beginning reform movement prompted him to enter a monastery in 1520 to obtain certainty about the Catholic faith but two years later he secretly left the monastery and returned to Basel, where the first wave of reform agitation was underway. Gradually Oecolampadius became the leader of the movement for reform. In 1523 he was appointed professor of theology at Basel, two years later preacher at St. Martin's, and minister at the Basel cathedral in 1529. During the Communion (q.v.) controversy Oecolampadius published two tracts against Martin Luther's (q.v.) understanding of the sacrament (q.v.). He was also responsible for the church order (q.v.) for Basel.

ORTHODOXY. In the context of early modern European Christianity this term refers to Protestant (q.v.) theology after the age of the Reformation, both in its Lutheran and in its Calvinist/Reformed (qq.v.) manifestations. Generally, this means that from the end of the 16th century, roughly 1580, to the end of the 17th century Protestant theology was so characterized. A number of Orthodox theologians can be found in the 18th century as well. The hallmark of Protestant Orthodoxy is the pivotal role Lutheran theologians attributed to Martin Luther (q.v.) and Calvinist theologians to John Calvin (q.v.). The teachings of these two reformers were seen as sacrosanct.

The Orthodox theologians were determined to see themselves as the faithful exegetes of these reformers. In the Lutheran tradition this affirmation of Luther must not obscure that in various ways Lutheran Orthodoxy was more indebted to Philip Melanchthon (q.v.) than to Luther. Thus the outcome of the Osiandrian controversy meant an affirmation of Melanchthon's forensic understanding of justification. Also, the emphasis on natural theology in Lutheran Orthodoxy was Melanchthonian, as was the new appreciation of Aristotle (whom Luther had despised), that is, the use of Aristotelian philosophy to understand the relationship between philosophy and theology.

While all Orthodox theologians shared certain common affirmations—the virtual canonization of the founding father being one—they distinctly separated into a Lutheran and a Reformed wing. Moreover, Lutheran Orthodoxy had to deal with, and resolve, the several internal theological controversies that were besetting the Lutherans: the controversy about the adiaphora; about the law (Antinomistic controversy); good works (Majoristic controversy); human participation in justification (Synergistic controversy); original sin (Flacius)—in each of which Gnesio-Lutherans and Philippists (qq.v.) feuded bitterly with each other. The Peace of Augsburg (q.v.) had given the territorial rulers authority to determine the religious affiliation of their territory even as only the Lutherans, and not the Reformed/Calvinists, had been recognized. This meant that the initial development after the peace suggested that the theological development would occur along territorial lines. In fact, a number of *corpus doctrinae*, individual territorial confessions (q.v.) of faith, were promulgated. By the same token, since the Lutherans were the only legally recognized alternative to Catholicism, much of the theological discussion of orthodoxy centered on the Augsburg Confession (q.v.), in both its original and altered form.

Fundamental to the theological discussions in Orthodox theology was the utter confidence in the possibility of attaining absolute truth. Protestant theologians found this truth in the Bible (q.v.) which, in order to buttress the truth claims that were made for one's own position, was seen as having been verbally inspired by God. Such inspiration before long encompassed the vowel marks of the original Hebrew Old Testament. This also meant that the essence of Christianity was seen as doctrinal truth. Orthodoxy was accordingly polemical since the entire century had been beset by doctrinal strife. The age of Protestant Orthodoxy was a fiercely polemical age, where the representatives of each ecclesiastical tradition polemicized with the other, Lutherans against Calvinists, Calvinists against Catholics, Catholics against Lutherans. Despite the strong confessional emphasis that characterizes the theologians of the Orthodoxy, none of them confused their own visible church with the church of Christ.

As regards specific theological foci, Lutheran Orthodoxy focused on the question of justification, whereas Reformed Orthodoxy wrestled with the topic of predestination (q.v.). Thus, both theological traditions underwent a change from within. The key word in all Protestant traditions was doctrine, since it was taken for granted that it was the most important assignment to delineate clearly the truth of one's own doctrinal position. Protestant theology during the period of the Orthodoxy took on some of the characteristics of scholastic theology.

OSIANDER, ANDREAS (1498-1552). Protestant (q.v.) reformer. Osiander studied at Ingolstadt and became priest at St. Lorenz in Nuremberg. In 1519 he attended the Leipzig disputation (q.v.), where he became a convert to Martin Luther's (q.v.) new theology. A few years later, he was instrumental in introducing the Reformation in Nuremberg. A thoughtful author, Osiander was an important participant both at the Marburg Colloquy (q.v.) of 1529 and the diet at

Augsburg (q.v.) the following year. In the 1530s and 1540s Osiander played an important role in the introduction of the Reformation in other territories and was principally responsible for the Brandenburg-Nuremberg church order (q.v.) of 1533. When the Interim (q.v.) was imposed after the War of Schmalkald (q.v.), Osiander accepted an invitation of Duke Albrecht to become pastor in Königsberg in East Prussia and also the first professor at the newly founded university there. Soon thereafter, in 1550, in his inaugural disputation at Königsberg, Osiander triggered a controversy within Lutheranism (q.v.). It is known as the Osiandrian controversy and lasted well beyond Osiander's death in 1552.

At issue was the doctrine of justification and Osiander's pointed notion, rejected by most Lutheran theologians, that in the act of justification the righteousness of Christ is implanted into the believer and becomes part of the believer. His main opponent was Philip Melanchthon (q.v.), who taught a "forensic" understanding of justification which held that there is no ontological change whatsoever in the believer as the result of his or her justification before God. According to Osiander, the declaration that the sinner was righteous in the eyes of God (justification) was merely the beginning of actually becoming just (sanctification). Undoubtedly, Osiander echoed authentic themes of Luther, though it was easy to denounce him as a mystic or Catholic. The Lutheran Formula of Concord (q.v.), which was to conciliate the various feuding theological factions in Lutheranism in the 1570s, rejected Osiander's teaching. Osiander was well learned in Hebrew and Jewish thought, had a strong eschatological bend but also saw to the publication (for which he provided a preface) of Nikolaus Copernicus's (q.v.) *De revolutionibus* (Concerning the Revolutions of the Heavenly Bodies), despite hesitancy on the part of both Luther and Melanchthon about the "hypothesis" of the book that the earth rotated around the sun.

OTTOMAN EMPIRE. The Ottoman Empire was, in a way, the successor to the Byzantine Empire, which ended with the conquest of Constantinople in May 1453 by Sultan Mohammed II. In the decades following the Turks expanded their hegemony throughout the Balkan peninsula, despite suffering a major defeat at Belgrade in 1456. Serbia was occupied in 1459, Bosnia in 1463. By the early 16th century Turkish forces stood ready to occupy Hungary. The successful battle at

Mohacs in 1526 brought the Turks to the outskirts of Vienna, foreboding an imminent intrusion into central Europe.

The European response oscillated between calls for renewed crusades against the Turks and the desire for pragmatic coexistence. As early as 1479, and then again in 1502, Venice had concluded treaties with the Ottoman Empire, which meant that it became part of the European political system. In 1523 France (q.v.) concluded a treaty with the Ottoman Empire to strengthen its hand against the Habsburgs (q.v.), a significant symbol for the end of the solidarity of Christian Europe. Throughout the 15th century calls for European unity against the Turks, such as by Pope Pius II, remained effective propaganda but without practical consequences.

The threatening presence of Ottoman forces outside Vienna was not without important consequences for the course of the Reformation in Germany (q.v.). Particularly in 1530, when Emperor Charles V (q.v.) sought to resolve the religious controversy at the diet at Augsburg (q.v.), he found that the Protestant estates were unwilling to provide military support against the Turks unless he was willing to afford the Protestants religious toleration (q.v.). The Ottoman Empire thus constituted an important indirect reality in the course of the German Reformation.

— P —

PACK CONSPIRACY. This event takes its name from a minor Saxon government official, Otto von Pack, who used a forged document in 1528 to confide to Landgrave Philip of Hesse (q.v.) that the Catholic territories had concluded an offensive military alliance against the evangelicals. Philip, who fully believed Pack because the notion of an imminent Catholic attack agreed with his own assessment of the political situation, sought to rally the evangelical estates and cities to a preventive war against the Catholics. When the forgery was recognized as such, and tempers cooled down, a great deal of mistrust had arisen between the Catholic and the Lutheran (q.v.) rulers.

PAMPHLETS. The term "pamphlet" refers to a highly popular genre of publications that was virtually unknown before the outbreak of the Reformation in Germany (q.v.) but gained immense popularity in the course of the early Reformation. The pamphlet was a brief treatise, usually 16 or 32 pages in length, which dealt with a single topic and was written in the German vernacular. While the illiteracy of the overwhelming majority of the people drastically limited readership, more people could read German than Latin so that the prospective audience of these German language pamphlets was bound to be significantly larger than would have been the case with Latin publications. The small size of the pamphlets made for a low price so that they turned into a cheap and effective means of propaganda. Printers found no dearth of authors, and the number of pamphlets published between 1519 and 1525 was enormous.

The pamphlets employed a variety of literary styles, of which the dialogue was the most popular. This approach allowed the author to express novel if not controversial opinions subtly by attributing them to one of the dialogue partners. Often, in early German Reformation pamphlets, a simple layman (occasionally a laywoman) plays the pivotal role. This importance assigned to the layperson found expression in dialogues and conversations in which the learned person, a priest or a monk, lost out in argumentation against a simple layman, frequently an artisan or a peasant, who had the more persuasive arguments and better biblical knowledge. The topics treated in the pamphlets varied, though religion and religious reform were most important.

In Germany pamphlets dominated the literary scene until the mid-1520s. Afterwards, the number of published pamphlets declined dramatically. This decline has been seen as a consequence of Martin Luther's (q.v.) loss of popularity after the Peasants' War (q.v.) but a more plausible reason lies in the change of theological agenda from the mid-1520s onward. After a decade or so of religious controversy, new ecclesiastical bodies needed to be structured, and systematic treatments of the controversial new theological issues had to be delineated. The need to persuade and rally the common people had passed. Outside Germany, wherever popular impulses for reform surfaced, pamphlets played the same kind of role,. Again, as in Germany, particular circumstances influenced topics and intensity of the publications. In England, Henry VIII (qq.v.) commissioned the writing of pamphlets in the 1530s as a propaganda effort among the English people. (See also LITERATURE; PRINTING).

PARACELSUS, THEOPHRASTUS (1493/94-1541). Philosopher. Born in Einsiedeln, Switzerland, Theophrastus Bombast of Hohenheim, who took on the name Paracelsus to denote his kinship with the ancient philosopher Celsus, studied in Italy and traveled extensively throughout Europe. After brief stays in Salzburg and Strasbourg, Paracelsus was appointed municipal physician and professor of medicine in Basel in 1527 with a tenure that lasted just about one year. Further peregrinations in South Germany and Austria followed, where Paracelsus always hovered on the margin of the Reformation turbulence. He died in Salzburg in 1541.

Foremost a physician, Paracelsus published detailed studies of specific illnesses, making experience a major criterion in the physician's diagnosis of illness and disease. He emphasized a chemotherapeutic approach to treating illnesses. As a philosopher Paracelsus not only echoed the timeless sentiment of philosophers to coin novel words and phrases but also used Neoplatonic notions to conceptualize an understanding of the cosmos which focused on the nature and structure of the universe and its parallels to humans and their organs. Theologically, Paracelsus may be said to have been a spiritualist who denounced all "churches with walls" but affirmed the use of the sacraments (q.v.) as an external catalyst to attain perfection of the inner spiritual human being.

PAUL III (1468-1549). Pope. Elected pope upon the death of Pope Clement VII (q.v.) in 1534, Paul III was born Alessandro Farnese. In his sixties when becoming pope, Paul had skillfully served six predecessor popes in a variety of administrative and diplomatic roles. He became a cardinal in 1493 but was not ordained to the priesthood until a quarter of a century later (1519). Prior to his ordination he had a mistress who gave birth to four children.

Paul III is generally credited with having committed himself to the cause of reform. While his nepotism continued (sons and grandsons were made cardinals), Paul saw that the path of reform was the best way to combat heresy. Several leading proponents of reform (Gasparo Contarini, Reginal Pole, Gian Pietro Carafa, and Jacobo Sadoleto) were made cardinals. A commission appointed by him was to take inventory of ecclesiastical shortcomings. Its findings, embodied in a 1537 document entitled *Consilium de emendanda ecclesia* (Counsel for the Improvement of the Church), candidly identified the needed areas of reform in the church. Paul doggedly pursued the convening of a general council, first in 1536 (to convene in Mantua the following year) but the ongoing conflict between France and Spain (qq.v.) made this impossible until the council eventually convened at Trent (q.v.).

Paul III astutely approved Ignatius of Loyola's new Society of Jesus (qq.v.).

Paul showed himself a great patron of the arts and learning in Rome, supporting the Vatican Library as well as Michelangelo. His ongoing nepotism and his temperamental indecisiveness made him, in the end, less influential that might have been the case.

PAUL IV (1476-1559). Pope. Born Gianpietro Carafa of a wealthy Neapolitan family, Paul made his first ecclesiastical mark when in 1524 he founded, together with St. Cajetan of Thiene, the Theatine order (q.v.) and became its first general superior. He was elevated to cardinal in 1536 and in 1555, at the age of 79, elected pope. At once he threw himself zealously into the task of reform and the eradication of heresy. During his pontificate the Inquisition (q.v.) became a powerful tool which did not hesitate to charge high churchmen, such as Cardinal Morone, previously a serious contender for the papacy, or Reginald Pole (q.v.), a leading figure at the Council of Trent (q.v.), of heresy.

PEASANTS' WAR. This is the customary term for the peasant uprisings in Germany (q.v.) and Austria, beginning in the late summer of 1524 and extending until 1525. The focus on an uprising of peasants has been recently argued to overlook the extensive turbulence in the cities and participation of townspeople in the uprising so that the alternate term "revolution of the common man" has been proposed. The term "common man" refers to all those, whether in the cities or in rural areas, who were deprived of meaningful participation in communal affairs.

The antecedents of the Peasants' War, which began with uprisings in the summer of 1524, must be sought in the long tradition of peasant restlessness and uprisings that is part and parcel of the social history of the later Middle Ages. Even in the early 16th century there had been uprisings, for example, that of the "poor Konrad" in Württemberg in 1514 and the Bundschuh movement in southwest Germany (the name Bundschuh was derived from the peasants' flag, which depicted a shoe with a long string attached to it). Whether or not the early 16th century brought a deterioration or an improvement in the economic condition of the peasants is not altogther clear but what is beyond dispute is that by the early 16th century the peasants manifested a new self-confidence which demanded an appropriate recognition in society and was aggrieved by the increasing restriction of communal self-government and the traditional use of common property. After the outbreak of the Reformation, the authorities were apprehensive that, in the wake of the controversy surrounding Martin Luther (q.v.), the common man might stage an uprising.

The connection between Luther, the Reformation, and the Peasants' War has been much debated. There should be little doubt, however, that a variety of impulses served to convey to the peasants (and the townspeople) that the cause of broad societal reform that was being advocated in hundreds of pamphlets and pronouncements was also theirs. Even Luther had addressed issues of societal reform in his 1520 *Letter to the Christian Nobility*. The uprising broke out in the southern part of the Black Forest in May and June 1524 and spread southeastward into Austria and northeastward into South Germany. Initially, the uprising or "war" had the character more of a series of demonstrations than an actual military uprising. Since the uprising soon began to be characterized by a measure of religious fervor, acts of violence against monasteries and churches occurred. Also, the need to feed the large throng of the peasant forces explains the confiscation, often brutal, of goods that became standard and the norm. Still, negotiation rather than confrontation was the hallmark of the early phase of the uprising.

A lengthy series of local grievance documents were formulated that set forth the specific grievances of the peasants. One such document actually found its way into print, the *Twelve Main Articles of the Common Peasantry*. In it, the influence of the Reformation is evident, for in addition to the traditional grievance for the restoration of the "old law," that is traditional custom and law, the *Twelve Articles* also spoke of the mandates of the divine law, that is, the principles pertaining to a community as found in Scripture. Initially, the peasants scored some successes. For example, the electors (q.v.) of Mainz and of the Palatinate were forced to accept the *Twelve Articles*. By early spring of 1525, however, the rulers had consolidated their forces, and in a series of skirmishes and battles in May and June 1525 in southwest and central Germany—the battle at Frankenhausen was disastrous for the central German peasants—the peasants were dramatically defeated. The wrath of the authorities fell on the survivors. All agreements that had been reached locally early on were declared to be null and void, and the estimates are that some 100,000 peasants lost their lives either in battle or afterwards. (See also EARLY BOURGEOIS REVOLUTION; MÜNTZER, THOMAS).

PHILIP II (1527-1598). Spanish king. Born in Valladolid as son of Charles V (q.v.) and Isabel of Portugal, Philip was brought up very much along the lines of his father's values of which the antagonism toward Protestantism (q.v.), an Erasmian kind of Christian Humanism (q.v.), and solid devotion to duty were important elements. Philip married no less than four times, each of his wives dying in childbed or of other natural causes (q.v.), as did Mary Tudor of England (qq.v.). At the death of his mother in 1539, Philip became regent of Spain (q.v.) for the periods of his father's extensive absences and king in 1556 upon his father's abdication. While he had spent several years abroad in the late 1540s, accompanying his father to the diet at Augsburg (q.v.) in 1548, after 1559 and the Peace of Cateau-Cambrésis (q.v.), Philip stayed in Spain, from where he ruled his vast dynastic inheritance, which included not only Spain (Castile and Aragon) but also the Low Countries (q.v.), Burgundy, Northern Italy, Naples, and Sicily.

Philip was a person of wide interests in the arts, music, and learning. He preoccupied himself with the administration of his vast domain, often with minutiae and trivia, complicated by his inability to make quick decisions. Convinced that there were formidable evil forces at work poised to destroy the Catholic Church and its faith, Philip rendered unequivocal support to the Catholic Church and its efforts to stamp out heresy with the help of the Inquisition (q.v.). Religion also played an important role in his foreign policy, alongside his determination to defend the dynastic rights of the house of Habsburg (q.v.). The revolt of the Low Countries (q.v.) lengthily consumed his attention, inconclusively at first, abortively at the end, and his attempt to defeat Elizabeth I (q.v.) and restore Catholicism to England with his mighty Armada (q.v.) proved to be a colossal failure.

PHILIP, LANDGRAVE OF HESSE (1504-1567). Son of Landgrave William II, who had secured Hesse's place as an increasingly important territory in Germany (q.v.), Philip succeeded his father as ruling landgrave in 1509. Contemporaries gave Philip the appellation "the magnanimous." It was to be of enormous significance both for Philip's life and the German Reformation that Philip became one of the first and most enthusiastic supporters of Martin Luther (q.v.) and one of the first territorial rulers in Germany to introduce the Reformation. A synod convened by Philip at Homburg in October 1526 (it was comprised of both secular and ecclesiastical representatives) decreed the abolition of papal practices. A committee drafted the Homburg Church Order (*Reformatio ecclesiarum Hassiae*), which defined the three ecclesiastical offices as that of bishop, deacon, and elder. Moreover, the church order (q.v.) stipulated that the truly committed believers should meet separately from the larger congregation. This Homburg Church Order was never put into practice, however, and in fact the Reformation was introduced in Hesse slowly.

Hesse was the first territory where the introduction of the Reformation meant the dissolution of the monasteries. Their wealth was used by Philip to establish a new university at Marburg (1527) and to establish four hospitals. Philip was strongly convinced that the new faith could only be sustained by the display of political and military strength among all adherents of the reform movement. The pointed division in the ranks of the reform movement seemed to render that impossible. Accordingly, Philip was the driving force to have Luther and Huldrych Zwingli (qq.v.) find common theological ground on this bitterly contested theological issue and at the same time make for a united Protestant front against the emperor. The colloquy at Marburg (q.v.) in 1529 was thus every bit as much a political as a theological event. When the colloquy failed to bring agreement between the two reformers, Philip continued his assertive role as leading spokesman for the Reformation cause. Eventually this led to the formation of the League of Schmalkald (q.v.). In 1534 Philip successfully restored Duke Ulrich as sovereign in Württemberg, which meant the introduction of the Reformation in Southwest Germany, a major achievement for the Hessian landgrave.

A few years later, in 1540, however, Philip became involved in the notorious scandal about his bigamy which dramatically paralyzed his leadership role in the League of Schmalkald. Married to the daughter of Duke George of Saxony, whom he did not love, Philip had a string of extramarital affairs which gave him scruples of conscience. Falling in love with a young woman at his court, Philip discovered (much as did Henry VIII [q.v.] in England) that the woman insisted on marriage (q.v.). Theologians who were consulted, including Luther, found that a second marriage was the solution preferable to divorce (q.v.), and accordingly Philip secretly married a second time in March 1540. This marriage was to have been kept a secret but word leaked out and Philip found himself in the difficult situation of having violated the imperial statute that enjoined monogamy. He eventually received the emperor's pardon but the price was high: Philip had to pledge secretly that he would thwart any further expansion of the League of Schmalkald (q.v.). It is difficult to say if this secret deal had consequences in 1547, when Charles V (q.v.) waged war against the league. The disaster of the war meant that Philip became the emperor's prisoner. His son Wilhelm had assumed rule in Hesse. Philip himself, once released, had lost his ebullience and vigor and played but a modest role in the course of events.

PHILIPPISTS. The term refers to the followers of Philip Melanchthon (q.v.), hence the appellation. The term was used particularly toward the end of the various theological controversies within Lutheranism (q.v.), especially after Martin Luther's (q.v.) death. The Philippists were opposed by the Gnesio-Lutherans (q.v.), who argued that they alone represented Luther's true legacy. (See also CONCORD, BOOK OF; CONTROVERSIES WITHIN LUTHERAN-ISM).

PIETY, CATHOLIC. In contrast to Protestant piety, Catholic piety appears immensely richer and also more specifically religious. In the late Middle Ages, Catholic piety found expression in devotion to relics (remains of saints), pilgrimages, mysticism, and a specifically religious literature which focused on legendary narratives of Jesus and the saints. With it went the insistence on meditation and contemplation and the ascetic life. The influential treatises of medieval devotional literature, the *German Theology* and the *Imitation of Christ*, convey this convergence of contemplation and the active life. It is still not clear to what extent the common people appropriated these ideals, though the traditional Protestant notion of unmitigated worldliness and perversion in the pre-Reformation church is surely incorrect. One must not forget that most people were illiterate and eked out a precarious existence. The church's insistence that the faithful receive the Lord's Supper (q.v.) at least twice a year was more often than not honored in the breach. In the 16th century Catholic piety had its eminent representatives in Ignatius of Loyola (q.v.) and his *Spiritual Exercises* together with Teresa of Avila (q.v.) and St. John of the Cross and their mysticism.

PIETY, PROTESTANT. Strictly speaking, Protestant (q.v.) piety is not a religious-theological but an ethical concept, even though Martin Luther (q.v.) had emphatically insisted that it was indeed religious. For Luther proper piety was essentially the proper self-awareness of one's sinfulness; Lutheran (q.v.) theologians more or less followed suit. On the popular level, however, it was different in that the virtuous life was taken to be the epitome of Christian spirituality as was the conviction that the last judgment would be rendered not by faith (q.v.) but by works. In short, there is a strong moralizing element in Protestant devotional writings and breviaries. Prayers—morning and evening as well as before and after meals—regular church attendance and periodic reception of the Lord's Supper (q.v.) (this meant receiving it more than twice a year which was deemed an improvement over Catholic practice) were, together with a morally upright life, the hallmarks of the devout Christian. The Calvinist (q.v.) tradition echoed this strong emphasis on Christian living, as did the Anabaptists (q.v.), without minimizing, however, an equally strong theological emphasis.

PILGRIMAGE OF GRACE. Henry VIII's (q.v.) break with Rome led to Parliament's decision to dissolve the (smaller) monasteries in 1536, whose property was used by the king to swell his own coffers or to pass on as gifts or attractive sales to favored barons, gentry, and townsmen. The dissolution, with its concomitant enormous transfer of wealth, accentuated the economic and social discontent in England (q.v.). There were obvious economic consequences for the communities in which the monasteries were located. Particularly in the north in Lincolnshire and Yorkshire this discontent led to an uprising spearheaded by gentry, abbots, and priests. Robert Aske, the leader, declared that the dissolution of the monasteries meant the ruin of religion in England and that the Act of Supremacy violated divine law. Some 9,000 rebels marched against York and returned monks and nuns to their monasteries and convents. When the rebels seemed successful, Aske entered into negotiations with the king, who thereby gained time to marshal his forces. The uprising was ruthlessly suppressed; Aske and many others were executed.

PIUS IV (1499-1565). Pope. Born Giovanni Angelo de' Medici, he studied law at Pavia and Bologna, then entered the curial administration. He became a cardinal in 1549 and was elected pope in 1559 in the hope that he would be able to effect permanent peace between the two rivals Spain and France (qq.v.), whose conflict seemed to thwart Catholic efforts at reform and combating Protestantism. His challenges were formidable in that both the curia and the eminent Catholic rulers, Philip II and Emperor Ferdinand (qq.v.), had different notions about how to deal with the Protestants (q.v.) and church reform. Ferdinand favored concessions to the Protestants, while Philip was adamantly opposed. Pius himself was quite open to certain changes, such as Communion (q.v.) under both kinds or even marriage for the clergy, as long as papal authority and power were not affected. His skill and determination brought about the reconvening of the Council of Trent (q.v.) in 1562 and its successful conclusion in December of the following year.

Pius continued to be convinced that doctrinal rapprochement with the Protestants was possible but his death less than two years after the adjournment of the council meant that those who were convinced that the differences were unbridgeable carried the day. Pius confirmed the decrees and canons of the council in the bull *Benedictus Deus* of January 1564 and was given the sole authority to interpret and enforce the decrees of the council.

PIUS V (1504-1572). Pope and saint. Pius V, whose pontificate ran from 1566 to 1572, was the first pontiff who presided over the renewal of the Catholic Church in the wake of the Council of Trent (q.v.). A Dominican, Antonio Michele Ghislieri introduced austerity to the papal court, did away with the blind nepotism of his predecessor, and rigorously suppressed all heretical tendencies, immorality, and desecration of holy days. At the same time he undertook an extensive array of reform measures, guided by the decrees and canons of the Council of Trent. For example, he issued a catechism (q.v.) for use by priests, the *Breviarium Romanum* (1568), and the *Missale Romanum* (1570). Pius vigorously undertook visitations (q.v.), including in Rome itself, established seminaries for the training of future priests, and employed new criteria and principles for the appointment of bishops. In everything Pius was intent on carrying out the determinations of the Council of Trent. Pius died on May 1, 1572. He was canonized in 1712.

POISSY, COLLOQUY OF. This colloquy, important in its own right, deserves note as the last of the great theological debates between Catholics and Protestants in the 16th century. It took place in Poissy, west of Paris, in September 1561. The Huguenot (q.v.) participants were led by Theodore Beza and Peter Martyr Vermigli (qq.v.), while the Catholic side was led by the cardinal of Lorraine, Charles of Guise, and Diego Lainez, successor to Ignatius of Loyola (q.v.) as general of the Society of Jesus (q.v.). Though neither side was greatly disposed to conciliation—Beza focused on persuading the French king to introduce the new faith in France (q.v.)—the theological issue dramatically separating the two sides was the interpretation of Christ's presence in the Lord's Supper (q.v.). (See also COLLOQUIES).

POLAND. In the early 16th century Poland, whose king was also the ruler of Lithuania, was one of the largest states in Europe. It comprised an area that extended westward to the Baltic and eastward far into Russia (then the Muscovite Dominion) and the Ukraine. This vast territory was variously divided—between Catholicism and Russian Orthodoxy, Central Europe and Eastern Europe, royal authority and authority of the nobility. In western Poland, Germans and Jews (q.v.) controlled much of the economy. In the east, the Ruthenians were part of the Russian Orthodox Church, whereas the Poles and the Lithuanians, the largest ethnic group in the land, were Catholic.

In the course of the 15th century the Polish nobility had increased its political power at the expense of king, towns, and peasants. The king was elected by the nobility, which hardly enhanced or stabilized the central power in the land. Culturally, Poland experienced in the 16th century a flourishing golden age, with learning and Renaissance ideas accepted as nowhere else. Politically and economically, however, the country was in a state of decline in prosperity and political power. In 1505 the Polish diet passed a statute that provided that the king could not have a standing army and that "nothing new" could be decided without the consent of the diet and the representatives of the regional diets of nobles. Thus, the center of governmental power moved to the diet, with the king simply acting as the executive branch of government.

Politically, Poland was in a precarious state early in the 16th century: threats came from Moscow and the Tartars in the east, and from the Ottoman Empire (q.v.) in the south, to which an ongoing conflict with the Habsburgs (q.v.) over Bohemia provided further challenges. The story of the Reformation in Poland intertwines with the opposition of the Polish nobility to the higher clergy and the sympathies of the German population in the western part of Poland with the cultural and religious currents in Western Europe. Understandably, a diversity of Protestant teaching found its way into Poland. Initially, of course, it was Lutheran (q.v.) sentiment but by the middle of the century Calvinist (q.v.) and incipient anti-Trinitarian (q.v.) notions had found their way into the country. By 1552 a Polish translation of the New Testament was completed. King Sigismund I (r. 1506-48) had followed the precedent of most European rulers and had sought to stamp out Lutheran sentiment. However, when he died in 1548, the presence of Protestant ideas was widespread enough to force the political authorities to decide seriously how the deal with Protestantism (q.v.).

Given the political power of the Polish nobles, it follows that they determined the religious policies adhered to in their own lands. At diets in 1547 and 1548 the nobles demanded that the Word of God be preached freely. By the same token, Catholicism showed itself strikingly sensitive to reform: both clerical marriage and the communion cup for the laity (q.v.) were discussed by Catholics as agenda items for possible reform. Efforts were made over the next few years to secure legal recognition for Protestantism. Complicated negotiations followed in the 1550s and 1560s, sometimes favoring Protestant recognition, sometimes supporting the Catholic cause.

When King Sigismund II accepted in 1564 the decrees and canons of the Council of Trent (q.v.) as binding for Poland, the diet in the following year declared all decisions of ecclesiastical courts null and void. This decision allowed Protestants to live peacefully for a decade. In the wake of Sigismund's death in July 1572, the Polish nobility successfully diminished royal power. The nobility also promulgated, in the Confederation of Warsaw, January 1573, religious freedom for Protestants, even though the language of the document lacked clarity (for example, if the anti-Trinitarians were included in the provision of the confederation). Stefan Bartory, who ruled until 1586, favored the Catholic cause but permitted religious freedom for Protestants. The succession of Sigismund III, who ruled until 1632, meant that a determined Catholic policy was pursued by a generally powerless king. Though neither Bartory nor Sigismund persecuted the Protestants, Protestantism began to lose its energetic vitality which seemed to be embodied in the revitalized and self-confident Tridentine Catholicism. By the time of Sigismund's death, Poland was once again a largely Catholic country.

POLE, REGINALD (1500-1558). English cardinal and archbishop of Canterbury. Educated at Oxford, Pole went to Italy in 1521 to study. Upon his return to England (q.v.) in 1527, he was elected dean of Exeter. After further studies at Paris (1529-30), Pole declined Henry

VIII's (q.v.) wish that he become archbishop of York. Disapproving the king's quest for royal supremacy over the English church, Pole returned to Padua in 1532. In response to a solicitation by Henry VIII in 1536 he wrote the lengthy treatise *Pro ecclesiasticae unitatis defensione* (A Defense of Ecclesiastical Unity), which denounced the king's position. That same year he became part of a papal commission to draw up comprehensive plans for the reform of the church. Made cardinal and papal legate, Pole unsuccessfully sought to effect an alliance against Henry VIII and, after Henry's death, effect the restoration of the English church to Rome.

When Mary Tudor (q.v.) succeeded to the English throne, Pole at long last returned to England, though not without political complications (Charles V [q.v.] did not want Pole to influence Mary concerning the marriage plans involving his son Philip [q.v.]). The difficulties in the effort to restore Catholicism in England, particularly from the ranks of those who had benefited from the dissolution of the monasteries, frustrated Pole, as did the personal animosity of Pope Paul IV (q.v.), who privately labeled Pole a heretic. Consecrated archbishop of Canterbury in March 1556, Pole died in November 1558, the same day Queen Mary died.

POLITIQUE. The term was coined during the French Wars of Religion to refer to those French who, in the turbulence of the wars, became convinced that the theological differences which had generated one bloody civil conflict after the other were less important than the unity of the French people and realm. The outstanding representatives were Jean Bodin (q.v.) and Duke Francis of Alençon. (See also FRANCE).

POPULAR RELIGION. The term refers to religious beliefs and practices held and carried out by the people in juxtaposition to official teaching and practice. Such religion can have several sources, such as a misunderstanding of the official teaching or the incorporation of elements alien to the official teaching. The methodological difficulty encountered when venturing to describe popular religion is that the sources are not easily appropriated. Thus, it is difficult to make meaningful comments about popular religion in the 16th century because the sources are sparse and evasive. It seems clear that the sophisticated theological debate, which characterized the Reformation controversy from the start, was beyond the comprehension of most people, though it seems equally clear that certain key concepts, such as "Word," "Christian freedom," or "by faith alone," could be understood and appropriated by the common people.

While there was undoubtedly, at least in Germany (q.v.), an initial groundswell of support for the reform message, it is impossible to make firm quantitative judgments in this regard. The various official visitations (q.v.) undertaken periodically wherever the Reformation was introduced reveal anything but a glowing picture of flourishing church life. People were frequently not even conversant with the most basic of Christian tenets, such as the Lord's Prayer and the Ten Commandments, nor did they seek to compensate for such ignorance by dynamic participation in the life and worship of the church. The Catholic Church wanted people to receive Communion at least twice a year but it seems clear that such an ideal was rarely realized. Throughout Europe, as had been shown most recently for England (q.v.), the people clung steadfastly to the beliefs of the Catholic Church.

It was not until late in the 16th century, when European societies began to demonstrate various forms of strict conformity, recently referred to as "confessionalization," that religious and theological competence appeared to have reached acceptable levels. By that time, of course, literacy (q.v.) had also increased significantly.

PRAETORIUS, MICHAEL (1571-1621). Musician and composer. Born in Thuringia, Praetorius was the eminent figure in Lutheran church music (q.v.) toward the end of the 16th century. After studies at Frankfurt/Oder, he became organist in that city and then entered the service of Duke Heinrich Julius of Braunschweig-Wolfenbüttel, becoming the director of court music in 1604. Several theoretical publications, notably *Syntagma musicum*, 1615, offered profound reflections about Protestant church music. In addition, Praetorius worked successfully as a composer. His nine volumes of *Musae sioniae*, published between 1605 and 1610, offered choral arrangements of Lutheran (q.v.) hymns. A contemporary of Monteverdi and Heinrich Schütz, Praetorius lacked their musical genius; by the same token, he offered a deep understanding of Protestant sacred music.

PREDESTINATION. This theological teaching refers to the decision about the eternal salvation or damnation which is not located in the human will but in a determination of God, namely that God determined whom he would choose to save and whom to condemn. A variant of this position is the notion of "foreknowledge," which holds that God "foreknows" whether or not a human being will seek salvation. In Western Christianity St. Augustine was the most pointed proponent of the predestinarian view, even though the subsequent medieval theological discourse did not follow him on this point.

In the Reformation the Protestant (q.v.) emphasis on divine grace (q.v.), rather than human works, meant a clear inclination to predestinarian views. Predestination was the presupposition for the utter helplessness of the human will for salvation. Martin Luther (q.v.) affirmed predestination in his *De servo arbitrio* (The Bondage of the Will), 1525, written against Desiderius Erasmus (q.v.), who affirmed the mainstream medieval consensus that faith (q.v.) formed by love, that is, good works, will bring salvation. However, Luther preferred not to dwell on the matter. John Calvin (q.v.), on the other hand, came to be the most emphatic protagonist of predestinarian views among the reformers. In his *Institutes of the Christian Religion* (q.v.) Calvin discussed the doctrine at length, distinguishing it from divine foreknowledge and defining predestination as the eternal decree of God by which he determined who should be saved and who should be damned. Calvin's important point of departure was the evident reality that not all humans have the opportunity to hear the gospel of Jesus Christ, nor do those who hear it respond in uniform fashion. Biblical passages undergirded this perspective, which related the doctrine to the emphasis on God's glory in his mercy to those whom he chooses to save and his justice to those whom he condemns.

PRINTING. The invention of movable type by Johannes Gutenberg in 1455 is generally referred to as the invention of printing as such. The difference must be noted, since it was the use of movable type which triggered the revolution in printing—a more efficient and speedier production of printed materials. Two consequences ensued almost immediately. One was the emergence of a new trade, namely book publishing, throughout Europe. The other was that the speedy means of publishing allowed a hitherto unknown popularization of learning. This added an important stimulus for increased literacy (q.v.) and therefore for education. Learning was laicized. The immense publication schedules of the emerging major publishing houses throughout Europe, such as Aldus in Venice, Froben in Basel, and Claxton in England, indicated the desire for information and education throughout Europe in the late 15th and early 16th centuries. Many of these publications were editions of classical authors, both Christian and Pagan.

The coming of the Reformation intensified a development that had been in the making for several decades. It did so dramatically because of the Protestant (q.v.) insistence on the laity (q.v.), which in turn meant the use of the vernacular. In addition, the early German Reformation triggered the use of a new format, called the pamphlet (q.v.): generally slender in size (16, 32, at most 64 pages in length) these pamphlets had the advantage of forcing the author to remain focused on one topic and of allowing a modest cost. It is instructive to note that Martin Luther's (q.v.) Latin treatises, even the important ones, such as the *Babylonian Captivity of the Church*, tended to have one or two reprints at most, whereas his German language pamphlets, such as the tract on *Christian Freedom*, saw two dozen and more reprints. Both the evolving printing trade and the fact that the heat of the controversy in the early Reformation witnessed a desire for all sorts of printed material, including some considered heretical or subversive, led to peregrinatic printshops, small-time printers, in other words, who printed on the run. The role of the printers in the Reformation controversy was critical. The printers were willing to risk potentially precarious investments, for example, in Protestant hymnals (q.v.).

PROFESSIO FIDEI TRIDENTINAE. This term refers to the Roman Catholic confession of faith which, as per the decree of the Council of Trent (q.v.), was promulgated by Pope Pius IV (q.v.) in 1564. This confession included the Nicean-Constantinopalitan creed, the major doctrinal points as affirmed by the Council (seven sacraments; original sin; justification; sacrifice of the Mass; purgatory; veneration of saints, and indulgences [q.v.]) and the general concurrence with all the "customs and traditions" of the church. Subscription to this *professio fidei Tridentinae* was mandatory for all Catholic priests.

PROTESTANTISM. The term Protestant, or Protestantism, has its origins in the "protest" lodged by the evangelical estates at the second diet at Speyer, 1529 (q.v.), against the imperial proposition which declared the recess of the diet at Speyer of 1526 (q.v.) to be null and void and prohibited any further ecclesiastical changes. The protest of the evangelical territories (notably Saxony, Hesse, Brandenburg, Anhalt, and Lüneburg, together with some 14 South German free imperial cities) argued that "in matters that pertain to the honor of God and the salvation of souls, each one must by himself be responsible before God."

The term "Protestant" soon came to be the common nomenclature for all advocates of reform, though officially another term—"the adherents of the Augsburg Confession (q.v.) (i.e., the Lutherans) and those who have kinship with them in matters of religion"—was used for some time. This more than cumbersome term hardly had a chance to become standard nomenclature. Originally, therefore, the term Protestant had the connotation of protest as its distinguishing characteristic, while after the Reformation an alternate Latin root-meaning of the term, to testify for something, became the favorite explanation of the meaning of the term.

The 16th century saw the emergence of several Protestant theological and religious traditions (Lutheran, Reformed/Calvinist, Anglican, Anabaptist, anti-Trinitarian [qq.v.]). Thus, Protestantism was never a homogenous entity. All the same, several identifying characteristics that all Protestant factions can be said to have in common have been noted. They are four: the affirmation that the Bible (q.v.) alone is the locus of authority (against the Catholic notion that Scripture and tradition constitute authentic sources of religious authority); the notion of the "priesthood of all believers" (against the Catholic notion that the priesthood has a special and an indelible character); the belief that salvation is solely attributable to God's grace (q.v.) (against the Catholic affirmation that God and humans work together); and the affirmation of two sacraments (q.v.), baptism and Communion (qq.v.) (against the Catholic affirmation of seven sacraments). Since Martin Luther (q.v.) and the other mainstream Protestant reformers vigorously rejected reformers who propounded a different theological perspective than they did, the suggestion has been made in scholarship to divide Protestantism into a mainstream and a radical wing, the latter nowadays referred to as the Radical Reformation (q.v.).

PURITANISM. Puritanism may be said to be both a timeless phenomenon in the history of Christianity and, as regards the age of the Reformation, a specific historical movement. As a timeless phenomenon in the history of Christianity, the "puritans" have been all those who, like the Cathari (which means, in fact, the "pure ones") in the Middle Ages, determinately and without hesitancy sought to establish a "pure" church with "pure" teaching. In the 16th century the Anabaptists (q.v.), and even before them Andreas Carlstadt (q.v.), manifested this kind of disposition. But the terms "Puritan" and "Puritanism" have been reserved in scholarship for the sentiment (and subsequent movement) that had its origins in England (q.v.) in the 1570s.

The catalyst of this English Puritan phenomenon was the Elizabethan settlement of religion (q.v.), even though the importance of the timeless factor just mentioned must also be noted. Queen Elizabeth I's (q.v.) settlement sought to return English religion to the beginning of her half brother Edward VI's (q.v.) reign, which entailed the reintroduction of the first *Book of Common Prayer* (q.v.) of 1549. This left the adamant Protestant reformers in England deeply disappointed, and from 1559 onward efforts were afoot to get the settlement of religion modified and to take the English church into a more pointedly Protestant, that is Calvinist (qq.v.), direction. In particular, the continuation of what was taken to be Catholic liturgy, namely the use of liturgical vestments and church music, was for these Marian exiles (q.v.) a deep thorn in the flesh. Two Oxford professors, Thomas Sampson and Laurence Humphrey, triggered what became known as the "vestiarian controversy" in which they and their supporters demanded "the authority of Scripture, the simplicity of the servants of Christ" and the "purity of the first and best churches." As early as 1567 followers of Sampson and Humphrey began to meet separately in so-called "prophecyings" which was an indication of separatist tendencies in the movement. They suspected that many in the church continued harboring Catholic beliefs, and they were unwilling to be in the same church with them.

A second phase in the Puritan controversy, carried forward by a younger and more determined group of clergy, had to do with a more scathing rejection of the Elizabethan church. At issue was not only the worship but also the ministry in the church. The battle lines were drawn in 1572 with the publication of the pamphlet (q.v.) *An Admonition to the Parliament*, which dealt with the proper biblical offices in the church. Then John Whitgift, a Cambridge don, published a defense of the status quo, entitled *An Answer to the Admonition*, to which his Cambridge colleague Thomas Cartwright, hewing the rigid Puritan line, responded with several *Replies to the Answer*. When Whitgift became archbishop of Canterbury in 1583 he made the eradication of Puritan sentiment in the Elizabethan church his major goal, suspending hundreds of priests who failed to subscribe to the official line. Cartwright, ever the staunch Puritan polemicist, began to find fault also with the absence of church discipline and published, together with William Travers, the *Holy Discipline*, which, with its rigorous insistence on how the Sabbath was to be kept, was signed by over 500 clergy. Thereby, the division between the mainstream Elizabethan church and its Puritan challengers had come to touch on moral issues as well.

Eventually, there were theological disagreements, focusing on the article on predestination (article 17) of the *Thirty-nine Articles* (qq.v.) and the mainstream church's insistence, first formulated by Bancroft, that the episcopal governance of the church was a matter of divine law (rather than an acceptable ecclesiastical practice). As far as the Puritans were concerned, the fundamental question facing all of them was if the Elizabethan church, despite its various shortcomings, could be reformed or if it could not. Those who gave the former response, and that included the majority of those of Puritan sentiment, had no problem staying in the church, while those who gave the latter response eventually had no choice but leave. This was the distinction between the Non-Separatist Puritans and the Separatist Puritans. But all were dependent on Calvinist notions including the rigid sort propagated by Theodore Beza (q.v.). By the 1590s it was clear that the Elizabethan church would not undertake further reform. In the 17th century, Puritanism, now significantly separatist, focused increasingly on moral issues, and that type is what has given the label "Puritan" its lasting meaning and definition.

— R —

RACOVIAN CATECHISM. Published in Racov, the center of Polish Socinianism, in 1603, this confession (q.v.) of faith of Reformation Socinianism actually included a small and a large catechism (q.v.). It was first published in Polish but subsequently also in German as well as in Latin. The confession is comprised of eight chapters, which, contrary to the traditional structure of Christian creeds, do not begin with a discussion of the doctrine of God but with a discussion of scripture, followed by "the way to salvation." Only the third chapter discusses the Socinian concept of God. The overall tenor of the document is anti-Trinitarian; its christology is adoptionist. (See also ANTI-TRINITARIANISM; SOZZINI, LAELIO).

RADICAL REFORMATION. The term "Radical Reformation" was coined by the Harvard church historian George H. Williams. It is to describe the congery of 16th-century reformers who cannot be subsumed under the rubrics of the three major Protestant traditions (Lutheran, Calvinist, Anglican [qq.v.]) that emerged in the Reformation. Since the theological reform proposals of some reformers were committed to the "roots" of the Christian faith far more so than those of the mainstream reformers, Williams suggested the appropriateness of the term "Radical Reformation." He argued that by venturing to go back to the earliest roots of Christianity, the radical reformers also rejected the Constantinian synthesis, that is, the identity of the civic and ecclesiastical community which came about through measures of the Emperor Constantine in the fourth century. According to Williams, all radical reformers disavowed the Christian's involvement in governmental affairs. Williams subsumed three basic groupings under the heading of the Radical Reformation, each one of them characterized by further subgroupings—the Anabaptists, the anti-Trinitarians, and the Spiritualists (qq.v.).

Williams's term has become widely accepted in Reformation scholarship, even though it begs a number of questions. Foremost, of course, is the fact that common parlance understands "radical" not so much as "going to the roots" but as "extreme" or "revolutionary." In a way, of course, the radical reformers were indeed more "radical" in the customary sense of the word than were the magisterial reformers, for example, in the Anabaptist repudiation of any connection between church and government but in other ways they were not. Moreover, it assuredly was the self-understanding of all reformers that they were going back to the "roots" as they perceived and understood them. The fact that Martin Luther (q.v.), for example, accepted the Nicene Creed was plainly due to his conviction that the creed was in conformity with biblical teaching, while the anti-Trinitarians saw it as a fourth century perversion. Underlying the concept of the "Radical Reformation" is the assumption that these three "radical" strands of the Reformation shared certain affirmations and presuppositions in such a way as to allow their being grouped together.

RAMUS, PETER (1515-1572). French Humanist (q.v.) and philosopher. Pierre de la Ramée was educated at the University of Paris, where he subsequently also taught. In his master's thesis of 1536 he pointedly attacked Aristotle, who provided the philosophical underpinnings of scholastic theology, and in the 1540s he published several important books on dialectic and Aristotle (such as *Aristotilae animadversiones*), which led to charges that he was undermining the foundations of theology. Nonetheless, Ramus was appointed professor at the Collège Royal, where he subsequently became dean. Under the influence of the Colloquy of Poissy (q.v.) Ramus converted to Protestantism (q.v.) in 1561-62. He left France in 1568 and joined the Calvinist (q.v.) congregation in Heidelberg in 1569.

His staunch opposition to any form of Protestant Aristotelianism brought him both opponents and supporters. When Theodore Beza (q.v.) insisted on the use of the term "substance" to describe the presence of Christ in the elements of bread and wine in Communion (q.v.), varying the content but not the method of the traditional Catholic teaching, Ramus objected vehemently. Beza's enmity closed the possibility of a teaching position in Geneva (q.v.), even as Ramus's advocacy of a more democratic congregational form of church government was rejected by the synod of the French Reformed Church in Nimes in 1572. Ramus's scholarly work focused on method, which was deductive, moving from the "general" to the "particular." His educational philosophy was widely influential in Calvinist/Reformed (q.v.) universities well into the 17th century. Ramus was murdered in the St. Bartholomew's Day Massacre (q.v.) in August 1572.

RECUSANCY, RECUSANTS. From the Latin term *recusare*, the term refers to the refusal, notably of Catholics, to participate in the worship of the Church of England during the reign of Elizabeth I (q.v.). It is nowadays generally taken for granted that even as late as the succession of Elizabeth, the majority of the English people had continued to be Catholic at heart so that the Elizabethan settlement (q.v.) of religion not only had to focus on the insistent demands of the adamant Protestants but also the evident Catholic majority in the country.

All the same, official policy until the late 1560s was fairly lenient until Mary Stuart's flight to England (q.v.) in 1568 raised the prospect of Catholics rallying behind Mary as legitimate heir to the English throne. Two years later Pope Pius V (q.v.) excommunicated Elizabeth and freed all English people from their allegiance to the queen. That triggered an intensification of the English domestic situation. In 1571 Parliament declared any questioning of the queen's rightful occupancy of the English throne or of her religion as heretical to be high treason.

Meanwhile William Allen had established the college at Douai (q.v.) for the express purpose of training English priests, and 10 years later Robert Parsons and Edmund Campion began the clandestine Jesuit (q.v.) mission to England. In the 1580s repression became more severe. Among English Catholics a heated debate took place as to whether or not mere external conformity (such as attending the services of the Anglican [q.v.] Church) was permissible. The confrontation between the Recusants and the English crown ended in a stalemate: the political loyalty of Catholics remained in doubt, while the Catholics in turn remained even over two generations adamant in their loyalty to the Catholic Church.

REFORM, IMPERIAL. The patent inability of the Holy Roman Empire (q.v.) early in the 15th century to defend itself in the face of the Hussite threat conveyed to many the weaknesses in the imperial constitution and furthered the calls for a comprehensive imperial reform. The major objective of such reform efforts was to assure law and order throughout the empire. But despite a plethora of reform proposals, no concrete reform followed. When, in the second half of the 15th century the Turkish threat against central Europe became formidable, deliberations about imperial reform received new urgency.

It was not until the succession of Emperor Maximilian I in 1493 that specific proposals—such as initiatives for the reform of taxation and the military—began to be discussed. At the diet at Worms, in 1495, several reform measures were adopted. Some of the measures, such as the creation of a Reichsregiment, as a standing representative body of the princes, failed to have practical import, while others, such as the establishment of a Reichskammergericht, or imperial supreme court, as an entity separate from the imperial court, proved to be enormously important. It was to be significant that this court used Roman Law to adjudicate its cases; the acceptance of Roman Law in Germany (q.v.) thus was dramatically furthered.

During the Reformation the imperial supreme court proved to be the agency called upon to settle the contested issue of church property in Protestant lands. Whenever, such as in the Peace of Nuremberg (q.v.), Protestants (q.v.) were given a temporary truce, one of the stipulations always was that all suits in religious matters before the court would be suspended for the time being. The financing of these activities was to be made possible through an empire-wide tax, the "common penny," which, since there was no appropriate administrative structure (not to mention the recalcitrance of many territories), was hardly ever collected. Not until the diet at Augsburg (q.v.) in 1555 did reform encompass a common military policy. This was done administratively by dividing the empire into 10 regions (*Kreise*) and giving each of them specific responsibilities for the common defense of the empire.

REFORMATION. The term "reform" *(reformatio)* was used in the latter Middle Ages to denote a return (as did the term "renaissance") to an earlier and better state of affairs and older principles. In 1308 the phrase "reform of the church and head and members" was first formulated, and it continued to be used until the 16th century. For Martin Luther (q.v.) "reformation" consisted not in practical reform measures so much as in the "liberation of consciences," that is, in a new theological orientation which was, however, declared to be the ancient and authentic biblical one.

Still, the self-understanding on the part of the Protestant (q.v.) reformers was that they were engaged in a Reformation of the church. In the political and legal deliberations leading to the Peace of Augsburg (q.v.), the Protestant churches were referred to as the "reformed churches". This included those territories and cities that were members of the League of Schmalkald (q.v.); theologically it meant those who subscribed to the Augsburg Confession (q.v.). Only when the Lutheran *Book of Concord* was introduced in 1580 did the term "reformed" come to be distinguished from the term "Lutheran" while the term "reformed" began to be used in Western Europe to describe, in contrast to the Catholic Church, all churches and theologies that were not Catholic. Historiographically, the term was used, together with the analogous terms "reformer" and "reform" already in the 16th century to describe what we have come to call "Reformation."

The German historian Leopold von Ranke introduced, early in the 19th century the notion of an "age of the Reformation" (which was then followed by an "age of the (Catholic) Counter Reformation" (q.v.) which usage continued until fairly recently, when the broader term "early modern Europe" began to be accepted. This latter term is based on the notion that one should see the Reformation of the 16th century as part of a much broader and longer development that began in the late 14th century and last until the early 18th century. This view questions much of the originality claimed for the Reformation by earlier scholarship and affirms much greater continuity between the 15th century and the 16th century. The implication of this view is to deny religion and theology the primacy which they had enjoyed when it was customary to speak about an "age of the Reformation."

Rcently, some scholars have begun to speak of "Reformations" in the 16th century using the plural to denote the diversity and multiplicity of reform initiatives.

REFORMED. This term denotes that Protestant tradition which resulted from the convergence of the Zwinglian and the Calvinist (qq.v.) Reformations. This coming together of these two quite similar theological traditions occurred in the 1549 agreement between Heinrich Bullinger and John Calvin (qq.v.) reached in the Consensus Tigurinus (q.v.). From then on the term "reformed," rather than "Calvinist" or "Zwinglian," expresses best the ecclesiastical tradition. (See also BULLINGER, HEINRICH; CALVIN, JOHN; CALVINISM; CONSENSUS TIGURINUS).

REMONSTRANTS. This faction of the Reformed church of the Low Countries received its appellation from the Remonstrance of 1610 presented to the Estates of West Friesland and Holland by the followers of Jacobus Arminius, who objected to the rigid Calvinist (q.v.) notion of predestination (q.v.).

RESIDENCY, EPISCOPAL. The late medieval church distinguished between the spiritual and the financial aspects of the episcopal office. It saw no problem if an incumbent received the financial benefits from his diocese, while not actually himself carrying out the actual episcopal functions. These were carried out by a substitute. This practice was severely attacked by the Protestant (q.v.) reformers. Pope Paul III (q.v.) began in 1540 to address the issue, issuing stricter regulations about bishops actually residing in their dioceses.

REUCHLIN, JOHANNES (1455-1522). Humanist (q.v.). Born in Pforzheim in southwest Germany, Reuchlin studied at Paris, Freiburg, and Basel; later he studied law at Orleans and Poitiers, which furthered his Humanist interests and inclinations. Several trips to Italy (1482, 1492, 1498) proved to be of significance for his intellectual formation. Reuchlin entered the service of Duke Eberhard of Württemberg, married well, and thus was able to pursue his literary, philosophical, and linguistic studies as an independent scholar. He quickly established himself as one of the foremost representatives of late 15th-century Neoplatonism.

Reuchlin began to study Hebrew in 1482 and published a Hebrew grammar (*Rudimenta linguae Hebraicae*) in 1506. This publication marked the beginning of serious Christian Hebrew scholarship in Europe. It was augmented during the ensuing decade by two further writings, *De verbo mirifico* (Concerning the Marvelous Word), 1514, and *De arte cabalistica* (Concerning the Art of the Cabalah), 1517, which were characterized by Reuchlin's appropriation of cabalistic notions.

The last decade of Reuchlin's life was overshadowed by his involvement in the controversy pertaining to the acceptability of Jewish books and writings. Reuchlin had affirmed this in a brief for Emperor Maximilian (1510), as well as in a polemical piece against Johann Pfefferkorn who, though himself a converted Jew, had vehemently argued that all Jewish books should be burned. While supported by virtually all Humanists, Reuchlin faced the adamant opposition of Dominican theologians. A suit against him resulted in his vindication, to which he added one of the great satires of the time, *The Letters of Obscure Men*, a biting and humorous indictment of the subtle and esoteric scholasticism of his opponents. The sharpness of his tone alienated the more irenic Humanists, such as Desiderius Erasmus (q.v.). While Reuchlin died soon after the outbreak of the Reformation controversy and thus had no opportunity to take sides, his significance for the Reformation lies in his providing a solid base for Protestant (q.v.) Hebrew scholarship. Virtually all of the Protestant Hebraeists of the first generation had been his pupils. (See also ANTI-SEMITISM).

ROTHMANN, BERND (c. 1495-1535). Anabaptist (q.v.) theologian. Rothmann was born in Stadtlohn near Münster (q.v.) in northwest Germany, studied at Mainz, was ordained to the priesthood in 1529, and became chaplain at one of the Münster town churches that same year. A brief period of study at Cologne followed but Rothmann soon came under the influence of Reformation thought. Münster merchants with similar inclinations financed a trip to Wittenberg. In 1532 Rothmann was instrumental in introducing the Reformation in Münster. During a visit to Strasbourg Rothmann encountered the Anabaptist notions of Melchior Hofmann (q.v.). Soon thereafter he embraced Anabaptist sentiment and, as the foremost reformer in

Münster, successfully took the city in the direction of a reform along Anabaptist lines.

In 1533 and 1534 Rothmann published several important tracts that summarized his own new theology, which was at once the theology of the Münsterite Anabaptists. Of these publications, *The Restitution* and *Concerning Wrath* were the most important in that they eloquently delineated Rothmann's view of salvation history and the place the city of Münster was to play in it. On January 5, 1534, Rothmann was baptized. The subsequent, more radical changes undertaken in Münster were at first opposed by him but then endorsed. Nothing is known about his death; he was undoubtedly killed when the besieging forces took Münster.

— S —

SACK OF ROME. On May 27, 1527, troops of Emperor Charles V (q.v.) under the command of Philibert, prince of Orange, and Georg von Frundsberg stormed Rome, took the pope prisoner, and ravaged the city, the famous *sacco di Roma*. Charles's army had been in northern Italy engaged in desultory fighting against the forces of the League of Cognac (q.v.), which was comprised, under the leadership of France (q.v.), of Venice, Florence, and the pope. Charles's mercenaries, who had not been paid for months, revolted and proceeded to Rome, after the attempt to storm Florence had been thwarted by the troops of the league. Pope Clement VII (q.v.) remained imprisoned in the castle of Sant' Angelo until the fall of 1528.

SACRAMENTS. The medieval church defined its sacramental teaching at the Council of Florence (1439). This meant the affirmation of seven sacraments (baptism, confirmation, marriage, extreme unction, Eucharist, penance, ordination). The Protestant reformers affirmed only two of those, namely baptism and the Lord's Supper (qq.v.), with the explanation that only those two could be shown to have been specifically instituted by Christ as sacraments, that is, vehicles of divine grace (q.v.). Moreover, the reformers rejected the notion of the automatic efficiency of the sacraments and argued that the sacraments were only beneficial for those who received them in faith. Martin Luther (q.v.) and a strand of the Anglican (q.v.) tradition were emphatic, all the same, in their assertion that the sacraments did serve as vehicles of divine grace if accompanied by the recipient's faith.

Among all reformers there was also strong agreement that the foremost vehicle of grace was the preached Word. Luther and the Lutheran (q.v.) tradition, while emphasizing the importance of the proclaimed Word, retained the notion of the sacraments of baptism and the Lord's Supper as such vehicles, objectively real but beneficial only to those in faith.

In contrast, the Zurich reformer Huldrych Zwingli (q.v.) rejected this notion of the "sacrament" as unbiblical. For him, baptism and the Lord's Supper were memorial signs and, even more so, public testimonials to one's faith. Luther's conviction that even as the proclaimed word the sacraments are vehicles of grace to be appropriated by the recipient by faith was alien to Zwingli. Zwingli's position was appropriated in modified form by John Calvin (q.v.), who argued that Jesus instituted the sacraments in order to seal and strengthen his word of salvation, that is, to strengthen the recipient's faith. In opposition to Lutheran theology Calvin rejected an independent autonomy of the sacrament as a vehicle of grace, arguing that the Word alone conveys salvation; the sacraments serve the function of being the seal of this Word. Still, something real takes place but only to those predestined. For all others, water, bread, and wine are simply natural elements, nothing more. In the Radical Reformation (q.v.) one may detect Zwingli's influence in that the term "sacrament" was rejected: the Lord's Supper was a memorial meal, while baptism denoted the public profession of one's faith.

SCHLEITHEIM CONFESSION. The "Brotherly Union" promulgated in the town of Schleitheim on the Swiss-German border in 1527 was the result of an effort to find common denominators for the Swiss-Austrian-South German Anabaptists (q.v.), who had splintered into various groupings since their origins in Zurich (q.v.) two years earlier. The confession emphasized essentially the position one may glean from the original Zurich group, including such principles as pacifism, the non-swearing of oaths, and the centrality of Scripture, which had not been emphasized by some Anabaptists who took the indwelling Holy Spirit as their authority. The confession thus laid the groundwork for a relatively cohesive Anabaptist movement in South Germany, Switzerland (qq.v.), and Austria.

SCHMALKALD, LEAGUE OF. The recess of the diet at Augsburg (q.v.) in 1530 had given the Protestants six months to return to the Catholic Church threatening them with legal and criminal proceedings before the imperial cameral court in case of their refusal to do so. The day after the recess was issued on September 22, the Saxon elector John indicated to the representatives of the South German cities that an alliance of all Protestant rulers and cities was desirable. When Charles V (q.v.) in turn invited the electors (q.v.) to meet in Cologne at the end of December to discuss the transfer of greater power and authority to his brother Ferdinand during his own absences from the Holy Roman Empire (q.v.), Elector John invited the Protestant rulers to convene at Schmalkald a week prior to the Cologne meeting to discuss the overall political situation prompted by the religious controversy. Both Ferdinand's election as Roman king and the threatened proceedings before the imperial cameral court were to be on the agenda. In the end, an alliance to resist the emperor's potential use of force against them was agreed upon at the meeting.

Officially, the league came into being in February 1531. Twenty-three territories and cities joined the league, which was to exist for six years; in 1537 the league was renewed for 10 years. However, it took until 1535 to reach agreement on the by-laws of the league, which dealt with such matters as the naming of a commander in chief in case of armed conflict, the financing of the common forces, etc. It bespeaks the intimate connection between religion and politics in the Reformation that the league was both an instrument for the defense of the Protestant (q.v.) faith and also an anti-Habsburg alliance. The explanation lies in the fact that the Protestants saw the Habsburgs as the principal menace to their faith. The key issue hovering over the beginnings of the league was the theological problem if political resistance against the emperor was in fact morally justified.

None other than Martin Luther (q.v.) initially had grave misgivings about such a resistance, being of the conviction that Christians had to suffer injustice rather than use force to have their way. The League of Schmalkald was a major factor in the German Reformation in the 1530s since its existence conveyed to the emperor and to the other Catholics that the Protestants could not be easily subdued. In the War of Schmalkald (q.v.) internal disagreements, which had been part and parcel of the league from the very beginning, precluded an effective strategy. After the emperor's victory the league was dissolved.

SCHMALKALD, WAR OF. By the early 1540s—after the series of abortive religious colloquies (q.v.)—it became evident to Emperor Charles V (q.v.) that his efforts to achieve conciliation with the

Protestants (q.v.) had failed. Charles began to prepare for a military showdown with the League of Schmalkald (q.v.) by consolidating his international involvement, particularly by concluding peace with France (q.v.). The Protestants were aware of the emperor's intention and undertook to strengthen their military preparedness. On July 20, barely six months after Martin Luther's (q.v.) death, Charles declared the Saxon elector and the landgrave of Hesse, the two main bulwarks of the League of Schmalkald, to be political outlaws for actions that in part had occurred in the distant past. The initial military confrontation between the emperor's forces and the League of Schmalkald occurred in South Germany in the summer. There was every reason for the league to retain the upper hand but the league did not utilize its superior military strength—the thinking of the league had been too much geared to a defensive, rather than offensive posture. In November, Duke Maurice of Saxony, officially a Protestant, joined the emperor's coalition and invaded Electoral Saxony. This forced the withdrawal of troops of the league from South Germany and the full surrender of South German Protestant cities and territories to the emperor.

The incisive military encounter of the war took place in Saxony in the spring of the following year, when the battle at Mühlberg on April 24 brought the decisive victory for the emperor. Soon thereafter, both the Saxon Elector John Frederick and the Hessian Landgrave Philip (q.v.) were taken prisoners. John Frederick lost not only half of his possessions but also the electoral title; Philip kept his territory but both remained the emperor's prisoners for five years. The war resulted in the end of the League of Schmalkald, and gave the emperor, at least for the time being, unchallenged power in the empire.

SCHWENCKFELD, CASPAR VON (1489-1561). Spiritualist (q.v.) reformer. A Silesian nobleman, Caspar von Schwenckfeld pursued an administrative career, became a committed follower of Martin Luther (q.v.) and, as such, was instrumental in the introduction of the Reformation in Liegnitz. His spiritualizing views of the Lord's Supper (q.v.), that is, he denied that the body and blood of Christ were truly present in the elements of bread and wine, together with the suspicion that he harbored Anabaptist (q.v.) views led to his expulsion from Silesia in 1529. Schwenckfeld's vision was that of apostolic Christianity and that meant for him that the Christian life, and the fruits of the Christian profession, were the most important aspect of

Christianity. Schwenckfeld settled in Strasbourg, where between 1529 and 1533 he formulated, in conversation with the Strasbourg reformers Martin Bucer and Wolfgang Capito (qq.v.) as well as Anabaptist leaders, his distinctive theology. In 1533 he was forced to leave Strasbourg and moved to Augsburg. In 1535 he briefly settled in Ulm but soon became unwanted because of his theological views.

The remaining two decades of his life were spent as a refugee, moving from place to place. All the while, Schwenckfeld wrote prolifically: over one hundred of his writings were printed, and many more circulated in manuscript form. In all, his appeal was to a spiritualistic, individualistic Christian faith, whose adherents lived their faith by themselves, divorced from the "creaturely church." He had a few followers who perpetuated his understanding of Christianity beyond the 16th century. (See also RADICAL REFORMATION).

SCOTLAND. In the 16th century Scotland was an independent kingdom, though intimate dynastic relations existed with England (q.v.) (Queen Margaret was the sister of Henry VIII [q.v.]). England had defeated Scotland in 1542 but Henry VIII's efforts to marry his son Edward to Mary Stuart (q.v.), daughter of Mary of Guise and James V of Scotland, proved unsuccessful. Mary was sent to France (q.v.) to marry Francis II but on his death in 1560 Mary found herself back in Scotland. She seemed to represent French interests, which, in turn, were bitterly opposed by the Scottish nobility. Moreover, and importantly so, the Reformation had made considerable headway in Scotland. The driving force was John Knox (q.v.) who, in 1558, had published a tirade entitled *The First Blast of the Trumpet against the Monstrous Regiment of Women*. It was directed against Mary and was an appeal for her to desist from her idolatrous religion. It also contained, rather subtly, the warning that a ruler who persecuted the true religion (as did Mary of Guise as queen regent in Knox's mind) could not command the loyalty of her subjects. Knox notwithstanding, a proclamation was issued in February 1559 that made any violation of ecclesiastical regulations punishable by death. This took Scotland to the brink of a civil war in which political and religious considerations intertwined. Politically, it was the specter of French domination of Scottish affairs; religiously, it was the aggressive effort to maintain Catholicism.

In 1560, after the death of the queen regent, both England and France removed their troops from Scotland. Parliament met and adopted a Protestant confession (qq.v.) of faith. Thus, in a way, the beginnings of Protestant Scotland can be put to 1560, even though Parliament had not been authorized to deal with religious matters, and it was not until 1567 that Queen Mary gave legal sanction to the new Protestant church. Mary Stuart's rule continued in a complicated fashion. An ill-fated marriage with Henry Stuart, Lord Darnley, together with an enigmatic relationship with her secretary David Riccio, led to Riccio's murder and Darnley's assassination. The Scottish nobility was fed up with a queen who had shown herself lacking in common sense and given to violent moods. In June 1567 she was arrested and forced to abdicate. She fled to England, soliciting Queen Elizabeth I's (q.v.) help against the disobedient rebels in her land. After years of imprisonment in England, Mary Stuart was convicted of having plotted against Queen Elizabeth and was beheaded in February 1587. By that time Calvinist (q.v.) Protestantism had established itself firmly in Scotland.

SERVETUS, MICHAEL (c. 1509-1553). Anti-Trinitarian (q.v.) reformer. Little is known about youth and background of this foremost anti-Trinitarian theologian of the 16th century. In 1530 he presented a fairly well developed understanding of the doctrine of the Trinity to the Basel reformer Johann Oecolampadius (q.v.), which suggests that he had extensive theological training. One year later Servetus published his first work entitled *De trinitatis erroribus* (Concerning the Errors of the Trinity), which was followed by two further treatises, also on the subject of the Trinity, *Dialogus de Trinitate* and *De justitita regni Christi* (Dialogue Concerning the Trinity and Concerning the Righteousness of the Kingdom of Christ). The simple premise of all three treatises was that neither the creeds of the early church nor the teachings of the reformers could be harmonized with the teaching of the Bible (q.v.).

Essentially, Servetus propounded a strictly monotheistic theology, in which Jesus, although imbued with the divine spirit, was merely a representation of the godhead. In addition, Servetus propounded a number of other notions, such as the assertion that one cannot speak of human sin before a person's 20th year, that baptism (q.v.) thus should be performed on adults, which added to the dismay and repudiation of his published work. Servetus found it appropriate to disappear from the public limelight but he resurfaced, in 1540, in Vienne, France, as personal physician to the local Catholic bishop, having changed his name to Villeneuve. Outwardly a devout Catholic physician, Servetus was prompted, by the publication of a Latin edition of the Bible, to reflect on the whole range of Christian theology. His findings were embodied in a manuscript entitled *Restitutio Christianismi* (The Restitution of Christianity).

In the mid-1540s Servetus engaged in correspondence with John Calvin (q.v.), seeking to convert the Genevan reformer to his views. In the process Servetus sent Calvin sections from his manuscript: and when, rather surprisingly, the manuscript was published in 1553, without an indication of its author, John Calvin was naturally aware of the author's identity. Possibly at Calvin's urging, a Calvinist refugee from France denounced Servetus to the Inquisition (q.v.) in Vienne. Servetus barely escaped arrest and, after a lapse of about three months, appeared of all places in Geneva (q.v.). He was immediately arrested, brought to trial, and sentenced to death for his theological errors. Burned at the stake, Servetus, who never rejected the deity of Jesus, only Jesus' eternal coexistence with the Father, became a symbol both for the repudiation of the orthodox doctrine of the Trinity but also for the inappropriateness of persecuting heretics with the sword.

SEXUALITY. The notions of human sexuality held in European Christendom may be said to go back to Augustine's interpretation of the relevant biblical passages. Thus, Augustine's long shadow falls even over the Reformation of the 16th century. Simply put, Augustine saw sexual intercourse as the reenactment of the Fall in the Garden of Eden in that the human inability to resist the sexual drive (the rebellion of body against the will, thus a rebellion of the lower against the higher) resembled the rebellion of the lower against the higher in Adam and Eve. Augustine cited anthropological observations to sustain his case that humans, under the burden of the Fall, are embarrassed both by their sexual organs, and cover them, and by the act of intercourse, which takes place in private.

The Protestant (q.v.) reformers, beginning with Martin Luther (q.v.), may be said to have been led a reinterpretation of human sexuality in a roundabout way. The point of departure was the repudiation of the ideal of celibacy, both because it was an expression of an elitist ethic meant for the few and also because it was unnatural and impossible. Consequently, the reformers extolled marriage (q.v.) as a divine order of creation, which meant embracing a pointedly positive understanding of human sexuality. However, the expression of human sexuality was strictly confined to marriage, and its function was procreation.

While one may find echoes of Augustine even in Luther, it is clear that the perspective had changed. The analogy of the understanding of human sexuality to the other orders of creation helps understand the reformers' position. Luther affirmed emphatically the Christian's responsibility to participate in the public realm as judge or soldier, fully realizing that the fallenness of creation placed the Christian into conflict situations, where the mandates of the Gospel seemed to be in conflict with the duties of a judge or soldier. Likewise, the exercise of sexuality does reverberate echoes of the Garden of Eden but at the same time expresses God's will not only of procreation but also of mutual love and affection between the spouses. In short, the Protestant Reformation brought a more emphatic affirmation of human sexuality than Catholic moral theology allowed; this new, more positive view was expressed even more positively in 17th-century English Puritanism (q.v.). (See also DIVORCE).

SIX ARTICLES ACT. The ecclesiastical changes occurring in England (q.v.) in the 1530s through a series of parliamentary statutes left theological considerations largely unconsidered. Understandably, the repudiation of papal supremacy and the designation of the king as the "supreme head of the church" gave impetus to the would-be Protestant (q.v.) reformers in England to seek more extensive theological changes along Protestant lines. Henry VIII (q.v.) himself was conservative, and the Six Articles Act, promulgated in 1539, officially the "act abolishing diversity in opinions," reflected his sentiment. The Six Articles were unmistakably conservative in nature, such as the re-iteration of clerical celibacy, which prompted Thomas Cranmer (q.v.) to send his wife back to her native Germany. The act of Parliament stipulated harsh punishments for violations. For example, the denial of transubstantiation was punishable by death. However, as long as Thomas Cromwell (q.v.) served as lord chancellor, the harsh measures were not implemented. After his fall (and execution), persecution was sporadic at best.

SIXTUS V (1521-1590). Pope. Successor to Pope Gregory XIII (q.v.), Felice Peretti combined the rigoristic mindset of Pius V with the diplomatic skills of Paul III (qq.v.). The five years of his pontifical rule (1585-1590) were characterized by his extensive reform measures in

Rome, restoring law and order to the city, and successfully salvaging papal finances. Above all, Sixtus undertook a comprehensive reform of the Roman curia, which had been (at papal insistence) left untouched by the otherwise ubiquitous reform measures of the Council of Trent (q.v.). In lieu of an unwieldy bureaucracy that was a legacy of the Middle Ages, Sixtus reorganized the curia along the lines of "congregations" in 1588. There were 15 of such "congregations," six of which were responsible for the administration of the Papal States, while the others dealt with churchwide matters (such as the Inquisition, the *Index of Prohibited Books* [qq.v.], diocesan councils, bishops, consistory, as well as the Vatican printing press). While in the Middle Ages the small number of cardinals in Rome had tended to force a claim of corule on the popes, the dramatic increase in the college of cardinals (the Council of Constance had limited the number of cardinals to 24) to no less than 70 enhanced the administrative functioning of the entire Catholic Church. At the same time, any claim to corule with the pope became practically meaningless.

Sixtus also deserves recognition for his many building projects in Rome, his intention being to make Rome into the most beautiful city in Christendom and thus the center of the religious world: most of the Roman buildings that have become the characteristic features of the "eternal city" go back to Sixtus (the dome of St. Peter's, St. Peter's Square, the Jesuit mother church Al Gesu, even the building of the Vatican library).

Sixtus's exuberance found its limitation in the revision of the Vulgate translation of the Bible (q.v.). The Council of Trent had ordered such a revision and a series of scholars had been at work ever since. Sixtus concluded that their work of revision was proceeding far too slowly and took it on himself to complete the work. The edition was printed in May 1590 and dispatched to leading Catholic rulers but it promptly became evident that it was (due to Sixtus's involvement) so replete with mistakes that it had to be withdrawn after Sixtus's death in August of that same year.

SOCIAL WELFARE. The term refers to the sum total of policies and practical initiatives that pertain to the social, physical, and economic well-being of the people in a community. Traditionally, in Europe this responsibility had been exercised in large measure by the church. This is understandable in that the care for the poor and the sick, two major components of any social welfare initiative, was integral to the moral teaching of the church. However, the second half of the 15th century increasingly manifested, particularly in the cities, a concern by city councils and secular authorities to assume far greater and comprehensive responsibility for the well-being of its citizens. Some of the tensions between church and secular authorities on the eve of the Reformation had to do precisely with this issue.

During the indulgences controversy (q.v.), when the true nature of the controversy was by no mean clear, a variety of social and economic reform proposals were put forward; Martin Luther (q.v.) himself, in his *Open Letter to the Christian Nobility*, 1520, wrote lengthily to issues of societal reform, making the long-standing German *gravamina* (q.v.) the focal point of his discourse. The first expression of social welfare reform in the context of the Reformation came at Wittenberg in 1522, when an *Order for the Common Chest* was promulgated. At issue was the care for the poor. Other similar orders invariably followed wherever the Reformation was introduced. Noteworthy was the close cooperation between church and political authority.

SOCIETY OF JESUS. Undoubtedly the most famous and important of the new expressions of Catholic monasticism in the 16th century, embodying the vision of one man, Ignatius of Loyola (q.v.), the Society of Jesus (Societas Jesu), or Jesuits, was formally approved by Pope Paul III (q.v.) in September 1540 with the bull *Regimini militantis ecclesiae*. The use of the name of Jesus in the appellation of the new society, quite offensive to many, was derived from the explanation given by Ignatius in Italy when first asked who they were: they were "Jesus' company." Ignatius and his companions wanted to do missionary work in the Holy Land but armed conflict forced them to fall back on their alternate objective, namely to go to Rome and offer their services to the pope. Their stern commitment evoked the suspicion of Lutheran (q.v.) heresy, while their formal recognition as a new monastic order, despite their small numbers, was complicated by the fact that the new order of the Theatines (q.v.) had virtually identical objectives as those proposed by Ignatius.

Within a few years of its formal approval, the Society of Jesus had spread across Europe and beyond. The society soon became the most powerful instrument of Catholic evangelism and spiritual renewal, not only in Europe but in places of European expansion as well. Particularly in the Americas (Brazil), the Jesuits played an important role in the European conquest and settlement. The Jesuits' engagement for a humane treatment of the native peoples in the Americas deserves special mention. Francis Xavier (q.v.) went to India and Japan and planned to go to China. In Europe, Jesuits increasingly occupied important positions in universities and as spiritual advisors to rulers. Jesuits came to be seen as the embodiment of the Counter-Reformation. At the time of Ignatius's death in 1556, the society had some one hundred houses with approximately 1,000 members, of whom only 35 were "professores." Ignatius had drafted a constitution for the society which had been in use ever since 1550. His successor Jacob Lainez saw to its formal adoption in 1558.

The key documents ordering the life of the Society are the *examen generale Societas Jesu* (for new members); the *Constitutiones* (the by-laws of the society); the *Declarationes* (the decisions of the various general congregations, or meetings of the society); the *Regulae* (the procedures and policies), and the *Ratio studiorum* (the prescribed course of study). These documents expressed the care with which new members were to be admitted to the society. For example, persons suspect of heresy and mentally disabled persons were to be excluded. Ignatius also was convinced that women were incapable of carrying out the kind of work he wanted the society to do so that no female branch of the Society of Jesus came into being.

The training of members followed the customary monastic pattern with the important difference that it was more extensive and rigorous. After two years of initial training the probationer took the customary "scholastic vows" (of poverty, celibacy, and obedience). For most "Jesuits" this ended their formal training and made them "secular coadjutors." A few specially selected members, the "scholastici approbati," continued their studies by entering a Jesuit seminary to pursue extensive theological studies. With their eventual ordination to the priesthood they became "spiritual coadjutors." A small number of those, in turn, were solicited to undertake further studies and, after a formal examination, were permitted to make the vow of special obedience to the pope. This last group is known as the "professores," in effect the inner core of the society.

In the strict sense the Society of Jesus is not a monastic "order" in that its members do not follow a daily "order," generally that of St. Benedict. Rather, the distinguishing mark of Jesuits was the obligation to engage once a year in doing the *Spiritual Exercises*, a four-week spiritual exercise or retreat. By the end of the 16th century members of the Society of Jesus increasingly occupied positions of influence and importance throughout Catholic Europe.

SOZZINI, FAUSTO (1539-1604). Anti-Trinitarian (q.v.) theologian. Born in Sienna to a family of distinguished jurists, Fausto early on come under the influence of manuscripts of his uncle Laelio Sozzini, (q.v.) who, in extensive travels throughout Switzerland and Germany (qq.v.), had been in contact with leading reformers of the time. These contacts helped sharpen his own theological position, which he put down in a number of unpublished manuscripts. Upon his death these manuscripts came to his nephew. Having been for over a decade in the service of the Florentine grand duke Cosimo, Fausto moved to Basel upon Cosimo's death in 1574. In Basel he pursued theological studies and wrote his major theological treatise entitled *De Jesu Christo Servatore* (Concerning Jesus Christ, the Saver). The strongly anti-Trinitarian sentiment of the book embroiled its author in controversy, and, finding Basel inhospitable, Fausto moved to Poland (q.v.), where anti-Trinitarian sentiment had found its way into Calvinist (q.v.) congregations, though characterized more by opposition to the traditional Trinitarian dogma than by a cohesive positive stand. Fausto succeeded in finding a common denominator for the Polish anti-Trinitarians. The anti-Trinitarian Minor Church was the result of his efforts, even though ironically his irenic position was found to be so compromising for some adamant anti-Trinitarians that he was never received into church membership.

When, after the turn of the century, the Minor Church began to consider the desirability of a confession (q.v.) of faith, Fausto's ideas formed the basis for the document that resulted in the *Racovian Catechism* (q.v.) in 1605. Already in 1598, however, he had removed himself from active involvement in church affairs and had settled in a small village. Fausto's significance lies less in his theology than in the application of his theological thought to the problems of practical churchmanship facing the Polish anti-Trinitarians toward the end of the 16th century.

SOZZINI, LAELIO (1525-1562). Anti-Trinitarian (q.v.) theologian. This lay theologian came from a family of Italian jurists. His father served as professor of law at various Italian universities. Though with broad interests, Laelio began the study of law but left Italy abruptly in 1547. Extensive travels to England and France (qq.v.) followed. In

1548-49 he debated John Calvin (q.v.) in Geneva (q.v.) on a number of theological points, notably the resurrection of the body. He moved to Zurich, where the Swiss theologians got ready to formulate the Consensus Tigurinus (q.v.). Again, Laelio caused consternation by his persistent questioning, this time regarding the teaching on the sacraments (q.v.) in the Consensus. In 1550 he traveled to Wittenberg to consult with Philip Melanchthon (q.v.). Back in Switzerland (q.v.) one year later, he quarreled with both Calvin and Heinrich Bullinger (q.v.). In 1555 appeared his only published work, *De sacramentis dissertatione* (Concerning the Sacraments). Three years later he traveled to Poland (q.v.), where he was in contact with Giorgio Biandrata (q.v.). He soon returned to Switzerland and died in 1562. His theological thought was mainly embodied in various manuscripts that on his death came to his nephew Fausto Sozzini (q.v.) whom they lastingly influenced. Particularly with regard to the sacraments and the Trinity Laelio developed distinctive notions. Alongside Michael Servetus (q.v.), Laelio clearly was the most important early representative of 16th-century anti-Trinitarian thought.

SPAIN. The Spanish peninsula, comprised (in addition to Portugal) of Aragon and Castile, was united under Ferdinand and Isabella, even though this union did not mean a real union of these two kingdoms. When Isabella died in 1506 Cardinal Ximenes de Cisneros became regent, and upon Ferdinand's death in 1516, his oldest son Charles of Burgundy assumed the crown as Charles I of Spain (q.v.) (subsequently Emperor Charles V [q.v.]). Charles's pursuit of the imperial crown upon the death of Emperor Maximilian meant a preoccupation with affairs other than those of Spain for stretches throughout his rule. The imposition of a new tax (*servicio*) in 1520 triggered a revolt which, for a while, seemed to mean the collapse of Charles's authority in Spain. Charles was saved by his willingness to make concessions.

Severe economic problems plagued Spain throughout the 16th century such as heavy taxation, required to finance Charles's wars, and the role of the Mesto, the powerful sheep-owners guild, whose flocks spoiled much of the cultivated land. Charles's abdication in 1555-56 was an indication of his own sense of frustration over the failure of his policies, not only as regards his attempt to reestablish the medieval concept of Christian unity under the aegis of pope and emperor but also in Spain, which, in his mind, was the true heart of his universal realm.

Under his son Philip II (q.v.), this realm ceased being Europe-wide and became a Spanish empire with a Castillian core. Even the bankruptcy of Spain in 1557 did not obscure the fact that the center of gravity had shifted from Central Europe to the West and that Spain was vying with England and the Low Countries (qq.v.) for the dominant role in the future.

SPEYER, 1526 DIET AT. Two important diets (q.v.) were held in Speyer, a city on the Rhine, roughly 50 miles south of Frankfurt. The first of these diets were held in 1526 in the wake of the German Peasants' War of 1524-25 (q.v.) and the unresolved enforcement of the Edict of Worms (q.v.) against Martin Luther (q.v.) and his followers. Emperor Charles V (q.v.) was absent from Speyer, though his victory at Pavia in 1525, and the peace of Madrid of the following year, seemed to give him that aura of strength necessary to bring the territories and cities that had undertaken religious reform into line. He was represented by his brother Ferdinand. However, the pointed determination of the evangelical territories and South German cities, led by the Strasbourg syndic Jakob Sturm, gave the evangelicals the political clout needed to argue that the administration of the Edict of Worms was impossible. The cities put forward the proposal to suspend the Edict of Worms and to draft a reform edict that would deal with the grievances against the church. This proposal was about to be accepted by the diet when Ferdinand presented secret instructions from his brother. These instructions prohibited any changes in religion until the convening of a general council.

The evangelical estates reiterated their position that it was outrightly impossible to administer the Edict of Worms. Their intransigence led to the famous recess of the diet, which stipulated that each territorial ruler should deal with the Edict of Worms in accord with his responsibilities toward God and the emperor. This provision dramatically strengthened the power and authority of the ruler in religious affairs, and thus proved to be of major significance for the subsequent course of events of the German Reformation, particularly since the evangelical estates and cities interpreted the recess as giving them authority to proceed to whatever change and reform they could "account before God and the Emperor." The Catholic estates, by the same token, took the meaning of the recess to deal simply with the question whether the Edict of Worms could presently be enforced or not. Even though the recess was meant as a temporizing provision; the majority of the diet was not willing to resolve the religious issue on that basis. Charles, whose political power had waned in the course of 1526 through the Turkish victory at the battle of Mohács and the formation of the anti-Habsburg League of Cognac (q.v.), accepted the recess.

SPEYER, 1529 DIET AT. The second diet (q.v.) convened in March 1529. Emperor Charles V's (q.v.) political fortunes had improved during the preceding three years, though he was again absent from Germany (q.v.) and the diet. Encouraged by the emperor's improved political strength, the Catholic estates were adamant that the evangelical estates had used the recess of 1526 as a means to introduce the Reformation wherever they wanted. They argued that the intent of the 1526 recess had been to offer a moratorium on administering the provisions of the Edict of Worms (q.v.). Ferdinand, who once again represented his brother, proposed that the recess of 1526 be rescinded and that no further ecclesiastical reforms be introduced anywhere.

The neat phrase used in Ferdinand's proposal was that no estate (which included the bishops) should be deprived of its customary honors and privileges. The evangelical estates (foremostly Saxony, Hesse, Brandenburg, Lüneburg, Anhalt, together with 14 South German cities) protested categorically on April 19 with the argument that a unanimous agreement, as had been reached in 1526, could by law and custom only be rescinded unanimously. Moreover, so the protest noted, in matters pertaining to the honor of God and the salvation of souls, each one must for himself give an account before God. The majority of the estates at the diet was unimpressed by that argument and rescinded the 1526 recess. The evangelicals were thereafter referred to as the "protesting" estates and, before long, as "Protestants." (See also PROTESTANTISM).

SPIRITUALISM. The term refers to the theology of individuals who dissented theologically both from the Catholic and the new Protestant (q.v.) churches. Unlike other theological movements in the 16th century, these individuals never coalesced into a sociological structure, church, or conventicle but propounded their thought in writing. Undoubtedly, there were many others who felt the way these literary individuals did but did not commit their thinking to print. The common denominator of these spiritualists or spiritualizers was their repudiation of all existing theologies and churches, both Catholic and Protestant, for the reason that they were preoccupied with sterile doctrinal and dogmatic matters. Deeply influenced by medieval mysticism, the spiritualists argued a sharp dichotomy between spiritual and material matters. Consequently, all external issues—including those doctrinal matters in dispute between Catholics and Protestants, or even among the Protestants themselves, such as the nature of the sacraments (q.v.)—were deemed to be secondary and insignificant.

The story of 16th-century spiritualism is thus not so much the story of a movement but the story of individuals, such as Sebastian Franck (q.v.), Sebastian Castellio, Jacob Acontius (q.v.), and Caspar von Schwenckfeld (q.v.), who were more concerned about piety (q.v.) and Christian living than theology. In many ways, these spiritualists anticipated modern notions, such as freedom of religion, the free church tradition, and the separation of church and state, even though historically these notions came to be recognized only through the English free churches of the 17th century and the French Revolution. (See also RADICAL REFORMATION).

ST. BARTHOLOMEW'S DAY MASSACRE. The Peace of Saint-German-en-Laye in 1570 had ended eight years of desultory fighting in France (q.v.). It gave the Huguenots (q.v.) freedom of conscience and the right to hold public office. Catherine de' Medicis, the mother of Charles IX, resented the increasing influence over her son exerted by Gaspard de Coligny (q.v.), Admiral of France, commander of the French infantry, and the foremost layperson among the French Calvinists (q.v.). In the early summer of 1572 Catherine plotted to get rid of Coligny but an assassination attempt failed. However, the Huguenots were incensed. Fearful and in panic, Catherine decided to eliminate all Huguenot leaders who were in Paris for the wedding of Henry of Navarre, the later Henry IV (q.v.), to Catherine's youngest daughter Margaret. Catherine had concluded that her policy of attempting to mediate between Catholics and Huguenots was weakening the throne and that a Protestant France was bound to encounter serious difficulties with the pope, Spain (q.v.), and the majority of the French people. Early on August 23, St. Bartholomew's Day, 1572, the wholesale killing of Huguenot leaders began.

The most prominent victim was Admiral Coligny (q.v.), whose body was mutilated beyond description. Between two and three thousand Huguenots were killed in Paris alone, with some 20,000 more killed throughout France. It is not clear if the massacre was spontaneous or astutely organized. Even though the elite of the

Huguenots had been murdered, the spirit of the movement was hardly broken. A formidable reaction in literary form forcefully argued against an illegal tyranny and cited historic precedent for the rights of the estates. They were called monarchomachs.

STOCKHOLM BLOODBATH (1520). The Union of Kalmar (1397), by which the nobility of Sweden (q.v.), Norway, and Denmark (q.v.) had agreed to unite under the Danish king, turned out to be only a dynastic union; each of the countries retained its governmental structure and its laws. When Christian II succeeded to the Danish crown in 1513, he sought to turn the Union of Kalmar into a reality. He undertook to force Sweden to accept his authority. A military confrontation ensued. In January 1520 Sten Sture, the head of the autonomous Swedish administration, who had been excommunicated by Pope Leo X (q.v.), was defeated by Christian's forces. However, his widow vigorously continued to defend the country against the Danish, until Christian promised a general amnesty. In November, Christian was crowned king of Sweden. Shortly thereafter he reneged on his promise of amnesty. The leaders of the Swedish opposition were arrested, summarily tried, and then executed in the market square of Stockholm. This "bloodbath" invigorated the Swedish resentment against Danish rule.

SWEDEN. The Union of Kalmar, 1397, proclaimed the union of Norway, Denmark, and Sweden, under Danish leadership. Throughout the 15th century conflict over issues of the union dominated the political picture of the three countries. In Sweden sentiment for independence from Danish rule was strong and triggered a century-long period of turmoil. Early in the 16th century, Gustavus Trolle, archbishop of Uppsala in Sweden, though himself a Dane, played a significant role in supporting Danish claims in Sweden. In December 1517 Trolle was arrested for his political involvement, and he was forced to petition the pope for his own removal from office. This communication was followed by a second one, however, in which he pleaded with the pope for help. As a result, toward the end of 1519 the pope excommunicated Sten Sture, leader of the Swedish opposition against Denmark, and placed Sweden under the interdict at the same time. The Danish king Christian II was determined to crush the Swedish opposition. Sture was killed in battle, and Christian was crowned king of Sweden on November 4, 1520. Three days later, the leaders of the Swedish opposition were denounced as heretics—seemingly at the urging of Gustavus Trolle—and summarily executed in Stockholm on November 8 and 9. Over one hundred people were executed in what became known as the Stockholm Bloodbath (q.v.).

The bloodbath, far from settling Danish claims of sovereignty in Sweden, however, only served to rally Sweden to the banner of Gustavus Vasa (q.v.), whose father had been executed in it. In 1523 Gustavus was proclaimed king of Sweden. The next four years were spent in an effort to deal with a troubling political and economic situation. Religiously, things were made complicated by the reverberations of the Reformation in Germany (q.v.), in particular by the evangelical preaching of Olaus Petri, who had studied in Wittenberg and become an enthusiastic follower of Martin Luther (q.v.). A second complication was Pope Clement VII's (q.v.) steadfast insistence that Gustavus Trolle be reinstated as archbishop of Uppsala. Since in the early 1520s most of the episcopal sees in Sweden were vacant, new appointments could be made with reform-minded incumbents while maintaining the historical episcopate.

In 1527 at the diet at Västerås, Gustavus announced his resignation as king—whether sincerely because of the seemingly insurmountable economic problems, or as a political ploy is impossible to say. The diet prevailed on him to stay and then dutifully passed legislation which put the property of the church under the control of the state; it was used to pay off the foreign debt accumulated during Gustavus's struggle for power (1520-23). Clergy were no longer to be exempt from civil law, and only the "pure Word of God"—that shorthand phrase of Reformation import—was to be preached. In a way, the provisions of the diet foreshadowed the subsequent course of events in England (q.v.) in the 1530s—a church, severed from the Roman see, with major control over it vested in the sovereign but also a new, Reformation church without significant doctrinal change. Accordingly, neither a new confession (q.v.) of faith nor any other doctrinal standard was promulgated at the time. Reformation teaching continued to make inroads in Sweden, even as the Swedish church showed its independence from the king in various ways. Gustavus Vasa responded by appointing a vice-gerent over the church with power to exercise jurisdiction on the king's behalf.

At the same time, the two leading reformers in the land, Olaus Petri and Laurentius Andreae, were accused of high treason, though without disastrous personal consequences. Under Gustavus's successor, Erik

XIV, who ruled for 18 troubled years from 1560 to 1568, not the least because of his mental instability, Laurentius Petri, brother of Olaus and archbishop of Uppsala, sought to introduce a Lutheran church order but the king's Calvinist (q.v.) sentiment made that impossible. When Erik was overthrown by his brother John, who ruled as John III from 1568 to 1592, a Lutheran church order (qq.v.) was formally introduced (1571) but without a formal confessional part. John, who considered himself a learned theologian, issued a book of worship (*Liturgia Suecanae Ecclesiae*) in 1576 which rescinded Petri's church order. The king secretly flirted with Catholicism, converted to it, and supported a clandestine Jesuit (q.v.) college operating in Stockholm for some time. In negotiations with the pope, John demanded that clergy be allowed to marry, that Mass be celebrated in the vernacular, and that communion be given under both kinds. When Pope Gregory XIII (q.v.) refused, John broke off contacts, and the prospect of Sweden becoming Catholic again faded. John's death in 1592 meant the succession of his Catholic son Sigismunt III Vasa. Sweden stood at the brink of turning Catholic.

Under the leadership of John III's younger brother a church assembly convened in Uppsala in 1593 which not only reinstated Petri's church order but also mandated that subscription to the Augsburg Confession (q.v.) was required of everybody, including the future kings of Sweden. This act effectively stymied a re-Catholizing of Sweden and allowed Sweden to remain Lutheran.

SWITZERLAND. In the early 16th century Switzerland was nominally still part of the Holy Roman Empire (q.v.) but in actual fact it was a loose confederation of 13 cantons that had their own diet and concluded their own international treaties. Much like Austria, for example, the Swiss Confederation was de facto an autonomous state within the empire until it reached its legal autonomy at the end of the Thirty Years' War in 1648. Historically, the confederation had grown from the original three cantons of Uri, Schwyz, and Unterwalden, which had formed a political union in 1291, to the situation early in the 16th century when, with the joining of Appenzell in 1513, all 13 cantons had joined the confederation. These 13 cantons had "associates" or "allies," such as the canton of Valais or, later, the city of Geneva (q.v.), which were allied with the 13 cantons for mutual military support. Early in the 16th century the confederation was bitterly divided internally. Swiss mercenaries served the great

European powers, which led to rivalries among them to dominate Swiss affairs, even though the increased use of artillery and cavalry in the early 16th century made the Swiss mercenaries less valuable. Particularly, the Papal States and France (q.v.) sought to extend their influence in Switzerland through bribes and the so-called "pensions," regular subsidies paid to influential citizens.

The course of the Reformation in Switzerland is intimately tied to Huldrych Zwingli's (q.v.) reform in Zurich (q.v.), which began in 1519 but evolved in the context of external and domestic Swiss rivalries. Zwingli always saw himself as a Swiss patriot with clear political goals and objectives. The successful introduction of the Reformation in Zurich by 1525 led to an intensification of tensions that already existed but also to parallel moves by other cantons in the direction of the Reformation. The powerful canton of Bern embraced the Reformation in 1528, and the city of Basel followed suit that same year. The outbreak of military hostilities between Zurich and the Catholic cantons in 1531, which led not only to Zwingli's death on the battlefield but also the peace of Kappel (q.v.), meant that both religious sides had to acknowledge the existence of the other. After 1531 it was evident that Switzerland would remain religiously divided.

SZLACHTA. Polish parliament, comprised of landed nobility, which played an extremely important role in both Polish political and religious history in the 16th century.

— T —

TAUSEN, HANS (1494-1561). Danish reformer who studied at Rostock, later in Wittenberg. Returning to Denmark (q.v.) in 1524, Tausen began to preach Reformation notions and was expelled from his monastic order (he belonged to the Order of St. John of Jerusalem) in 1526 but received appointment as preacher to King Frederick I that same year. In 1529 Tausen became minister at the important St. Nicolaj Church in Copenhagen, from which position he played an important role in facilitating the introduction of the Reformation in Denmark. When, in 1536 the new king Christian III officially introduced the Reformation in Denmark, Tausen became the leading spokesperson for the Lutheran (q.v.) cause. After a stint as professor of Hebrew, he was elected bishop of Ribe in Jutland in 1541. Tausen published prolifically, including a widely used *Postille*, a book of sermons for use by pastors. Theologically he was a committed Lutheran who embraced certain of Philip Melanchthon's (q.v.) notions concerning the relationship of the ecclesiastical and temporal realm as well as John Calvin's (q.v.) notion of church discipline.

TERESA OF AVILA (1515-1582). Spanish mystic. Born into a noble family in Castile, Teresa entered the Carmelite Convent of the Incarnation in Avilla in 1535. For the next decade Theresa was torn between her love of the world and her devotion to God but eventually found her spiritual vocation. Increasingly mystical in her spirituality, herself characterized by keen intuition, clarity of thought, and intellectual brilliance, not to mention organizational and administrative talent, Teresa employed these qualities to establish convents of Carmelites throughout Spain (q.v.), some 14 by the time of her death. Her instruction and exhortations to the Carmelite nuns turned into her writings, notably *El camino de la perfección* (The Path of Perfection), *Las Moradas o el castillo interior* (The Interior Castle), and *El Libro de su fundaciones* (The Book of the Foundations). These are characterized by a mystical individualism, christological orientation, and a structured manner of spirituality. Her rich literary work also includes her spiritual autobiography, *El libro de su vida* (The Book of Her Life).

TETRAPOLITAN CONFESSION. Drafted by Martin Bucer and Wolfgang Capito (qq.v.), this confession "of the four cities" was submitted by the South German cities of Constance, Memmingen, Lindau, and Strasbourg to Emperor Charles V (q.v.) at the diet at Augsburg (q.v.) in 1530 in response to the emperor's general solicitation to hear "everybody's opinion." Strasbourg was unwilling to agree to the Lutheran (q.v.) interpretation of the Lord's Supper (q.v.), which meant that a separate confession (q.v.) of faith had to be submitted. Rejected by the emperor, the Tetrapolitan Confession nonetheless remained the formal confession of Strasbourg until the middle of the century.

TETZEL, JOHANN (1465-1519). Dominican monk and indulgences (q.v.) preacher. Tetzel had a fairly distinguished career in the church (prior of a Dominican monastery, inquisitor for Poland, doctor of theology) before serving, in 1517, as indulgences preacher for Albert of Brandenburg, thereby triggering Martin Luther's (q.v.) Ninety-five Theses. Tetzel defended his preaching against Luther but died before the controversy over Luther's theses had reached its formidable stage. (See also INDULGENCES CONTROVERSY).

THEATINES. Catholic religious order. This order was approved by Pope Clement VII (q.v.) in 1524. It was the work of Gaetano de Thiene (1480-1547) with support of Gianpietro Carafa, later Pope Paul IV (q.v.). The name of the new order came from "Theate," the Latin for "Chieti," Carafa's former bishopric. The members of the new order committed themselves to absolute poverty (they were not even to beg) and devoted themselves to preaching and the administration of the sacraments (q.v.). In so doing, they sought to be models for the secular clergy. They founded hospitals and orphanages. The founding of the Society of Jesus (q.v.) meant a certain competition between the two orders with virtually identical goals; however, the Jesuits built on a strikingly different internal model.

THEOLOGY. While the Protestant Reformation of the 16th century clearly was a convergence of several societal forces and factors, theology was crucially important and ostensibly the determinant of the decision to separate from the Catholic Church. The outcome of the extensive theological polemic was the emergence of a new theological system, namely Protestantism (q.v.), which, despite sundry antecedents prior to the 16th century and a lack of full agreement among its adherents, represented a new understanding of the Christian faith. The major theological issues debated in the course of the Reformation controversy were the question of authority (Bible vs. the Church); justification (by faith vs. by faith and works); the sacraments (q.v.) (seven vs. two); and the church (the visible church vs. the invisible church). Among the various manifestations of Protestantism, the foremost contested issues were the Lord's Supper and baptism (qq.v.). (See also CALVINISM; LUTHERANISM).

THIRTY-NINE ARTICLES. The Thirty-nine Articles of the Church of England were part of the Elizabethan settlement (q.v.) of religion. The origins of the document lay in a prior document, the Forty-two Articles (q.v.), which had been promulgated, under the auspices of Thomas Cranmer (q.v.), then archbishop of Canterbury, in 1552. (See also ENGLAND).

TITIAN (c. 1487-1576). Painter. Tiziano Vecellio, born in northern

Italy, dominated Venetian painting in the mid-16th century with portraits, altar pieces, and paintings of the Madonna. Portraitist of both Emperor Charles V and Pope Paul III (qq.v.), Titian's mature work is characterized by its monumental dimension and brilliant use of color.

TOLERATION. The term refers to the willingness to accept opinions and positions contrary to one's own. The presupposition is that definitive truth cannot be known or that truth embraces even seemingly contradictory positions. Since the Middle Ages held that truth can be known and that religious truth was the pathway to eternal salvation, understandably tolerance was a concept not embraced by that time. The same must be said, as a matter of fact, about the Reformation. Virtually all of the protagonists in the fierce controversy were blatantly intolerant, sometimes (as in the case of the old Martin Luther's [q.v.] tirades against the Jews [q.v.]) even excessively so. Early in the Reformation controversy, Luther argued rather forcefully (and understandably) that the secular authorities had no role in adjudicating religious and theological matters. Soon, however, the traditional understanding of truth reasserted itself, and ecclesiastical as well as theological uniformity was a hallmark of Protestant (q.v.) no less than of Catholic societies. Alongside this notion there was another important consideration for pre-modern European society: neither the Protestant reformers nor their Catholic counterparts were able to envision a society that was not religiously homogeneous.

TRENT, COUNCIL OF. The notion of a general council to deal with both the existing abuses in the church and the issues triggered by the Reformation controversy was based on the historical reality that councils had in the past played precisely such a role. It was advanced soon after the indulgences controversy (q.v.) erupted in 1517. While seemingly an attractive means to deal with the growing problem, the obstacles were several, not the least the fact that Martin Luther (q.v.), in the Leipzig Debate (q.v.), had argued that even councils can be in error. The implication of that sentiment was a lack of urgency on the part of the reformers who were ambivalent about whether they wanted a council. They feared, moreover, that a council convened by the pope would only do the pope's bidding. There was also lack of specific clarity as to what a council should do—deal with abuses in the church or address the tricky topic of a theological conciliation between Catholic and Protestant (q.v.) theology? The several popes of the early years of the Reformation, in turn, were concerned that a vigorous and activist council might revive the strength of conciliarism and thus undermine papal power and authority. Others, such as Emperor Charles V (q.v.), were adamant believers in what a council might do in order to alleviate the religious controversy that was rending Christendom asunder.

It was not until the mid-1540s that Pope Paul III (q.v.) finally convened an ecumenical council in the North Italian town of Trent. The first session took place in December 1545 but was transferred — since Trent was considered to be a site under the emperor's influence— by papal instruction in March 1547 to Bologna. It adjourned in September 1549. While important decisions were made during the sessions at Trent, not much of importance took place in Bologna. A second period of the council commenced in September 1551 and lasted until April 1552. During this second period, several Protestant representatives appeared in Trent, and substantive, albeit abortive, discussions took place between the two sides. After adjournment the council did not resume and complete its work until 10 years later. The third and final period began in January 1562 and lasted until December of the following year.

The achievements of the council, which clearly stood under papal influence, were truly significant. When the council first convened in 1545 it was faced with the controversial question of whether doctrinal issues or matters of church reform should be considered first (a decision on that question had obvious implications for what the council thought about the relationship with Protestants). The council fathers decided on a compromise—both would be considered concurrently. During the first period of sessions the council decided several important theological topics: the relationship of tradition to Scripture, the doctrine of justification, original sin. In general, the council sought to find intra-Catholic compromises on doctrine rather than seek compromise with the Protestant position. The third period of sessions of the council was characterized by intense internal disagreements. Council fathers from Spain, France, and Germany (qq.v.) were intent on not enhancing papal authority in the church. But they were bitterly divided among themselves so that no uniform front against the papacy emerged.

As regards practical issues of church reform, the council addressed a large number of reforms, some of which were forward looking, such as its endorsement of polyphonic church music (q.v.), while others, such as the insistence that Jerome's Vulgate translation of the Bible (q.v.) was the authentic text of Scripture, were bound to cause problems later on. Both the council itself, and the various Catholic rulers, such as Philip II (q.v.) or Ferdinand, showed by their bitter divisions that there was anything but unity in the Catholic Church regarding the question how the church might be best reformed and how the Protestant heresy could be best dealt with. By the same token, the canons and decrees of the council constituted, both in spirit and in content, a splendid manifestation of restored Catholic self-confidence in the second half of the 16th century. The influence of the Council of Trent lasted until the second Vatican Council of the 1960s.

TWELVE ARTICLES OF THE COMMON GATHERING OF THE PEASANTS. Written by the Memmingen (South Germany) furrier Sebastian Lotzer, and given a theological twist by the Zwinglian preacher Christoph Schappler, these articles summarized the grievances of the peasants in the context of the German Peasants' War (q.v.) in the 1520s. In addition to several economic grievances, such as the demand to have the right to fish, hunt, and cut wood in the common forests, together with relief from excessive feudal dues and rents and the abolition of the inheritance tax, the Twelve Articles also addressed religious issues. The document insisted on the right of a congregation to elect its minister, while the 12th article expressed willingness to withdraw any demand found to be contrary to the Word of God.

The striking feature of the Twelve Articles lay in this affirmation, which tied them directly to the Reformation. Prior to the 1520s, peasant grievances had always been expressed in terms of the insistence that the "ancient law" be restored. The peasants demanded a return to conditions and practices that had once existed but been changed by the lords and rulers. The Twelve Articles echoed this appeal to the "ancient law" but at the same time expressed something new. The demand that serfdom be abolished was based on the premise that "Christ made all men free." It was therefore not based on ancient statutes but reflected the peasants' sense of the divine law. In other words, the new element in the Twelve Articles was that they expressed a vision of society based on the principles of Scripture.

Since the document, replete as it was with Bible (q.v.) citations, clearly reflected the influence of the Reformation, and the peasants had, moreover, called on Martin Luther (q.v.), and others, to serve as arbiters with respect to their demands, Luther responded with a treatise entitled *Friendly Admonition to Peace* in which he denounced the peasants for their use of the Bible in order to attain worldly goals. The specific economic and social grievances needed to be heard by experts; he was merely a theologian without competence in worldly matters. A second tract, *Against the Murdering and Robbing Hordes of the Peasants*, denounced the peasants vehemently for their insurrection against duly ordained governmental authority. (See also THOMAS MÜNTZER).

TWO KINGDOMS. In the Age of the Reformation the notion of the "two kingdoms" (or "two regiments," "two realms") was most pronouncedly represented by Martin Luther (q.v.). Drawing on Augustine's distinction between the kingdom of God and the kingdom of the world, Luther found that these two realms were differentiated both by their principles and their members. As regards principles, the two realms express God's rule through both regiments, the one through the gospel and the mandates of Jesus, the other through secular government. In a way, Luther reacted against the medieval understanding of these two realms, expressed most poignantly in the papal bull *Unam Sanctam* of 1302, in which the pope laid out the claim that both the secular and the spiritual realm were under the aegis of the pope who had turned over the administration of the secular realm to secular rulers. For Luther this constituted a confusion of the two realms by blurring the two ways in which God rules the world. The duty of secular government is to maintain peace and punish evildoers; the task of the kingdom of God is to proclaim the gospel and establish the rule of God in the hearts of people. A Christian must be subject to that secular authority, even participate in it, albeit not blindly. Obedience has its limit whenever government acts unjustly.

Luther's distinction of the two realms was put severely to the test in the German Peasants' War (q.v.) in 1524-25, when the Twelve Articles (q.v.) of the peasants advocated a whole series of reforms and societal changes based on their reading of the Scriptures. Luther's responses to the Twelve Articles took the form of three treatises which differed dramatically in tone but expressed a pointed consistency. The grievances of the peasants had to be adjudicated before secular courts, by lawyers and other experts: the gospel has nothing to say about worldly and secular issues. Undoubtedly, the peasants' document exposed a weak point in Luther's argumentation—what to do if under the guise of economic, social, or political issues some fundamental biblical notions are violated. That is to say, the question posed by the peasants fundamentally was if the Bible (q.v.) has absolutely nothing to say about the social and political order.

A second weakness in Luther's argument came to the fore in 1530, when the stalemate with respect to the religious controversy at the diet of Augsburg (q.v.) suggested the formation of a political alliance in order to defend the new faith against a possible military attack by the emperor. Luther modified his earlier notion of a purely passive resistance on the part of the Christian with a more active notion which he derived, however, more from German constitutional law than from the Bible: hereditary rulers have a right to oppose the emperor, if the emperor oversteps the bounds of his authority and power. In the Calvinist (q.v.) tradition, the Lutheran (q.v.) distinction of the two realms was essentially retained, even though John Calvin (q.v.) was far more insistent on affirming the complementarity of the spiritual and the secular realm than was Luther. Church and state worked far more harmoniously in Geneva (q.v.) than in Lutheran territories, at least from the perspective of the clarity of the Calvinist confessions (q.v.). These left no doubt but that secular government played an incisive role in ecclesiastical affairs.

TYNDALE, WILLIAM (c. 1494-1536). English reformer. Tyndale was educated at Oxford, possibly studied at Cambridge, and in the early 1520s translated Desiderius Erasmus's (q.v.) *Enchiridion* into English. Tyndale then went to study at the University of Wittenberg (q.v.) and by 1525 had translated the New Testament into English. The translation evoked severe negative reactions in England (q.v.), prompting Tyndale to continue on the Continent. He went to Antwerp. Several important Reformation pamphlets (q.v.) issued from his pen during the next few years—*The Parable of the Wicked Mammon* and *The Obedience of the Christian Man*, both of 1528. Tyndale was betrayed near Brussels, arrested, and found guilt of heresy. He was executed in 1536. His achievement lay in his work as a translator possessing outstanding linguistic skills. His theology, which was greatly influenced by Martin Luther (q.v.), remained fragmentary, undoubtedly because of his clandestine existence during the last 10 years of his life.

— U —

UNIVERSITIES. The decades immediately preceding the Reformation had witnessed the establishment of a number of new universities. This meant in fact that the old European universities, such as Paris or Bologna, which had drawn students from all over Europe, faced competition from these new national universities. Another major change in early modern university life, in addition to the proliferation of institutions, was the increasing influence of Humanism (q.v.) and Humanist faculty. In Scotland, Aberdeen (1494) and Glasgow (1450) were founded; in northern Europe, Uppsala (1477) and Copenhagen (1478); while in Germany, new universities were founded at Tübingen (1477), Mainz (1477), and Wittenberg (1502), to name the most important ones. In each instance, the interests of the territorial ruler, either secular or ecclesiastical, were major motivating factors in the creation of these new universities, even though undoubtedly the new learning associated with the Renaissance played an incisive role as well. It was a dramatic blossoming of higher learning.

The new universities received the requisite imperial or papal privileges that were the hallmark of the medieval university and were thus equal to the older institutions. As regards structure and courses of studies, the new universities followed the models of Paris and Bologna. The study of the liberal arts led through the study of the Trivium (mainly grammar and rhetoric) and the Quadrivium (mainly arithmetic) to the bachelor and the master's degrees. North of the Alps, such liberal arts degrees were deemed the prerequisite for studying theology, law, or medicine, while Italian universities did not have such formal prerequisites. Despite their acknowledged eminence, they were considered diploma mills.

Universities played a notable role in the course of the Reformation: Archbishop Albrecht asked the theologians at the University of Mainz to assess Martin Luther's (q.v.) Ninety-five Theses, and Duke George of Saxony sent the minutes of the Leipzig Debate (q.v.) to the universities of Paris and Cologne for their appraisal. Henry VIII (q.v.) undertook a grandiose canvass of European universities in order to establish if his marriage with Catherine of Aragon (q.v.) was valid. More important, however, was the fact that many Protestant (q.v.) reformers were university faculty and, moreover, encouraged the establishment of new institutions of higher learning. The argument can well be made that the Reformation was a university movement, particularly since new universities were established in Protestant places (such as Marburg or Geneva [q.v.]). (See also WITTENBERG, UNIVERSITY OF).

URSULINES. Established by Angeli Merici (1474-1540) at Brescia in 1535 and formally approved by Pope Paul III (q.v.) in 1544, the Ursuline order (officially Ordo Sanctae Ursulinae) was a female order which focused on education, especially of youth. Initially, the members of the order lived with their own families at home, having taken the customary three monastic vows of poverty, chastity, and obedience. Carlo Borromao called the members of the new order to Milan in 1568, and this meant the beginning of a cloistered life for the members of the order. The statutes for the order were confirmed by Pope Gregory XIII (q.v.) in 1582. The geographic site of activity of the Ursulines remained at first confined to northern Italy but at the turn of the century spread to France (q.v.). Not unlike the Jesuits (q.v.), the Ursulines made a fourth vow, which was the express commitment to further the Christian education of girls. The Ursuline Order is actually comprised of several branches: the order of St. Ursula, which is characterized by solemn vows in cloistered independent convents; the congregations of Ursulines without solemn vows; and the Societas sanctae Ursulae whose members continue to live in their own families. (See also MONASTICISM).

— V —

VADIAN (1483/84-1551). Swiss Humanist. Joachim von Watt, in Latinized form Vadianus, was born at St. Gall, where he spent most of his life. He studied medicine in Vienna, where he was rector in 1516-17 and published a number of historical and geographic writings. Upon his return to his hometown he became municipal physician and, in 1526, mayor. While he initially embraced Desiderius Erasmus's Humanism (qq.v.) and notion of the Christian religion, the influence of Huldrych Zwingli (q.v.) turned him into a committed proponent of the Reformation. He was crucial in introducing the Reformation in St. Gall. In the 1530s he actively supported the efforts to reach theological consensus in the Swiss Reformation which led to the First Helvetic Confession (q.v.) of 1536.

VASA, GUSTAVUS (1496-1560). Swedish king. Gustavus Ericksson, who took the name Vasa from the sheaf on the family coat of arms, succeeded in driving out the Danish forces from Sweden (q.v.) in 1521. Two years later, in June 1523, he was elected king by the Swedish diet meeting at Strengnäs. Sweden was in dire straits, with the church holding two-thirds of the land and refusing to pay taxes and the nobility owning the remaining land and likewise not paying taxes. Gustavus, not unaware of the strong resentment against the church for having supported the Danish king, had Lutheran sympathies and facilitated the spread of Lutheranism (q.v.) in Sweden. When Adrian VI and Clement VII (q.v.) insisted that Gustavus Trolle, deposed archbishop of Uppsala, be restored—Trolle had been deposed by a national diet as the "Swedish Judas Iscariot" for his support of the Danish king—Gustavus adamantly refused, obtained a loan from the Swedish church, and insisted that no foreigner occupy a position of authority in the church in Sweden. Clement confirmed Gustavus's candidate for the archbishopric of Uppsala, Johan Magnusson, which meant that subsequent Swedish (Lutheran) clergy and bishops stood in apostolic succession through Magnusson.

At the Diet at Västerås in 1527 Gustavus dramatically announced his abdication when the bishops failed to accept his insistence that the wealth of the church be used to restore fiscal integrity to Sweden. The majority of the diet prevailed on Gustavus to stay, and the recess of the diet stipulated that all "superfluous means" of the church should be turned over to the king and that all clergy should preach only the "pure word of God." In subsequent years Gustavus showed himself a strong advocate of the Reformation, while at the same time making sure that he controlled the church; the Protestant (q.v.) faith had turned into a tool to maintain the absolute power of the king. A rebellion in the south of Sweden in 1542 proved to be a serious threat to the king. In 1544 the diet meeting at Västerås proclaimed Sweden a Protestant realm. Gustavus's ecclesiasti
cal policy oscillated several times, but at his death in 1560 Sweden was solidly Lutheran which it remained since then.

VERMIGLI, PETER MARTYR (1499-1562). Protestant (q.v.) theologian and Humanist (q.v.). Born in Florence, Vermigli joined the Augustinian order and later studied at the University of Padua, where he received the doctorate. Later he served as abbot of monasteries in Naples and Spoleto. In 1542 Vermigli came to accept Protestant notions and fled to Switzerland (q.v.), then to Strasbourg. In 1547, at the invitation of Archbishop Thomas Cranmer (q.v.), he went to Oxford. The succession of Mary Tudor (q.v.) caused his return to the Continent. A learned and prolific scholar, Vermigli is primarily remembered for his three-volume *Loci Communes* (Common Places) of 1580 which saw over a dozen editions.

VISITATIONS. The term refers to official delegations which "visit" local parishes for the twofold purpose of taking inventory of the parish and of providing constructive recommendations for needed improvement. Such visitations, carried out by ecclesiastical functionaries, generally the bishop, had a history long preceding the 16th century. In the decades immediately prior to the Reformation the practice of visitations had fallen into neglect. Once in the 1520s new evangelical churches began to be organized, the obvious need to take stock of the overall state of affairs suggested the inauguration of systematic and comprehensive visitations for that purpose.

In contrast to the medieval visitations, however, the new Lutheran and subsequent Protestant (qq.v.) visitations were undertaken, understandably, on the initiative of the secular authorities: the state was concerned about order in the churches. Generally, the visitation committees consisted of both clerical and governmental officials, the latter government lawyers, an understandable involvement in that questions of finance and property were always included in the visitors' queries. In the course of the century, different types of visitations emerged: general visitations which involved the entire territory; special visitations which focused on a special problem, generally a doctrinal one; and local visitations, undertaken within a deanery or a particular locale. The visitors used a questionnaire and tended to examine the local minister (possibly other important members of a parish as well) with a focus on theological competence, doctrinal correctness, and moral probity.

When Bishop John Hooper (q.v.) undertook a visitation in England (q.v.) in the 1550s, his visitors queried the clergy about their competence in the Ten Commandments, the Lord's Prayer, and the Apostle's Creed. In Electoral Saxony, the first comprehensive Lutheran visitation was undertaken in the fall of 1528. It lasted intermittently until 1531. Two years later a new visitation got underway, and further ones followed at somewhat less than regular intervals. The same process was followed in other Protestant territories, such as Hesse,

Württemberg, Pomerania, and Brandenburg. The same happened in other European countries, notably in England. A royal writ vested visitations in the hands of the king in 1535. This led to the visitations of the monasteries, which were dissolved as a result. The following year the bishops were authorized, however, to resume their episcopal visitations, which, particularly during the reign of Edward VI (q.v.), focused on the local conformity to the religious legislation that had been enacted.

As far as the Catholic Church was concerned, the 16th century was characterized by a revitalization of visitations as well. This was formally delineated by the Council of Trent (q.v.), which affirmed in 1563 the episcopal obligation to undertake visitations. The visitations, Protestant and Catholic alike, left an enormous documentary record— the so-called "visitation records." While one must recognize the nature of these materials (the visitors were understandably seeking to ferret out deviation from doctrine or morals and were not greatly disposed to affirm the positive), these records do offer a unique insight into actual church life in the 16th century.

VITORIA, FRANCISCO (c. 1490-1546). Catholic jurist and theologian. Vitoria began his studies in his hometown of Burgos, Spain (q.v.). He joined the Dominican order, then studied in Paris, where he joined the faculty and taught until 1522, the year he received the doctorate in theology. Between 1523 and 1526 Vitoria taught in Valladolid, and from 1526 onward he was professor of theology at the University of Salamanca. His fame rests on his willingness to address contemporary questions and issues, notably the discussion over the various implications of the Spanish conquest in America. Two of his lectures, *De Indis noviter inventis* (Concerning the Newly Discovered Indies), and *De jure Hispanorum in barbaros* (Concerning the Use of Spanish Law among the Uncivilized) of 1538/39 laid the foundation for a more humane treatment of the native Americans and of modern international law. (See also DISCOVERIES).

VIVES, JUAN LUIS (1492?-1540). Spanish Humanist (q.v.). Of Jewish parentage, Vives was baptized as a child and studied in Paris. He became enamored by the Humanistic ideal and moved to Brugge, where he became part of a circle of Erasmian Humanists. Living mainly in the Low Countries (q.v.), with intermittent stays in England (q.v.), where he taught at Oxford, Vives became a prolific writer, beginning with an extensive commentary on Augustine's *City of God* and including such works as his pathbreaking work on poor relief (*De subventione pauperum*) and on women (*De institutione feminae Christianae*). Much like his mentor Desiderius Erasmus (q.v.) Vives stayed aloof from the theological controversies triggered by the Reformation and focused on devotional writings that could be read by Catholics and Protestants alike.

— W —

WEDDINGS. The late Middle Ages were characterized by several important features with respect to the performance of weddings. For one, marriage (q.v.) was understood as a sacramental celebration. The Catholic Church spelled out the various aspects of marriage in canon law, thus insisting on its exclusive right to supervise who was able to get married, and how. However, apart from such formal considerations, there was also discernible a considerable neglect by couples to get formally married in the church, which entailed enormous complications with respect to issues of property and inheritance.

The reformers rejected the exclusive claims of the church to regulate marriages; they also rejected the notion that marriage was a sacrament (q.v.). While in the medieval period clandestine weddings were numerous, and church weddings were by no means the rule—the free agreement made by a couple to marry was deemed to be crucial—the Protestant reformers insisted that weddings be formal, not secret, and in church rather than at other sites. Some reformers, notably Martin Luther (q.v.), insisted that secret weddings be considered invalid. (See also MARRIAGE).

WITCHCRAZE. The rise of the European witchcraze late in the 15th century and lasting until well into the 17th is one of the most important features of Central Europe during that time. The catalyst was the promulgation, in 1484, of the papal bull *Summis desiderantes,* which was meant to provide support for two Dominican inquisitors, Heinrich Institoris and Jakob Sprenger, in their effort to identity and ferret out witches. The bull affirmed the connection between magic and heresy. In 1489 Institoris and Sprenger published the *Malleus maleficarum* (The Witchhammer), which elaborated in great detail all the aspects of the phenomenon of witches. Undoubtedly, the common people saw the "witch" as an explanation of disasters and misfortunes, both personal and societal, while the educated classes understood the realities in the context of a Neoplatonic-dualistic world view.

The Catholic Church had earlier been hostile to the notion of witches but began to accept it under the influence of Thomas Aquinas. In the course of the 15th century, and culminating with *The Witchhammer*, a systematic sharpening of focus occurred, which saw the exercise of magic as a female phenomenon. Undoubtedly the traditional low view of women (q.v.) in the Christian tradition played an important role. *The Witchhammer*, as a matter of fact, derived the word "femina" (woman) by way of crude etymology from *fides* and *minus*, "without faith." The immediate practical consequences of the publication of *The Witchhammer* were modest, however, even though the book was promptly perceived to have legal ramifications which found their way into legal statutes.

Not until the middle of the 16th century did the witchcraze begin in earnest and on a Europe-wide scale. Thereby, the collective noun "witch" emerged as referring to a female magician who took nightly and damaging flights, involving intercourse with the devil and travels on brooms and into chimneys. It also involved the celebration of Witches' Sabbaths, gatherings of witches. A number of theories have been advanced as explanation. For one, it seems clear that the delay between the publication of *The Witchhammer* and the onset of real persecution—just about half a century—not only indicated that there was no popular thirst for persecuting witches (if anything, notions of magic, as long as magic was good, were widely accepted) but also that social control in communities was still loose. The terrible climactic conditions in the middle of the century, with the concomitant bad harvests, have been suggested as the catalyst for the real onset of the persecution of witches.

WITTENBERG CONCORD. The failure of the Marburg Colloquy (1529) (q.v.) to attain agreement between the Saxon and Swiss reformers, Martin Luther and Huldrych Zwingli (qq.v.), concerning the presence of Christ in the elements of bread and wine in the Lord's Supper (q.v.), meant that Protestantism (q.v.) was a house divided, a fact not only with evident political consequences but theological ramifications as well. In the 1530s Strasbourg reformer Martin Bucer (q.v.), aware of both realities, strove relentlessly to find a formula of agreement between the disagreeing parties. He took his cue from Luther's notion of "sacramental union," namely that the presence of

Christ in Communion was a mystery, not separate from the elements of bread and wine but not removed from them either.

In 1532 Bucer persuaded the South German cities (and their theologians) to subscribe to the Augsburg Confession (q.v.) and thereby facilitated their admission to the League of Schmalkald (q.v.). Bucer and Philip Melanchthon (q.v.) were able to reach an agreement in Kassel (1534) because Bucer, once again the key figure in the deliberations, was willing to accept Luther's position as delineated in his *Confession Concerning the Lord's Supper*. In May 1536 Bucer and several other South German theologians traveled to Wittenberg, where they signed the Wittenberg Concord.

This document dealt with three topics: the Lord's Supper, baptism (q.v.), and absolution (of sins). On the issue of baptism, the concord affirmed infant baptism, and regarding absolution it acknowledged the value of private confession. As regards the Lord's Supper, the concord manifested, despite some compromise formulations, a Lutheran orientation. The so-called *"manducatio indignorum"* ("eating of the unworthy"—the notion that even the "unworthy" ingest the body of Christ) was affirmed in the concord as was the incisive phrase "through sacramental union the bread is the body of Christ." The concord was rejected by the more adamantly Zwinglian South German theologians. Its importance must be seen in the fact that it had proved possible to find conciliatory language and that, as far as the Lutheran theologians were concerned, the Augsburg Confession was identified as the benchmark against which the authentic Lutheran interpretation of the gospel was measured.

WITTENBERG, UNIVERSITY OF. The division of Saxony into an Ernestine and an Albertine Saxon line in 1485 meant that the University at Erfurt belonged to Albertine Saxony, and Ernestine Saxony no longer had a university. This prompted Elector Frederick the Wise to establish a new university at Wittenberg (together with Torgau one of his two residences) in 1502. Emperor Maximilian bestowed all traditional rights and privileges on the new university; papal appropriation was received in 1507. Initially, the new university had a faculty of 15. Twelve of the professors were supported by benefices at All Saints Church in Wittenberg, while the three remaining professorships were supported by the Franciscan and Augustinian orders.

The young university modeled itself after the University at Tübingen and succeeded in attracting a number of outstanding faculty (Johann von Staupitz, Andreas Bodenstein von Carlstadt, Nikolaus Amsdorf, Martin Luther [qq.v.]). A striking consensus existed among the faculty of the young university to be in the forefront of university reform. This was the case not only in theology, under Luther's leadership but also in law, medicine, and the liberal arts. The university soon became one of the largest in Germany; some 2,000 students were enrolled at the time the indulgences controversy (q.v.) erupted (in a town of only 3,000). The university remained for decades the citadel of Lutheranism (q.v.), though at the time of the intra-Lutheran theological controversies the charges of crypto-Calvinism were variously leveled against faculty members. When, at the end of the Thirty Years War, Saxony had to cede part of its territory, the university was transferred to Halle. (See also UNIVERSITIES).

WOLSEY, THOMAS (1472-1530). English churchman and cardinal. Wolsey was the son of an innkeeper and wool merchant of Ipswich. He was educated at Oxford for an ecclesiastical career. Entering royal service in 1508 he was admitted to the royal council three years later. The new king Henry VIII (q.v.) was impressed by Wolsey, whose career advanced spectacularly after 1509. By 1515 Wolsey was archbishop of York, a cardinal, and lord chancellor of England (q.v.). His skill in managing the English military foray into France (1513) (q.v.) and his negotiation of the treaty with France (1514) bore fruit.

In 1518 Wolsey became a papal legate, which effectively placed the entire English church under his control. This legatine authority was given for life in 1524. While these ecclesial titles reflected Wolsey's important role in the church, which he exercised for example by convening the heads of the monastic orders in England in 1519 to discuss reform, his eminent involvement was in English domestic and international politics. In the latter, he sought to pursue a policy of balance of power between the two major Continental powers, Spain (q.v.) and France, though supporting the election of Charles I of Spain as German Emperor Charles V (q.v.). Wolsey strove to be elected pope upon the death of Leo X but Charles threw his support behind his former confessor, Adrian. Henry VIII allowed Wolsey to run English politics, both at home and abroad, with little interference. When, in 1527, the king began to seek an annulment of his marriage to Catherine of Aragon (q.v.), Wolsey naturally was the one to gain the pope's approval in the matter. By the spring of 1529 it was clear, however, that Wolsey had failed, that is, no papal decision in accord with the king's wishes was forthcoming from Rome. Moreover, a faction of the nobility, led by the dukes of Suffolk and Norfolk, resented Wolsey's enormous power and conspired against him.

In October 1529 Wolsey was dismissed from the office of lord chancellor, to be succeeded by Thomas More (q.v.). One year later, he was arrested and charged with high treason but the king's trusted servant died on November 29, 1530, before he could be brought to trial.

WOMEN. The generalization that women have always been closely tied to religion but that religion has not always been tied to women applies to the 16th century as well. In medieval theology women were viewed with considerable ambivalence, inferior to men, weaker than men, more than men given to fleshly passion. In the medieval church women had been excluded from leadership roles in the church hierarchy ever since the synods of Orange (441) and Orleans (533). The place of women in the church was in the monastic world, where they possessed their own space, including positions of power. Even though the Italian Renaissance may be said to have articulated a new view of womanhood—mundane, learned, active in politics and economics—in some ways this new ideal was but the traditional ideal of the woman religious in the convent.

The Protestant (q.v.) Reformation presented the ideal of the bourgeois burgher woman whose role was defined as that of wife and mother. Martin Luther (q.v.) identified such womanhood as one of the "estates." Luther extolled the "estate" of marriage (q.v.)—which now became the normative role model for women—as one of chastity and an affirmation of love and the cross. This notion of women having their calling in this estate meant that nothing (or very little) was made of women as active participants in the spiritual and ecclesial work of the church. A few exceptions can be noted. In the early German Reformation several tracts were specifically addressed to women, such as Ambrosius Blarer's (q.v.) *Sendbrief an die christliche Gemeinde* (Letter to the Christian Congregation) of 1532, and a few women were literary protagonists of the new evangel, such as Argula von Grumbach (q.v.) or Katherina Zell. After 1566 Geneva (q.v.) organized conferences of deaconesses in Cleves and Amsterdam.

Since the Reformation abolished monasteries and convents, the autonomous space which medieval women (if they chose the religious vocation) possessed, disappeared. It did not find a home in the Protestant tradition until the 17th century (Quakers) and the various forms of late 17th- and 18th-century Pietism. In the 16th century Reformation the early Anabaptist (q.v.) conventicles anticipated the development in that Anabaptist women appear to have played important roles. Certainly, Anabaptist martyr books bespeak an important role for women as Anabaptist martyrs and witnesses.

WORMS, DIET OF (1521). Emperor Charles V (q.v.), who had been elected in 1519, convened a diet (q.v.) to meet in Worms in January 1521. This was his first diet (q.v.) as newly elected emperor, and a number of important issues were on the agenda. Foremost was the clarification of how imperial authority should be exercised in Germany (q.v.) during the emperor's absence from Germany. But the controversy surrounding Martin Luther (q.v.) was making its way into the deliberations of the German estates. By the time the diet was to convene the ecclesiastical verdict against Luther had not been issued. In this uncertainty, Charles promised the Saxon elector Frederick III (q.v.) in November to give Luther a hearing at the diet. Luther's condemnation, in the bull *Decet Romanum pontificem*, dramatically altered the situation as far as the church was concerned, and accordingly the papal nuncio Aleander insisted at the diet, once it had convened, that a condemned heretic could not be given a hearing. The estates in turn expressed concern that the restlessness among the common people would increase if Luther were not given a hearing at the diet. And Elector Frederick argued that Luther had to be given a hearing since Charles's election agreement stipulated that no German could be sentenced without a proper hearing.

If in the end the estates and Frederick had their way, despite the preponderance of ecclesiastical rulers sitting in the diet, then it was because citing Luther to Worms was the most expedient thing to do: the fervent Catholics understood it as merely giving him a formal opportunity to recant (in March Aleander had seen to the publication of an imperial mandate against Luther which ordered the burning of his writings and noted that his citation to Worms was to give him an opportunity to recant formally). The reform-minded estates saw it as a means to further the cause of reform, however understood, while the estates generally saw it as an opportunity to convey to the new emperor that he had to reckon with the importance of the power and authority of the estates and could not proceed unilaterally as he himself wished.

Luther's citation to Worms, issued early in March, was vague as to the purpose of his appearance at Worms. When Luther appeared before the diet, on April 17 and 18, he was indeed only asked to recant. In a famous response Luther declared himself to be bound by his conscience and Scriptures and refused to recant. Subsequent private negotiations with Luther proved unsuccessful, particularly when he refused to accept the decisions of a general council as binding on him. On April 26 Luther left Worms, having been informed of the emperor's determination to proceed against him as became his imperial obligation as defender of the church.

On his return to Wittenberg, Luther was spirited away by soldiers of Elector Frederick to the Wartburg, a desolate castle near Eisenach, where he spent the better part of the ensuing year in hiding, removed from the emperor's reach. Most thought that Luther had been killed by the emperor who issued the Edict of Worms (q.v.) against Luther and his followers late in May and then left Germany because of imminent danger of war with France (q.v.). He was to be gone for almost a decade.

WORMS, EDICT OF. The Edict of Worms (q.v.) was promulgated by Emperor Charles V (q.v.) on May 25, 1521, against Martin Luther (q.v.) and his followers. It placed Luther and his followers under the imperial ban. This meant that Luther and his followers were political outlaws, to be arrested by anyone, and, after a perfunctory trial (since he had already been convicted of heresy), sentenced to death. Furthermore, Luther's writings were to be burned. The edict was in its way the routine conclusion of the proceedings against Luther that had led to his condemnation as a heretic by the church in January of that year. However, the promulgation of the edict was accompanied by a variety of procedural errors, which helps explain its failure to play a significant role in the subsequent course of events.

— X —

XAVIER, FRANCIS (1506-1552). Jesuit missionary. Born of a noble family in Navarre, Francis studied at the University of Paris, where Ignatius of Loyola (q.v.) was his roommate. Converted by Ignatius, Francis began to study theology and then joined Ignatius and the other "companions" in Italy. In 1542 he set out for India, where he stayed for three years. A second journey came in 1547. In 1549 he went to Japan. Three years later he sought to enter China but died before he had succeeded, on an island off the China coast. At these places Francis batpized thousands of converts. Francis was canonized in 1622. (See also SOCIETY OF JESUS).

— Z —

ZURICH. Zurich became a member of the Swiss Confederation in 1351 and was directly under the jurisdiction of the emperor. The Swiss Confederation of which Zurich was a member was a weak union, which meant that for all intents and purposes Zurich was ruled autonomously. The city itself was governed by a great and a small council in which the 13 city guilds played an important role. Ecclesiastically, the city was dominated by two important foundations, the Fraumünster and the Großmünster. The latter was a collegiate church whose canons exercised considerable say in the city. The Reformation in Zurich was aided by several incisive factors. One was that a school had been created at the Großmünster in the late Middle Ages, which turned harmoniously into what might be called a Protestant seminary after the Reformation had been established in Zurich. Moreover, Huldrych Zwingli (q.v.) succeeded in delineating a concept of reform that was harmoniously tailored to the political and social conditions of Zurich, in which, contrary to Martin Luther's (q.v.) notion of reforming the church, the political and the religious institutions were taken to be harmoniously intertwined.

The formal catalyst of the introduction of the Reformation in Zurich were two disputations (q.v.) held in 1523 at the behest of the city council. The first of these was to address the contested issues between the reformers and the Catholic Church but few Catholics actually participated, since they argued that the Zurich city council did not have the authority to convene such a disputation. This is precisely what the council did in the end: the city council declared it as part of its authority to determine the religious configuration of the city. The second disputation, in October, dealt with the necessary changes in the religious life of the city now that the decision in favor of reform had been made. In the wake of the introduction of the Reformation changes in the political power structure of Zurich occurred; when they were completed, Zwingli and his evangelical supporters possessed the power to sustain the religious changes even in the face of conservative opposition.

The political tensions with the Catholic cantons triggered by Zurich's acceptance of the new evangelical faith eventually led to the (second) War of Kappel (q.v.), which not only brought Zwingli's own death on the battlefield but also stymied any notion that Protestantism (q.v.) might be uniformly accepted in the Swiss Confederation. Zwingli's 27-year-old successor, Heinrich Bullinger (q.v.), was initially confronted with the backlash against Zwingli's convergence of religious and political goals, expressed by a city council which had become nervous about Zwingli's intrusion into the "worldly realm," but with a steady hand he consolidated the workings of the Reformation in Zurich. Bullinger was responsible for the Zurich synodical church order (q.v.) of 1532, which provided a permanent structure for the Zurich church and its relationship to the Zurich power structure. Under his leadership Zurich continued to play an important role in European Protestantism, especially after the Consensus Tigurinus (q.v.) tied Zurich to the ever more ebullient Calvinism (q.v.). (See also SWITZERLAND).

ZWICKAU PROPHETS. The term refers to two weavers from the town of Zwickau, Nikolaus Storch and Thomas Drechsel, who arrived in Wittenberg late in 1521 (while Martin Luther [q.v.] was on the Wartburg) and announced, together with Philip Melanchthon's (q.v.) former student Thomas Stübner, that they had received direct revelations from the Holy Spirit to guide them in religious truth. Also, the world would soon be radically changed by the imminent coming of the kingdom of God; and, finally, the baptism (q.v.) of infants was an abomination. The notion that the inspiration of the Spirit was more important than the written Word radically challenged the emerging Reformation notion of the centrality of the Word.

ZWINGLI, HULDRYCH (1484-1531). Swiss reformer. Zwingli was born in Wildhaus, where his father was bailiff. He matriculated at the University of Vienna in 1498 and four years later moved to the University of Basel. At both universities he encountered a school of thought which sought to combine Thomistic scholasticism and Humanism (q.v.), rationalism and ethics, which characterized his thought throughout his life. He received his master's degree in 1506 and began the study of theology. His appointment as priest in Glarus, a town of about a thousand, precluded formal studies but afforded him ample time for studies on his own. Theologically, Zwingli was self-taught. At Glarus he became involved in Swiss politics as an ardent opponent of French hegemonic notions; his first literary work was a patriotic poem in which he warned his fellow Swiss of the French efforts to hire Swiss mercenaries.

His political activism on behalf of papal interests earned him a papal pension but the victory of the French in the battle of Marignano meant that the French party in Glarus became dominant and jeopardized Zwingli's position, and in November 1516 Zwingli received a three-year leave. He spent it at Einsiedeln, a pilgrimage center, where he actively participated in traditional pilgrimage activities, including going on a pilgrimage of his own. Two years later he became a candidate for the position of "people's priest" in Zurich (q.v.) at the Great Münster, a position funded by the Zurich city council for the purpose of regular preaching at that church.

By that time Zwingli was significantly influenced by Erasmian notions, and his views of church and theology were essentially Erasmian. Zwingli began his appointment in Zurich—which almost came to naught because of word that he had violated his vow of celibacy in Glarus—with a program of preaching consecutively from the Gospel of Matthew. Also in 1519 Zwingli became acquainted with Martin Luther's (q.v.) writings, distributed them, and spoke enthusiastically about them to friends, although a few years later he steadfastly and categorically denied that Luther had in any serious way influenced him. Undoubtedly, political considerations prompted Zwingli to minimize his connection with the excommunicated professor at Wittenberg. Moreover, an almost fatal illness (the plague) and a seemingly miraculous recovery have been seen as the theological turning point, comparable to Martin Luther's "evangelical experience," though it seems more accurate to observe that the illness proved a deeply spiritual maturation. In 1520 Zwingli ceased accepting the papal pension which he had been receiving, a step that can be seen either as an expression of his determined notion of neutrality or as another indication of a break with the papal church.

The open break between Zwingli and the church occurred during Lent, 1522, when a group of Zurich citizens broke the fast and consumed a few sausage links. Zwingli, who was present but did not eat the "forbidden fruit," subsequently published a sermon as his first Reformation treatise, *Concerning the Choice and Freedom of Food*. In rapid succession followed a series of additional Reformation treatises which accompanied the determined effort to undertake reform and change in Zurich. The key elements were clerical celibacy and the freedom to preach the pure Word of God. On October 10, 1522, Zwingli formally resigned his position as priest and was promptly appointed a "preacher" by the city council.

At the two Zurich disputations (q.v.) of 1523 (January; October), which had been convened at Zwingli's urging by the Zurich city council, the groundwork was laid for the repudiation of the papal authority and the introduction of an "evangelical" form of Christianity. The January disputation, in which mainly supporters of Zwingli were present, was a lame affair: Zwingli himself had written the *Sixty-seven Theses* which, arguing the matter on the basis of "solely the gospel of Christ," rejected papacy, the Mass, intercession of the saints, monasticism (q.v.), celibacy, and even general councils. The October disputation, in turn, proved to be a hotly contested affair, since the advocates of immediate and drastic reform rose to challenge Zwingli's seemingly slow approach to religious and liturgical change: the celebration of the Mass and the images in the churches were the contested topics.

The Zurich city council's determination of the outcome of the disputation favored the slow approach. For some of Zwingli's impatient followers, notably the future Anabaptist (q.v.) leader Conrad Grebel (q.v.), the outcome meant that Zwingli had succumbed to the dictates of the city council. Alienation began, which was to end with the emergence of an "Anabaptist" conventicle in Zurich in January 1525. It was, in fact, not until the spring of 1525 that more extensive changes—such as the replacement of the Mass by a simple communion service—were undertaken in Zurich.

In subsequent years Zwingli guided Zurich through the full ramifications of ecclesiastical change, notably the introduction of the Marriage Court Order, of 1525, which like all other ecclesiastical orders of this sort was in fact promulgated by the city council, which acted on the part of a Christian congregation identical with the civic community. One year later the functions of this Marriage Court were expanded to entail a comprehensive monitoring of the moral and religious lives of the Zurich citizens (the court was comprised of six members, two of whom were clerics, while the remaining four were representatives of the city council). A theological seminary was established in 1525, while Zwingli himself established the "prophecy" (*prophezei),* a daily session at which all clergy in the city as well as older students were required to be present. Zwingli exegeted the Old Testament both for the "in-service" training of the clergy and also the progress on what eventually came to be known as the Zurich Bible, a German version of the Bible (q.v.) in the Swiss dialect.

Between 1525 and 1529 Zwingli's theological orientation was dominated by his controversy with Luther over the interpretation of the Lord's Supper (q.v.). Triggered by a letter of the Dutchman Cornelis Hoen, Zwingli concluded that the words of institution ("This is my body. . . this is my blood") should be understood figuratively so that the presence of Jesus in Communion was a spiritual one. This was a far cry from the notion of the "real" presence of Christ in the elements, which Luther, despite his repudiation of the scholastic interpretation of "transubstantiation," had retained. A series of treatises exchanged fierce and bitter polemics, involving not only Luther and Zwingli but just about every reformer of note.

The colloquy of Marburg (q.v.) of 1529, convened by Landgrave Philip of Hesse (q.v.), was to attempt a conciliation of the two perspectives. Despite some compromise formulations in the agreement signed by all present, the colloquy marked what proved to be a major and permanent theological division in Protestant (q.v.) ranks. Moreover, the failure to agree isolated Zwingli and Zurich politically as well. When Emperor Charles V (q.v.) solicited presentations of the theological positions at the diet of Augsburg (q.v.) in 1530, Zwingli was not included. Desperately he sought to bolster the work of Reformation in Zurich by pursuing international alliances with Hesse, Strasbourg, and even with France (q.v.).

But an internal Swiss dispute determined Zwingli's fate. Zwingli was intent on expanding the Reformation beyond Zurich and the other cantons which had turned Protestant. He pushed for armed confrontation with the Catholic cantons but the first step was an embargo against them. Since they were dependent on grain from South Germany and the Alsace the embargo presented them with mortal danger.

In October 1531 the Catholic cantons declared war on Zurich. Despite Zwingli's agitation for war, the city was ill prepared. On October 11, two days after the declaration of war, Zurich frantically and belatedly mobilized its army. The battle took place near Kappel (q.v.) that day. Zurich was defeated. Zwingli, who had accompanied the Zurich military contingent into battle as a soldier, died on the battlefield.

His early death meant that his legacy as a reformer was limited. There can be little doubt, however, that he was the progenitor of that major Protestant tradition which was to bear the name of "that Frenchman" John Calvin (q.v.), who arrived in Geneva (q.v.) half a decade after Zwingli's death. The Consensus Tigurinus (q.v.) brought agreement between Zwinglian and Calvinist theology, and through Calvinism and the Reformed (q.v.) tradition Zwingli's influence persisted beyond the 16th century. (See also SWITZERLAND).

Bibliography

Bibliographical Note

The first comment to be made about the literature pertaining to the Reformation and Catholic Reform in the 16th century is that over the years Reformation scholarship has been one of the most active and prolific areas of study in European history. The reasons are not that difficult to ascertain and have to do with the important role the Reformation has been perceived to have played in several national histories and the more scholarly fact that not only historians but also theologians have had a notable interest in it.

For many years, most of this scholarship was done in Europe, notably by German scholars, but more recently this picture has changed. American scholars have become active participants in the scholarly discourse. This has meant that the traditional preponderance of materials in German or French has in recent years been replaced by a huge number of English-language publications, some of which are the very best publications on the topic in any language. American Reformation scholarship has come into its own. Consulting this bibliography will quickly convey that numerous entries are in English. This bibliography has sought to acknowledge the richness of English-language literature but has also, whenever appropriate, included publications in other languages as well. Also, this bibliography has sought to give preference to scholarly monographs, rather than journal articles, even though quite a few groundbreaking works have been published in journals. A practical reason determined this preference: monographs are much easier to obtain than are articles in scholarly journals.

There are several bibliographical tools that will make access to the most recent literature easier. One is the annual literature survey of the *Archive for Reformation History (Archiv für Reformationsgeschichte)*, which strives to compile all pertinent literature pertaining to the entire 16th century in slightly annotated form. It is a most helpful research tool indeed. An important electronic on-line tool is the journal index of the American Theological Libraries Association (ATLA). While this survey, which includes book reviews as well, concentrates on articles (and books) dealing with religion, it is most helpful precisely for this area.

Other important electronic tools accessible through the World Wide Web are the catalogues of the large research libraries of the world such as the Library of Congress and the British Museum. Enormously important for works from the 16th century is the Herzog August Bibliothek in Wolfenbüttel, Germany, whose catalogue is also accessible on the Web. There is no doubt but that the Web has significantly enhanced, and eased, a researcher's work. Also available, though only through websites of subscribers, is OCLC WorldCat, a kind of "national union catalogue" listing the library holdings of specific titles.

The *Oxford Encyclopedia of the Reformation* (1996), in four volumes, is the most comprehensive detailed reference work on the age of the Reformation. It includes useful bibliographies, both of primary and secondary works. Two mammoth German reference works, both probably in some 20 volumes, are in the process of being published: the *Theologische Realenzyklopädie* and the *Lexikon für Theologie und Kirche*. While their respective scopes go far beyond the 16th century, the articles pertaining to the Reformation are most useful.

Mention must also be made of a number of ambitious and formidable source editions that make primary materials from the 16th century available. Several of them had their beginning in the 19th century, such as the edition of Martin Luther's writings, the *Weimar Edition*, and the edition of the works of Huldrych Zwingli and John Calvin in the *Corpus Reformatorum*. There also is the edition of Anabaptist source materials, primarily of court and interrogation records of individual Anabaptists, the so-called *Täuferakten* that has reached almost 30 volumes.

In addition, there are also editions of political and diplomatic documents. For Germany there are the proceedings of the several diets in the 16th century, *Deutsche Reichstagsakten, Jüngere Reihe*, while for England we have the *State Papers*.

There are several additional research tools. The Center for Reformation Research in St. Louis has microfilms of the entire political archive of Landgrave Philip of Hesse. Luther Seminary in Minneapolis is presently engaged in an ambitious microfilming project of works of 16th-century reformers. The project has made considerable progress.

There is a microfiche edition of German-language Reformation pamphlets.

The best overall introductions to the 16th century in English probably are the books by Dickens, Cameron, and Spitz, together with the *Handbook* edited by Brady, Oberman, and Tracy. The various Luther biographies tend to cover the early years of the German Reformation as well: the biographies of Bainton, Haile, and Oberman must be mentioned. The annual literature survey of the Archive for Reformation History allows a convenient exposure to the most recent publications.

Bibliography ♦ 225

I. Bibliographies and Guides

ALAND, Kurt. *Hilfsbuch zum Lutherstudium.* 3rd rev. ed. Witten: Luther-Verlag, 1970.

ANDERSON, C. *Augsburg Historical Atlas of Christianity in the Middle Ages and Reformation.* Minneapolis: Augsburg Publishing House, 1967.

Archiv für Reformationsgeschichte: Literaturbericht [annual survey of publications]. Gütersloh: Verlagshaus Gerd Mohn.

BAKER, D., ed. *The Bibliography of the Reform 1450–1648 Relating to the United Kingdom and Ireland, for the Years 1955–70.* Oxford: Oxford University Press, 1975.

BENZING, Josef. *Lutherbibliographie: Verzeichnis der gedruckten Schriften Martin Luthers bis zu dessen Tod.* Baden-Baden: Heitz, 1966–1994.

BURCHILL, C. J. "The Urban Reformation and its Fate: Problems and Perspectives in the Consolidation of the German Protestant Movement," *History Journal* 27 (1984): 997–1010.

CROSS, F. L., ed. *The Oxford Dictionary of the Christian Church.* Oxford: Oxford University Press, 1997.

DICKENS, A. Geoffrey, and TONKIN, John M.. *The Reformation in Historical Thought.* Cambridge: Cambridge University Press, 1985.

GREEN, Lowell C. "Luther Research in English-Speaking Countries since 1970," *Lutherjahrbuch* 44 (1977), 105–26.

GREYERZ, Kaspar von. "Stadt und Reformation: Stand und Aufgaben der Forschung," *Archiv für Reformationsgeschichte* 76 (1985): 6–64.

HILLERBRAND, Hans J., ed. *The Oxford Encyclopedia of the Reformation.* 4 vols. New York: Oxford University Press, 1996.

HSIA, Ronnie P., ed. *The German People and the Reformation*. Ithaca, NY: Cornell University Press, 1988.

―――. *Social Discipline in the Reformation: Central Europe 1550– 1750*. London: Routledge, 1989.

KIEMPFF, D. *A Bibliography of Calviniana 1959–1974*. Leiden: Brill, 1975.

McGRATH, Alister E. *Reformation Thought: An Introduction*. Oxford: Oxford University Press, 1988.

―――. *Encyclopedia of Medieval, Renaissance and Reformation Thought*. Oxford: Blackwell, 1995.

OZMENT, Steven E., ed. *Reformation Europe: A Guide to Research*. St. Louis, MO: Center for Reformation Research, 1982.

PIPKIN, H. Wayne, ed. *A Zwingli Bibliography*. Pittsburgh: Pittsburgh Theological Seminary Press, 1972.

ROBBERT, George S., ed. "A Checklist of Luther's Writings in English," *Concordia Theological Monthly* 36 (1965): 772–92, and 41 (1970): 214–20; *Concordia Theological Journal* 4 (1978): 73– 77.

RUBLACK, H.-C. "Forschungsbericht Stadt und Reformation," in Bernd Moeller, ed. *Stadt und Kirche im 16. Jahrhundert*. Gütersloh: Gerd Mohn, 1978, 9–26.

SCOTT, Tom. "The Peasants' War: A Historiographical Review," *History Journal* 22 (1979): 693–720, 953–74.

1. Sources and Editions

BUCER, Martin. *Martini Buceri Opera Omnia*. F. Wendel, E. Staehelin, R. Stupperich, J. Rott, and R. Peter, ed. Gütersloh: Gerd Mohn, 1960–.

——. *Common Places of Martin Bucer*. Ed. and trans. D. F. Wright. Nashville, TN: Abingdon, 1972.

——. *Correspondance de M. Bucer*. Ed. Jean Rott. Leiden: Brill, 1979.

BULLINGER, Heinrich. *The Decades of Henry Bullinger*. 4 vols. Trans. H. I. and ed. T. Harding, Parker Society. Cambridge: Cambridge University Press, 1849–52.

CALVIN, John. *Ioannis Calvini Opera Quae Supersunt Omnia*. Ed. G. Baum, E. Cunitz, and E. Reuss. (*Corpus Reformatorum*. Vols. 29–87). Braunschweig and Berlin: Schwetschke, 1853–1900.

CASTELLIO, Sebastian. *Concerning Heretics; Whether They Are to Be Persecuted and How They Are to Be Treated*. Ed. Roland H. Bainton. New York, Columbia University Press, 1935.

ERASMUS, Desiderius. *Erasmi Epistolae*. 12 vols. Ed. P. S. and H. M. Allen. Oxford: Oxford University Press, 1906–58.

——. *Collected Works of Erasmus*. 66 vols. Toronto: University of Toronto Press, 1988–.

MELANCHTHON, Philip. *Philippi Melanchthonis Opera Quae Supersunt Omnia. Corpus Reformatorum*. Ed. C. G. Bretschneider et al. Vols. 1–28. Halle: Schwetschke, 1834–60. *Supplementa Melanchthoniana*. 4 vols. Leipzig, 1910–29 [works omitted in the *Corpus Reformatorum* edition].

——. *Melanchthons Werke in Auswahl*. Ed. Rudolf Stupperich. Gütersloh: Gerd Mohn, 1951–.

——. *Melanchthon on Christian Doctrine: Loci Communes 1555*. Ed. and trans. Clyde L. Manschreck. New York: Abingdon, 1965.

——. *Melanchthons Briefwechsel: Kritische und kommentierte Gesamtausgabe*. Ed. Heinz Scheible. Stuttgart: Frommann-Holzboog, 1977–.

MÜNTZER, Thomas. *The Collected Works of Thomas Müntzer*. Ed. and trans. Peter Matheson. Edinburgh: T. & T. Clark, 1988.

OECOLAMPADIUS, Johann. *Briefe und Akten zum Leben Oekolampads*. 2 vols. Ed. E. Staehelin. Leipzig, M. Heinsius Nachfoger, 1927–34.

OSIANDER, Andreas. *Andreas Osiander: Gesamtausgabe*. 8 vols. Ed. Gerhard Müller and Günther Seebass. Gütersloh: Gerd Mohn, 1975–.

POTTER, G. R., and GREENGRASS, M., eds. *John Calvin*. London: St. Martin's, 1983.

ZWINGLI, Huldrych. *Huldreich Zwinglis Werke*. 8 vols. Ed. M. Schuler and J. Schulthess. Zürich, 1828–42.

———. *Huldreich Zwinglis sämtliche Werke*. Corpus Reformatorum. Vol. 88 ff. Ed. E. Egli et al. Berlin, Leipzig, and Zürich: Schwetschke, 1905–.

2. Collections of Sources

BAYLOR, Michael G., ed. *The Radical Reformation*. Cambridge: Cambridge University Press, 1991.

Die Bekenntnisschriften der Evangelisch-Lutherischen Kirche. Hrsg. im Gedenkjahr der Augsburgischen Konfession. Göttingen: Vandenhoeck & Ruprecht, 1976 [includes Augsburg Confession and Apology, Luther's Catechisms, and the Formula of Concord].

COCHRANE, Arthur C. *Reformed Confessions of the 16th Century*. Philadelphia: Westminster, 1966.

Conciliorium Oecumenocorum Decreta. 3rd ed. Ed. G. Alberigo et al. Bologna: Istituto per le scienze religiose, 1973.

DICKENS, A. Geoffrey, and CARR, D., eds. *The Reformation in England to the Accession of Elizabeth I.* New York: St. Martin's Press, 1967.

ENGLANDER, David, et al., eds. *Culture and Belief in Europe 1450–1600.* 1990.

FERRELL, Lori Anne, and CRESEY, David, eds. *Religion and Society in Early Modern England: A Sourcebook.* New York: Routledge, 1996.

FRANZ, Günther, ed. *Quellen zur Geschichte des Bauernkrieges.* Munich: Oldenburg, 1963.

KIDD, Beresford J., ed. *Documents Illustrative of the Continental Reformation.* Oxford: Oxford University Press, 1911. Also London: SPCK, 1966.

SEHLING, Emil, ed. *Die evangelischen Kirchenordnungen des XVI. Jahrhunderts.* 5 vols. Leipzig, 1902–13; Repr. 5 vols. Tübingen: Mohr, 1955.

3. Textbooks, Surveys, Essays

BATORI, Ingrid, ed. *Städtische Gesellschaft und Reformation.* Stuttgart: Klett, 1980.

BLICKLE, Peter. *Die Reformation im Reich.* Ulm: Ulmer Verlag, 1985.

————, ed. *Revolte und Revolution in Europa: Referate und Protokolle des internationalen Symposiums zur Erinnerung an den Bauernkrieg 1525.* Historische Zeitschrift, Neue Folge Beiheft 4, 1975.

————, ed. *Bauer, Reich und Reformation: Festschrift Günther Franz.* Stuttgart: Ulmer Verlag, 1982.

————, ed. *Zwingli und Europa: Referate und Protokolle des internationalen Kongresses aus Anlass des 500. Geburtstages von Huldrych Zwingli, 1984.* Göttingen: Vandenhoeck & Ruprecht, 1985.

BONNEY, Richard. *The European Dynastic States, 1494–1660.* Oxford: Oxford University Press, 1991.

BOSSY, John. *Christianity in the West 1400–1700.* Oxford: Oxford University Press, 1985.

BRADY, Thomas A., OBERMAN, Heiko A., and TRACY, James, eds. *Handbook of European History 1400–1600.* 2 vols. Leiden: Brill, 1994.

BROOKS, Peter N., ed. *Reformation Principle and Practice: Essays in Honour of Arthur Geoffrey Dickens.* London: Scolar Press, 1980.

BUCK, Lawrence P., and ZOPHY, Jonathan W., eds. *The Social History of the Reformation.* Columbus: Ohio State University Press, 1972.

CAMERON, Euwen. *The European Reformation.* Oxford: Oxford University Press, 1991.

CARGILL THOMPSON, W. D. J. *Studies in the Reformation: Luther to Hooker.* Ed. C. W. Dugmore. London: Athlone, 1980.

CHAUNU, Pierre, ed. *The Reformation.* Trans. V. Acland et al. Gloucester: Sutton, 1989.

DAVIS, Natalie Z. *Society and Culture in Early Modern France.* Stanford, CA: Stanford University Press, 1975.

DELUMEAU, Jean. *Naissance et affirmation de la réforme.* 3rd ed. Paris: Fayard, 1973.

DICKENS, A. Geoffrey. *The German Nation and Martin Luther.* New York: Harper & Row, 1974.

ELTON, Geoffrey R., ed. *The Reformation 1520–1559*. 2nd ed. The New Cambridge Modern History. Cambridge: Cambridge University Press, 1990.

FEBVRE, Lucien. *Au coeur religieux du XVIe siècle*. Paris: S.E.V.P.E.N., 1957.

FRIEDMAN, Jerome, ed. *Regnum, Religio et Ratio: Essays Presented to Robert M. Kingdon*. Kirksville, MO: Sixteenth Century Journal Publishers, 1987.

GREENGRASS, Mark. *The Longman Companion to the European Reformation, c. 1500–1618*. London: Longman, 1998.

GREYERZ, Kaspar von, ed. *Religion and Society in Early Modern Europe 1500–1800*. London: German Historical Institute, 1984.

HILLERBRAND, Hans J. *Christendom Divided*. New York: Macmillan, 1972.

HSIA, Ronnie P., ed. *The German People and the Reformation*. Ithaca, NY: Cornell University Press, 1988.

HUGHES, Michael. *Early Modern Germany, 1477–1806*. London: Macmillan, 1992.

ISERLOH, Erwin, GLAZIK, J., and JEDIN, Hubert. *Reformation and Counter Reformation*. Vol. 5 of *History of the Church*. Ed. H. Jedin and J. Dolan. Trans. A. Biggs and P. W. Becker. London: Crossroad, 1980.

KARANT-NUNN, Susan. *The Reformation of Ritual: An Interpretation of Early Modern Germany*. New York: Routledge, 1997.

KÖHLER, Hans-Joachim, ed. *Flugschriften als Massenmedium der Reformationszeit: Beiträge zum Tübinger Symposion 1980*. Stuttgart: Klett-Cotta, 1981.

KOURI, E. I., and SCOTT, T., eds. *Politics and Society in Reformation Europe: Essays for Sir Geoffrey Elton on His Sixty-Fifth Birthday.* London: Macmillian, 1987.

LAU, Franz, and BIZER, Ernst. *A History of the Reformation in Germany to 1555.* Trans. B. A. Hardy. London: Black, 1969.

LEONARD, Emile G. *A History of Protestantism.* 2 vols. Ed. H. H. Rowley. Trans. M. H. Reid and R. M. Bethell. London, 1965–67.

LORTZ, Joseph. *The Reformation in Germany.* London and New York: Herder and Herder, 1968.

MACKENNEY, Richard. *Sixteenth Century Europe.* London: Macmillan, 1993.

MOMMSEN, Wolfgang. J., and SCRIBNER, Robert W., eds. *Stadtbürgertum und Adel in der Reformation: Studien zur Sozialgeschichte der Reformation in England und Deutschland.* Stuttgart: Klett, 1979.

OBERMAN, Heiko A. *The Dawn of the Reformation.* Edinburgh: T. & T. Clark, 1986.

OLIN, John C., SMART, D. S., and McNALLY, R. E., eds. *Luther, Erasmus and the Reformation.* New York: Fordham University Press, 1969.

OZMENT, Steven E. *The Age of Reform 1250–1550: An Intellectual and Religious History of Late Medieval and Reformation Europe.* New Haven, CT: Yale University Press, 1980.

————, ed. *The Reformation in Medieval Perspective.* Chicago: Quadrangle, 1971.

PRESTWICH, M. ed. *International Calvinism 1541–1715.* Oxford: Oxford University Press, 1985.

ROBINSON-HAMMERSTEIN, Helga, ed. *The Transmission of Ideas in the Lutheran Reformation.* Dublin: Irish Academy Press, 1989.

SCHILLING, Heinz. *Aufbruch und Krise: Deutschland 1517–1649*. Berlin: Siedler, 1988.

SCRIBNER, Robert W. *The German Reformation*. Atlantic Highlands, NJ: Humanities Press, 1986.

———. *Popular Culture and Popular Movements in Reformation Germany*. London: Hambledon, 1987.

SKINNER, Quentin. *The Foundations of Modern Political Thought*. 2 vols. Cambridge: Cambridge University Press, 1978.

SPITZ, Lewis W. *The Protestant Reformation 1517–1559*. New York: HarperCollins, 1986.

———. ed. *The Reformation: Basic Interpretations*. Lexington, MA: Heath, 1972.

II. Late Medieval Religion

1. General Surveys

DOBSON, R. B., ed. *Church, Politics, and Patronage in the 15th Century*. Gloucester: A. Sutton, 1984.

HARPER-BILL, C. *The Pre-Reformation Church in England 1400–1530*. London: Longman, 1989.

McGRATH, Alister E. *Intellectual Origins of the European Reformation*. Oxford: Blackwell, 1987.

OAKLEY, Francis. *The Western Church in the Later Middle Ages*. Ithaca, NY: Cornell University Press, 1979.

OBERMAN, Heiko A. *The Harvest of Medieval Theology: Gabriel Biel and Late Medieval Nominalism*. Cambridge, MA: Harvard University Press, 1963.

————, ed. *Forerunners of the Reformation: The Shape of Late Medieval Thought Illustrated by Key Documents.* 2nd ed. Philadelphia: Fortress, 1981.

SOUTHERN, R. W. *Western Society and the Church in the Middle Ages.* Harmondsworth: Penguin, 1970.

SWANSON, R. N. *Church and Society in Late Medieval England.* Manchester: Manchester University Press, 1989.

2. Popular Religion

ABRAY, Lorna J. *The People's Reformation: Magistrates, Clergy, and Commons in Strasbourg, 1500–1598.* Ithaca, NY: Cornell University Press, 1985.

BOSSY, John. "The Mass as a Social Institution 1200–1700," *Past and Present* 100 (1983): 29–61.

DOUGLASS, Jane D. *Justification in Late Medieval Preaching: A Study of John Geiler of Kaysersberg.* Leiden: Brill, 1966.

GALPERN, A. N. *The Religions of the People in 16th-Century Champagne.* Cambridge: Cambridge University Press, 1976.

GINZBURG, Carlo. *The Cheese and the Worms: The Cosmos of a 16th-Century Miller.* New York: Penguin, 1982.

————. *Night Battles: Witchcraft and Agrarian Cults in the 16th and 17th Centuries.* New York: Penguin, 1985.

KAMINSKY, H. *History of the Hussite Revolution.* Berkeley: University of California Press, 1967.

MOELLER, Bernd. "Religious Life in Germany on the Eve of the Reformation," in Gerald Strauss, ed., *Pre-Reformation Germany.* London: Macmillan, 1972.

MONTER, E. William. *Ritual, Myth and Magic in Early Modern Europe*. Brighton: Ohio University Press, 1983.

MUCHEMBLED, R. *Popular Culture and Elite Culture in France 1400–1750*. Trans. L. Cochrane. Baton Rouge: Louisiana State University Press, 1985.

OBELKEVICH, J., ed. *Religion and the People, 800–1700*. Chapel Hill: University of North Carolina Press, 1979.

O'NEIL, M. "Magical Healing: Love, Magic and the Inquisition in Late 16th-Century Modena," in S. Haliczer, ed., *Inquisition and Society in Early Modern Europe*. Totowa, NJ: Barnes & Noble, 1987.

POST, R. R. *The Modern Devotion: Confrontation with Reformation and Humanism*. Leiden: Brill, 1968.

RUBIN, Miriam. *Corpus Christi: The Eucharist in Late Medieval Culture*. Cambridge: Cambridge University Press, 1991.

SCRIBNER, R. W., JOHNSON, Trevor, eds. *Popular Religion in Germany and Central Europe, 1400–1800*. London: Macmillan, 1996.

STRAUSS, Gerald, ed. *Manifestations of Discontent in Germany on the Eve of the Reformation*. Bloomington: Indiana University Press, 1972.

TENTLER, Thomas N. *Sin and Confession on the Eve of the Reformation*. Princeton, NJ: Princeton University Press, 1977.

THOMAS, Keith. *Religion and the Decline of Magic: Studies in Popular Beliefs in 16th- and 17th-Century England*. London: Penguin, 1971.

TOUSSAERT, J. *Le Sentiment religieux en Flandre à la fin du moyen-âge*. Paris: Plon, 1963.

TRINKAUS, Charles, and OBERMAN, Heiko A., eds. *The Pursuit of Holiness in Late Medieval and Renaissance Religion.* Leiden: Brill, 1974.

3. Ecclesiastical Life

BLACK, A. *Council and Commune: The Conciliar Movement and the 15th-Century Heritage.* London: Burnes & Oates, 1979.

BOWKER, Margaret. *The Secular Clergy in the Diocese of Lincoln 1495–1520.* Cambridge: Cambridge University Press, 1968.

———. *The Henrician Reformation: The Diocese of Lincoln under John Longland 1521–47.* Cambridge: Cambridge University Press, 1981.

HAY, Dennis. *The Church in Italy in the 15th Century: The Birkbeck Lectures 1971.* Cambridge: Cambridge University Press, 1977.

HEATH, Peter. *The English Parish Clergy on the Eve of the Reformation.* London: Routledge, 1969.

THOMPSON, A. Hamilton. *The English Clergy and Their Organization in the Later Middle Ages.* Oxford: Oxford University Press, 1947.

THOMSON, J. A. F. *Popes and Princes 1417–1517: Politics and Piety in the Late Medieval Church.* London: Longman, 1980.

4. Theology

O'MALLEY, John W. *Giles of Viterbo on Church and Reform: A Study in Renaissance Thought.* Leiden: Brill, 1968.

OZMENT, Steven E. *Homo Spiritualis: A Comparative Study of the Anthropology of Johannes Tauler, Jean Gerson, and Martin Luther 1509–16 in the Context of Their Theological Thought.* Leiden: Brill, 1969.

PELIKAN, Jaroslav J. *Reformation of Church and Dogma 1300–1700.* Vol 4 of *The Christian Tradition.* Chicago: University of Chicago Press, 1984.

STEINMETZ, David C. *Miseriacordia Dei: The Theology of Johannes von Staupitz in Its Late Medieval Setting.* Leiden: Brill, 1968.

ULLMANN, K. H. *Reformers Before the Reformation.* Trans. R. Menzies. 2 vols. Edinburgh, 1855 [useful extracts from primary sources].

5. Renaissance and Humanism

BOYLE, Margaret O'R. *Rhetoric and Reform: Erasmus' Civil Dispute with Luther.* Cambridge: Cambridge University Press, 1983.

MENCHI, Silvia Seidel. *Erasmus als Ketzer: Reformation und Inquisition im Italien des 16. Jahrhunderts.* Leiden: Brill, 1993.

OVERFIELD, J. H. *Humanism and Scholasticism in Late Medieval Germany.* Princeton, NJ: Princeton University Press, 1984.

PAYNE, John B. *Erasmus: His Theology of the Sacraments.* Richmond: John Knox, 1970.

RUMMEL, Erika. *The Humanist-Scholastic Debate in the Renaissance and Reformation.* Cambridge, MA: Harvard University Press, 1997.

SPITZ, Lewis W. *The Religious Renaissance of the German Humanists.* Cambridge, MA: Harvard University Press, 1963.

STADTWALD, Kurt. *Renaissance Popes and German Patriots. Antipapalism in the Politics of the German Humanist Movement from Gregor Heimberg to Martin Luther.* Geneva: Droz, 1996.

TRACY, James D. *Erasmus of the Low Countries.* Berkeley: University of California Press, 1996.

TRINKAUS, Charles. *The Scope of Renaissance Humanism*. Ann Arbor: University of Michigan Press, 1983.

III. Catholicism in the 16th Century

DeMOLEN, RICHARD L., ed. *Religious Orders of the Catholic Reformation: In Honor of John C. Olin on His Seventy-Fifth Birthday*. New York: Fordham University Press, 1994.

EVENETT, H. O. *The Spirit of the Counter-Reformation*. Ed. with postscript J. Bossy. Notre Dame: University of Notre Dame Press, 1970.

GLEASON, Elisabeth. *Gasparo Contarini: Venice, Rome, and Reform*. Berkeley: University of California Press, 1993.

JEDIN, Hubert. *A History of the Council of Trent*. 2 vols. St. Louis, MO: Herder, 1957.

JONES, Martin D. W. *The Counter Reformation. Religion and Society in Early Modern Europe*. Cambridge: Cambridge University Press, 1995.

MEISSNER, W. W., SJ. *Ignatius of Loyola: The Psychology of a Saint*. New Haven, CT: Yale University Press, 1992.

O'MALLEY, John W., SJ, ed. *Catholicism in early Modern History: A Guide to Research*. St. Louis, MO: Center for Reformation Research, 1988.

―――. "Was Ignatius Loyola a Church Reformer? How to Look at Early Modern Catholicism," *Catholic Historical Review* 77 (1991): 177–93.

―――. *The First Jesuits*. Cambridge, MA: Harvard University Press, 1993.

RANFT, Patricia. *Women and the Religious Life in Premodern Europe*. New York: St. Martin's Press, 1997.

SHAW, Christine. *Julius II: The Warrior Pope*. Oxford: Blackwell, 1993.

SOERGEL, Philip. *Wondrous in His Saints: Counter-Reformation Propaganda in Bavaria*. Berkeley: University of California Press, 1993.

WICKS, Jared, SJ, ed. *Cajetan Responds: A Reader in Reformation Controversy*. Washington, DC: Catholic University of America Press, 1978.

IV. The Reformation

1. General Surveys

BLICKLE, Peter. *Kommunalisierung und Christianisierung: Voraussetzungen und Folgen der Reformation 1400–1600*. Berlin: Duncker & Humboldt, 1989.

DYKEMA, Peter A., and OBERMAN, Heiko A., eds. *Anticlericalism in Late Medieval and Early Modern Europe*. Leiden: Brill, 1993.

GEORGE, Timothy. *Theology of the Reformers*. Nashville: Broadman, 1988.

GRITSCH, Erich W. and JENSON, R. W. *Lutheranism: The Theological Movement and Its Confessional Writings*. Philadelphia: Fortress, 1976.

MATHESON, Peter. *The Rhetoric of the Reformation*. Edinburgh: T & T Clark, 1998.

OBERMAN, Heiko A. *Masters of the Reformation: The Emergence of a New Intellectual Climate in Europe*. Trans. D. Martin. Cambridge: Cambridge University Press, 1981.

PELIKAN, Jaroslav. *The Reformation of the Bible/The Bible of the Reformation*. New Haven, CT: Yale University Press, 1996.

REARDON, B. M. G. *Religious Thought in the Reformation*. London: Longman, 1981.

2. Martin Luther and Lutheranism

ALTHAUS, Paul. *The Theology of Martin Luther*. Trans. R. C. Schultz. Philadelphia: Fortress, 1966.

BAINTON, Roland H. *Here I Stand: A Life of Martin Luther*. New York: Abingdon, 1950.

BORNKAMM, Heinrich. *Luther in Mid-Career 1521–1530*. Ed. Karin Bornkamm. Trans. E. T. Bachmann. Philadelphia: Fortress, 1983.

BRECHT, Martin. *Martin Luther, I: His Road to Reformation 1483–1521*. Minneapolis: Augsburg, 1985.

————. *Martin Luther, II: Shaping and Defining the Reformation 1521–1532*. Minneapolis: Augsburg, 1990.

————. *Martin Luther, III: The Preservation of the Church 1532–1546*. Minneapolis: Augsburg, 1993.

Confessions of the Evangelical Lutheran Church. Philadelphia: Fortress, 1959.

EBELING, Günther. *Luther: An Introduction to his Thought*. Philadelphia: Fortress Press, 1970.

EDWARDS, Mark U. *Luther and the False Brethren*. Stanford, CA: Stanford University Press, 1975.

————. *Luther's Last Battles*. Ithaca, NY: Cornell University Press, 1983.

FIFE, R. H. *The Revolt of Martin Luther*. New York: Columbia University Press, 1957.

GERRISH, Brian A. *Grace and Reason: A Study in the Theology of Luther.* Oxford: Oxford University Press, 1962.

GRANE, Leif. *The Augsburg Confession: A Commentary.* Minneapolis: Augsburg, 1987.

————. *Martinus Noster: Luther in the German Reform Movement 1518–1521.* Mainz: Zabern, 1994.

HAILE, H. G. *Luther: An Experiment in Biography.* Princeton, NJ: Princeton University Press, 1980.

HARRAN, Marilyn. J. *Luther on Conversion: The Early Years.* Ithaca, NY: Cornell University Press, 1983.

JANZ, Denis. *Three Reformation Catechisms: Catholic, Anabaptist, Lutheran.* New York and Toronto: Edwin Mellon, 1982.

KOLB, Robert. *For All the Saints: Changing Perceptions of Martyrdom and Sainthood in the Lutheran Reformation.* Macon, GA: Mercer University Press, 1987.

LOEWENICH, Walther von. *Luther's Theology of the Cross.* Minneapolis: Augsburg, 1976.

LOHSE, Bernd. *Martin Luther: An Introduction to His Life and Thought.* Edinburgh: T. & T. Clark, 1987.

LUTHER, Martin. *Werke: Kritische Gesamtausgabe.* Weimar: Böhlau, 1883–1948. 58 vols. There are separate series for Letters *(Briefwechsel).* 12 vols.; the German Bible *(Die Deutsche Bibel)*; the "Table Talks" *(Tischreden).* 6 vols.

McGRATH, Alister. E. *Luther's Theology of the Cross: Martin Luther's Theological Breakthrough.* Oxford: Blackwell, 1985.

OBERMAN, Heiko A. *Luther: Man between God and the Devil.* New Haven, CT: Yale University Press, 1989.

PELIKAN, Jaroslav, and LEHMANN, Helmut T., eds. *Luther's Works, American Edition*. 55 vols. Philadelphia and St. Louis, MO: Fortress and Concordia, 1955–.

RUPP, E. Gordon. *The Righteousness of God: Luther Studies*. New York: Philosophical Library, 1953.

————, and DREWERY, B. J. *Martin Luther*. London: Edward Arnold, 1970.

SCHARFFENORTH, Gerta. *Becoming Friends in Christ: The Relationship between Man and Woman As Seen by Luther*. Geneva: Lutheran World Federation, 1983.

SCHORN-SCHÜTTE, Luise. *Evangelische Geistlichkeit in der Frühneuzeit*. Gütersloh: Güterloher Verlagshaus, 1996.

SCRIBNER, Robert W. *Popular Culture and Popular Movements in Reformation Germany*. London: Hambledon, 1987.

SIEMON-NETTO, Uwe. *The Fabricated Luther: The Rise and Fall of the Shirer Myth*. St. Louis, MO: Concordia, 1995.

SIGGINS, Ian. *Martin Luther's Doctrine of Christ*. New Haven, CT: Yale University Press, 1970.

3. John Calvin and Calvinism

BOUWSMA, William J. *John Calvin: A 16th-Century Portrait*. New York: Oxford University Press, 1988.

DUFFIELD, Gervase, ed. *John Calvin*. London: Duffield, 1966.

EIRE, Carlos M. N. *War Against the Idols: The Reformation of Worship from Erasmus to Calvin*. Cambridge: Cambridge University Press, 1986.

GANOCZY, Alexandre. *The Young Calvin*. Trans. D. Foxgrover and W. Provo. Edinburgh: T. & T. Clark, 1987.

GERRISH, Brian A., ed. *Grace and Gratitude: The Eucharistic Theology of John Calvin*. Minneapolis: Fortress, 1993.

HÖPFL, H. *The Christian Polity of John Calvin*. Cambridge: Cambridge University Press, 1982.

KENDALL, R. T. *Calvin and English Calvinism to 1649*. Oxford: Oxford University Press, 1979.

MONTER, William. *Calvin's Geneva*. New York: Wiley, 1967.

NAPHY, William G. *Calvin and the Consolidation of the Genevan Reformation*. Manchester: Manchester University Press, 1994.

NIESEL, Wilhelm. *The Theology of Calvin*. Philadelphia: Westminster, 1956.

PARKER, T. H. L. *John Calvin*. London: Dent, 1975.

WENDEL, Francois. *Calvin: The Origins and Development of His Religious Thought*. Trans. P. Mairet. New York: Harper & Row, 1963.

4. Other Reformers

BROOKS, Peter N. *Thomas Cranmer's Doctrine of the Eucharist*. London: Macmillan, 1965.

EELLS, Hastings. *Martin Bucer*. New Haven, CT: Yale University Press, 1931.

FURCHA, E. J., ed. *Huldrych Zwingli, 1484–1531: A Legacy of Radical Reform*. Montreal: Faculty of Religious Studies, 1985.

GÄBLER, Ulrich. *Huldrych Zwingli im 20. Jahrhundert*. Zürich: Theologischer Verlag, 1975.

GREAVES, Richard. *Theology and Revolution in the Scottish Reformation: Studies in the Thought of John Knox.* Grand Rapids, MI: Christian University Press, 1980.

KITTELSON, James M. *Wolfgang Capito: From Humanist to Reformer.* Leiden: Brill, 1975.

KLAASSEN, Walter. *Michael Gaismeier: Revolution and Reformation.* Leiden: Brill, 1978.

LOCHER, Gottfried W. *Zwingli's Thought: New Perspectives.* Leiden: Brill, 1981.

MANSCHRECK, Clyde L. *Melanchthon, the Quiet Reformer.* New York: Abingdon, 1958.

McNAIR, Philip. *Peter Martyr in Italy: An Anatomy of Apostasy.* Oxford: Oxford University Press, 1967.

POTTER, George R. *Zwingli.* Cambridge: Cambridge University Press, 1976.

RUPP, Gordon E. *Patterns of Reformation.* Philadelphia: Fortress, 1969.

SIDER, Ronald J. *Andreas Bodenstein von Karlstadt: The Development of His Thought 1517–1525.* Leiden: Brill, 1974.

STEPHENS, William P. *The Holy Spirit in the Theology of Martin Bucer.* Cambridge: Cambridge University Press, 1970.

———. *The Theology of Huldrych Zwingli.* Oxford: Clarendon, 1986.

———. *Zwingli. An Introduction to His Thought.* Oxford: Clarendon, 1992.

WRIGHT, David F., ed. *Martin Bucer: Reforming Church and Community.* Cambridge: Cambridge University Press, 1994.

5. Reformation and Society

ANGERMEIER, H. *Die Reichsreform 1410–1555: Die Staatsproblematik in Deutschland zwischen Mittel-alter und Gegenwart.* Munich: Beck, 1984.

BAK, Janos., ed. *The German Peasant War of 1525.* London: Cass, 1975.

BLICKLE, Peter. "Peasant Revolts in the German Empire in the Late Middle Ages," *Social History* 4 (1979): 223–39.

————. *The Revolution of 1525: The German Peasants' War from a New Perspective.* Baltimore, MD: Johns Hopkins University Press, 1981.

————. *Communal Reformation: The Quest for Salvation in 16th-Century Germany.* Atlantic Highlands, NJ: Humanities Press, 1992.

CARSTEN, Francis L. *Princes and Parliaments in Germany from the Fifteenth to the Eighteenth Century.* Oxford: Oxford University Press, 1959.

FISHER-GALATI, Stephen A. *Ottoman Imperialism and German Protestantism.* Cambridge: Cambridge University Press, 1959.

FRANZ, Günther. *Der deutsche Bauernkrieg.* Darmstadt: Wissenschaftliche Buchgemeinschaft, 1977.

RÖSSLER, Hans, ed. *Der deutsche Adel 1430–1555.* Darmstadt: Wissenschaftliche Buchgemeinschaft, 1965.

SCOTT, Tom. "Reformation and Peasants' War in Waldshut and Environs: A Structural Analysis," *Archiv für Reformationsgeschichte* 69 (1978): 82–102, and 70 (1979): 40–68.

SCRIBNER, Robert W., and BENECKE, G., eds. *The German Peasant War of 1525: New Viewpoints.* London: Allen and Unwyn, 1979.

6. The Reformation and the Cities

ABRAY, Lorna J. *The People's Reformation: Magistrates, Clergy and Commons in Strasbourg 1500–1598*. Oxford: Oxford University Press, 1985.

BARON, Hans. "Religion and Politics in the German Imperial Cities during the Reformation," *English Historical Review* 52 (1937):, 405–27, 614–33.

BRADY, Thomas A. *Ruling Class, Regime and Reformation at Strasbourg, 1520–1559*. Leiden: Brill, 1978.

————. *Turning Swiss: Cities and Empire, 1450–1550*. Cambridge: Cambridge University Press, 1985.

CHRISMAN, Miriam U. *Strasbourg and the Reform: Study in the Process of Change*. New Haven, CT: Yale University Press, 1967.

————. *Conflicting Visions of Reform: German Lay Propaganda Pamphlets, 1519–1530*. Atlantic Highlands, NJ: Humanities Press, 1996.

GOERTZ, Hans-Jürgen. *"Pfaffenhass und gross Geschrei": Die reformatorischen Bewegungen in Deutschland 1517–1529*. Munich: Oldenburg, 1987.

GREYERZ, Kaspar von. *The Late City Reformation in Germany: The Case of Colmar, 1522–1628*. Wiesbaden: Steiner, 1980.

GUGGISBERG, Hans R. *Basel in the 16th Century*. St Louis, MO: Center for Reformation Research, 1982.

HALL, Basil. "The Reformation City," *Bulletin of the John Rylands Library* 54 (1971): 103–48.

HAMM, Berndt. *Bürgertum und Glaube. Konturen der städtischen Reformation*. Göttingen: Vandenhoeck & Ruprecht, 1996.

KARANT-NUNN, Susan. *Zwickau in Transition 1500–1547: The Reformation as an Agent of Change.* Columbus: Ohio State University Press, 1987.

MOELLER, Bernd. *Imperial Cities and the Reformation: Three Essays.* Ed. and trans. H. C. E. Midelfort and M. U. Edwards. Philadelphia: Fortress, 1972.

———. "Zwinglis Disputationen: Studien zu den Anfängen der Kirchenbildung und des Synodalwesens im Protestantismus," *Zeitschrift der Savigny-Stiftung für Rechtsgeschichte, Kanonistische Abteilung* 56 (1970): 275–324; 60 (1974): 213– 364.

———. "Stadt und Buch: Bemerkungen zur Struktur der reformatorischen Bewegung in Deutschland," in Wolfgang J. Mommsen and Robert W. Scribner, eds. *Stadtbürgertum und Adel in der Reformation: Studien zur Sozialgeschichte der Reformation in England und Deutschland.* Stuttgart: Klett, 1979, p. 25–39.

NAEF, Henri. *Les Origines de la réforme à Genève.* 2 vols. Geneva: Droz, 1968.

NAUJOKS, Eberhard. *Obrikeitsgedanke, Zunftverfassung und Reformation: Studien zur Verfassungsgeschichte von Ulm, Esslingen und Schwäbisch Gmünd.* Stuttgart: Kohlhammer, 1958.

OZMENT, Steven E. *The Reformation in the Cities: The Appeal of Protestantism to 16th-Century Germany and Switzerland.* New Haven, CT: Yale University Press, 1975.

RUBLACK, Hans-Christoph. *Gescheiterte Reformation: Frühreformatorische und protestantische Beweg-ungen in süd- und ostdeutschen geistlichen Resi-denzen.* Stuttgart: Klett, 1978.

SCHILLING, Heinz. "The Reformation in the Hanseatic Cities," *16th Century Journal* 14 (1983): 443–56.

SCHMIDT, Heinrich-Richard. *Reichsstädte, Reich und Reformation: Korporative Religionspolitik 1521–1529.* Stuttgart: Franz Steiner, 1986.

STAFFORD, William S. *Domesticating the Clergy: The Inception of the Reformation in Strasbourg 1522–1524.* Missoula, MT: Scholars Press, 1976.

STRAUSS, Gerald. *Nuremberg in the 16th Century.* New York: Wiley, 1966.

VOGLER, Günther. *Nürnberg 1524–1525: Studien zur Geschichte der reformatorischen und sozialen Bewegung in der Reichsstadt.* Berlin, 1982.

WALTON, Robert C. *Zwingli's Theocracy.* Toronto: University of Toronto Press, 1967.

WARMBRUNN, Paul. *Zwei Konfessionen in einer Stadt: Das Zusammenleben von Katholiken und Protestanten in den paritätischen Reichsstädten Augsburg, Biberach, Ravensburg und Dinkelsbühl von 1546–1648.* Wiesbaden: F. Steiner, 1983.

WHALEY, Joachim. *Religious Toleration and Social Change in Hamburg.* Cambridge: Cambridge University Press, 1985.

7. England

ASTON, Margaret. *The King's Bedpost: Reformation and Iconography in a Tudor Group Portrait.* Cambridge: Cambridge University Press, 1995.

BRAY, Gerald ed. *Documents of the English Reformation.* Minneapolis: Fortress, 1994.

BRIGDON, Susan. *London and the Reformation.* Oxford: Oxford University Press, 1992.

CLEBSCH, William A. *England's Earliest Protestants 1520–1535.* New Haven, CT: Yale University Press, 1964.

COLLINSON, Patrick. *The Elizabethan Puritan Movement*. Berkeley: University of California Press, 1967.

———. *The Religion of Protestants: The Church in English Society 1559–1625*. Oxford: Clarendon, 1982.

———. *The Birthpangs of Protestant England: Religious and Cultural Change in the 16th and 17th Centuries*. London: St. Martin's, 1988.

CROSS, Claire. *Church and People 1450–1660*. Atlantic Highlands, NJ: Humanities Press, 1976.

DICKENS, A. Geoffrey. *The English Reformation*. 2nd ed. University Park: University of Pennsylvania Press, 1991.

———. "The Shape of Anti-clericalism and the English Reformation," in E. I. Kouri and Tom Scott, eds. *Politics and Society in Reformation Europe: Essays for Sir Geoffrey Elton on his Sixty-Fifth Birthday*. New York: St. Martin's, 1987.

DUFFY, Eamon. *The Stripping of the Altars: Traditional Religion in England 1400–1580*. New Haven, CT: Yale University Press, 1992.

ELTON, Geoffrey R. *Policy and Police: The Enforcement of the Reformation in the Age of Thomas Cromwell*. Cambridge: Cambridge University Press, 1972.

———. *England Under the Tudors*. London: Methuen, 1969.

GUY, John. *Tudor England*. Oxford: Oxford University Press, 1988.

HAIGH, Christopher, ed. *The English Reformation Revised*. Cambridge: Cambridge University Press, 1987.

HOULBROOKE, Richard. *Church Courts and the People during the English Reformation 1520–1570*. Oxford: Oxford University Press, 1979.

KNOTT, John R. *Discourses on Martyrdom in English Literature, 1563–1694*. Cambridge: University Press, 1993.

LITZENBERGER, Caroline. *The English Reformation and the Laity: Gloucestershire, 1540–1580*. Cambridge: Cambridge University Press, 1997.

LOADES, Donald. *Revolution in Religion: The English Reformation 1530–1570*. Cardiff: University of Wales Press, 1992.

MacCULLOCH, Diarmaid. *The Later Reformation in England*. New York: St. Martin's Press, 1990.

MARTIN, J. W. *Religious Radicals in Tudor England*. London: Hambledon, 1989.

MORGAN, John. *Godly Learning: Puritan Attitudes Toward Reason, Learning and Education, 1560–1640*. Cambridge: Cambridge University Press, 1986.

O'DAY, Rosemary. *The English Clergy: Emergence and Consolidation of a Profession, 1558–1642*. Atlantic Highlands, NJ: Humanities Press, 1979.

———. *The Debate on the English Reformation*. London: Methuen, 1986.

SCARISBRICK, John. J. *The Reformation and the English People*. Oxford: Blackwell, 1984.

SHEILS, William J. *The English Reformation 1530–1570*. London: Longman, 1980.

8. France

BAUMGARTNER, Frederic. *France in the Sixteenth Century*. London: Macmillan, 1996.

———. *Louis XII*. London: Macmillan, 1996.

CHRISTIN, Olivier. *La Paix de Religion: L'autonomisation de la raison politique au XVIe siècle.* Paris: Senil, 1997.

GREENGRASS, Mark. *France in the Age of Henri IV. The Struggle for Stability.* London: Longman, 1984.

———. *The French Reformation.* Oxford: Blackwell, 1987.

HELLER, Henry. *The Conquest of Poverty: The Calvinist Revolt in 16th-Century France.* Leiden: Brill, 1985.

KELLEY, Donald R. *The Beginning of Ideology: Consciousness and Society in the French Reformation.* Cambridge: Cambridge University Press, 1982.

KIM, Seong-Hak. *Michel de L'Hôpital: The Vision of a Reformist Chancellor during the French Religious Wars.* Kirksville, MO: Sixteenth Century Journal Publishers, 1997.

KNECHT, Robert J. *Francis I.* Cambridge: Cambridge University Press, 1982.

———. *Renaissance Warrior and Patron: The Reformation of Francis I.* Cambridge: Cambridge University Press, 1994.

———. *The French Wars of Religion 1559–1598.* London: Longman, 1996.

———. *Catherine de' Medici.* London: Longman, 1998.

POTTER, David. *French Wars of Religion: Select Documents.* London: Macmillan, 1998.

SALMON, J. H. M. *Society in Crisis: France in the 16th Century.* London: Methuen, 1975.

SUTHERLAND, Nicola Mary. *The Massacre of St. Bartholomew and the European Conflict, 1559–1572.* New York: Barnes and Noble, 1973.

————. *The Huguenot Struggle for Recognition.* New Haven, CT: Yale University Press, 1980.

WOLFE, Michael. *The Conversion of Henri IV: Politics, Power, and Religious Belief in Early Modern France.* Cambridge: Cambridge University Press, 1993.

9. Propaganda

CHRISMAN, Miriam U. *Lay Culture, Learned Culture: Books and Social Change in Strasbourg, 1480–1599.* New Haven, CT: Yale University Press, 1982.

EDWARDS, Mark U., Jr. *Printing, Propaganda, and Martin Luther.* Berkeley: University of California Press, 1994.

EISENSTEIN, Elizabeth. *The Printing Press as an Agent of Change.* 2 vols. Cambridge: Cambridge University Press, 1979.

FEBVRE, Lucien, and MARTIN, H.-J. *The Coming of the Book.* Trans. D. Gerard. London: Verso, 1976.

GAWTHROP, Richard, and STRAUSS, Gerald. "Protestantism and Literacy in Early Modern Germany," *Past and Present* 104 (1984): 31–55.

HIRSCH, Ruth. *Printing, Selling and Reading 1450–1550.* Wiesbaden: Harrassowitz, 1974.

MOXEY, Keith. *Peasants, Warriors, and Wives: Popular Imagery in the Reformation.* Chicago: University of Chicago Press, 1989.

RUSSELL, Paul A. *Lay Theology in the Reformation: Popular Pamphleteers in Southwest Germany 1521–1525.* Cambridge: Cambridge University Press, 1986.

SCRIBNER, Robert W. *For the Sake of Simple Folk: Popular Propaganda for the German Reformation.* Cambridge: Cambridge University Press, 1981.

10. Political Thought

CARGILL THOMPSON, W. D. J. *The Political Thought of Martin Luther*. Ed. Philip Broadhead. Totowa, NJ: Barnes & Noble, 1984.

OLSON, Oliver K. "Theology of Revolution: Magdeburg, 1550–1555," *16th Century Journal* 3 (1972): 56–79.

SHOENBERGER, C. G. "The Development of the Lutheran Theory of Resistance, 1523–1530," *16th Century Journal* 8 (1977): 61–76.

SKINNER, Quentin. *The Foundations of Modern Political Thought*. 2 vols. Cambridge: Cambridge University Press, 1978.

V. Fringe Groups of the Reformation

BAUMGARTNER, Mira, ed. *Die Täufer und Zwingli: Eine Dokumentation*. Zurich: Theologischer Verlag, 1993.

BAYLOR, Michael G., ed. and trans. *The Radical Reformation*. Cambridge: Cambridge University Press, 1991.

BENDER, Harold S. *Conrad Grebel, c. 1498–1526, the Founder of the Swiss Brethren, Sometimes Called Anabaptists*. Goshen, IN: Mennonite Historical Society, 1950.

BLANKE, Fritz. *Brothers in Christ: The History of the Oldest Anabaptist Congregation, Zollikon, Near Zurich, Switzerland*. Trans. J. Nordenhaug. Scottdale, PA: Herald Press, 1961.

BOYD, Stephen. *Pilgram Marpeck: His Life and Social Theology*. Durham, NC: Duke University Press, 1992.

BUBENHEIMER, Ulrich. *Consonantia Theologiae et Iurisprudentiae: Andreas Bodenstein von Karlstadt als Theologe und Jurist zwischen Scholastik und Reformation*. Tübingen: J. C. B. Mohr, 1977.

CLASEN, Claus-Peter. *Anabaptism: A Social History, 1525–1618.* Ithaca, NY: Cornell University Press, 1972.

DEPPERMANN, Karl. *Melchior Hoffmann: Social Unrest and Apocalyptic Visions in the Age of the Reformation.* Edinburgh: T. & T. Clark, 1987.

FURCHA, Edward. J., ed. *The Essential Carlstadt.* Waterloo, ON: Herald, 1995.

GOERTZ, Hans-Jürgen. *Die Täufer: Geschichte und Deutung.* Munich: Oldenburg, 1980.

————, ed. *Umstrittenes Täufertum, 1525–1975: Neue Forschungen.* Göttingen: Vandenhoeck & Ruprecht, 1975.

————. ed. *Profiles of Radical Reformers: Biographical Sketches from Thomas Müntzer to Paracelsus.* Kitchener, ON: Herald, 1982.

GRITSCH, Erich. *Thomas Müntzer: A Tragedy of Errors.* Minneapolis: Augsburg, 1989.

GROSS, T. Leonard. *The Golden Years of the Hutterites: The Witness and Communal Thought of the Communal Moravian Anabaptists during the Walpot Era, 1565–78.* Scottdale, PA: Herald, 1980.

GUGGISBERG, Hans R. *Sebastion Castellio. Humanist und Vorkämpfer der religiösen Toleranz im konfes-sionellen Zeitalter.* Göttingen: Vandenhoeck & Ruprecht, 1997.

HILLERBRAND, Hans J. "'The Radical Reformation': Reflections on the Occasion of an Anniversary," *Mennonite Quarterly Review* 67 (1993): 408–20.

KEENEY, William E. *The Development of Dutch Anabaptist Thought and Practice from 1539 to 1564.* Nieuwkoop: B. de Graaf, 1968.

KLAASSEN, Walter, ed. *Anabaptism in Outline: Selected Primary Sources.* Waterloo, Ont.: Herald Press, 1981.

KOT, Stanislaus. *Socinianism in Poland: The Social and Political Ideas of the Polish Anti-Trinitarians.* Trans. E. M. Wilbur. Cambridge, MA: Harvard University Press, 1957.

LIENHARD, Marc, ed. *The Origins and Characteristics of Anabaptism.* The Hague: Nijhoff, 1977.

McLAUGHLIN, R. Emmet. *Caspar Schwenckfeld, Reluctant Radical: His Life to 1540.* New Haven, CT: Yale University Press, 1986.

PACKULL, Werner O. *Hutterite Beginnings: Communitarian Experiments during the Reformation.* Baltimore, MD: Johns Hopkins University Press, 1996.

PATER, Carl A. *Karlstadt as the Father of the Baptist Movements: The Emergence of Lay Protestantism.* Toronto: University of Toronto Press, 1984.

REMPEL, John D. *The Lord's Supper in Anabaptism: A Study in the Christology of Balthasar Hubmaier, Pilgram Marpeck, and Dirk Philips.* Waterloo, Ont.: Herald Press, 1993.

RUPP, E. Gordon. *Patterns of Reformation.* London: Epworth, 1969.

SCOTT, Tom. *Thomas Müntzer: Theology and Revolution in the German Reformation.* London: St Martin's, 1989.

SIDER, Ronald J. *Andreas Bodenstein von Karlstadt: The Development of His Thought 1517–1525.* Leiden: Brill, 1974.

STAYER, James M. *Anabaptists and the Sword.* Lawrence, Kan.: Coronado, 1972.

WILBUR, Earl M. *A History of Unitarianism: Socinianism and Its Antecedents.* Cambridge, MA: Harvard University Press, 1946.

WILLIAMS, George H. *The Radical Reformation.* 3rd ed. Kirksville, MO: 16th Century Journal Publishers, 1992.

VI. Sixteenth-Century Confessionalism

1. Germany

CLASEN, Claus-Peter. *The Palatinate in European History 1559–1660.* Oxford: Oxford University Press, 1963.

JUNGKUNTZ, Theodore R. *Formulators of the Formula of Concord: Four Architects of Lutheran Unity.* St. Louis, MO: Concordia, 1977.

Kolb, Robert. *Nikolaus von Amsdorf 1483–1565: Popular Polemics in the Preservation of Luther's Legacy.* Nieuwkoop: De Graaf, 1978.

NISCHAN, Bodo. "The Second Reformation in Brandenburg: Aims and Goals," *16th Century Journal* 14 (1983): 173–87.

————. *Prince, Protestantism, and Confession: The Second Reformation in Brandenburg.* Philadelphia: University of Pennsylvania Press, 1994.

SCHILLING, Heinz. *Konfessionskonflikt und Staatsbildung: Eine Fallstudie über das Verhältnis von religiösen und sozialen Wandel in der Frühneuzeit am Beispiel der Grafschaft Lippe.* Gütersloh: Gerd Mohn, 1981.

————. *Religion, Political Culture and the Emergence of Early Modern Society: Essays in German and Dutch History.* Leiden: Brill, 1992.

SCHMIDT, Heinz-Richard. *Konfessionalisierung im 16. Jahrhundert.* München: Oldenbourg, 1992.

SPITZ, Lewis W., and LOHFF, Wenzel, eds. *Discord, Dialogue and Concord: Studies in the Formula of Concord.* Philadelphia: Fortress, 1977.

2. European Countries

BUCSAY, Mihály. *Der Protestantismus in Ungarn 1521–1978.* 2 vols. Vienna: Köln, 1977–79.

CAMERON, James K. *The First Book of Discipline.* Edinburgh: T. & T. Clark, 1972.

COHN, Henry J., ed. *Government in Reformation Europe 1520–1560.* New York: Harper & Row, 1971.

COLLINSON, Patrick. *The Elizabethan Puritan Movement.* London: Cape, 1967.

————. *Archbishop Grindal 1515–1583: The Struggle for a Reformed Church.* London: Cape, 1980.

————. *"Godly People": Essays on English Protestantism and Puritanism.* Oxford: Blackwell, 1989.

————. *From Cranmer to Bancroft: English Religion in the Age of the Reformation.* Oxford: Blackwell, 1997.

COWAN, Ian B. *The Scottish Reformation: Church and Society in 16th-Century Scotland.* New York: St. Martin's, 1982.

CREW, Phyllis M. *Calvinist Preaching and Iconoclasm in the Netherlands, 1544–1569.* Cambridge: Cambridge University Press, 1978.

DAVIES, Norman. *God's Playground: A History of Poland.* 2 vols. Oxford: Oxford University Press, 1982.

DIEFENDORF, Barbara. *Beneath the Cross: Catholics and Huguenots in 16th-Century Paris.* New York: Oxford University Press, 1991.

DONALDSON, Gordon. *The Scottish Reformation.* Cambridge: Cambridge University Press, 1960.

DUKE, Alastair. *Reformation and Revolt in the Low Countries.* London: Hambledon, 1990.

DUNKLEY, E. H. *The Reformation in Denmark.* London: SPCK, 1949.

FEDORORWICZ, J. K., BOGUCKA, M., and SAMSONOWICZ, H., eds. *A Republic of Nobles: Studies in Polish History to 1864.* Cambridge: Cambridge University Press, 1982.

GRELL, Ole Peter, ed. *The Scandinavian Reformation: From Evangelical Movement to Institutionalisation of Reform.* Cambridge: Cambridge University Press, 1995.

HAIGH, Christopher. *English Reformations: Religion, Politics, and Society under the Tudors.* Oxford: Clarendon Press, 1993.

HIGMAN, Francis. *La Diffusion de la Réforme en France 1520–1565.* Geneva: Droz, 1992.

HINSON, Edward, ed. *Introduction to Puritan Theology: A Reader.* Grand Rapids, MI: Baker Book House, 1976.

HUDSON, Winthrop S. *The Cambridge Connection and the Elizabethan Settlement of 1559.* Durham, NC: Duke University Press, 1980.

JONES, Norman L. *Faith by Statute: Parliament and the Settlement of Religion 1559.* London: Royal Historical Society, 1982.

KINGDON, Robert M. *Geneva and the Coming of the Wars of Religion in France 1555–1563.* Geneva: Droz, 1956.

———. *Geneva and the Consolidation of the French Protestant Movement 1564–1572.* Geneva: Droz, 1967.

KIRK, James. *The Second Book of Discipline.* Edinburgh: T. & T. Clark, 1980.

————. *Patterns of Reform: Continuity and Change in the Reformation Kirk.* Edinburgh: T. & T. Clark, 1989.

LAKE, Peter. *Moderate Puritans and the Elizabethan Church.* Cambridge: Cambridge University Press, 1983.

MACZAK, Antoni, SAMSONOWIOZ, H., and BURKE, Peter, eds. *East-Central Europe in Transition from the 14th to the 17th Century.* Cambridge: Cambridge University Press, 1985.

PARKER, Geoffrey. *The Dutch Revolt.* London: Penguin, 1977.

PETTEGREE, Andrew, et al., eds. *Calvinism in Europe 1540–1620.* Cambridge: Cambridge University Press, 1997.

RABE, Horst. *Reichsbund und Interim: Die Verfassungs- und Religionspolitik Karls V. und der Reichstag zu Augsburg 1546–48.* Cologne: Böhlau, 1971.

REDDAWAY, William F., et al. *The Cambridge History of Poland to 1696.* Cambridge: Cambridge University Press, 1950.

ROBERTS, Michael. *The Early Vasas: A History of Sweden, 1523–1611.* Cambridge: Cambridge University Press, 1968.

WIESFLECKER, Hermann. *Kaiser Maximilian I.: Das Reich, Österreich und Europa an der Wende der Neuzeit.* 5 vols. Munich: Oldenburg, 1971–86.

WILLIAMS, Patrick. *Philip II.* London: Macmillan, 1998.

WORMALD, Jenny. *Court, Kirk and Community: Scotland 1470–1625.* London: Edward Arnold, 1981.

VII. Society

1. Women and Family

BAINTON, Roland H. *Women of the Reformation in Germany and Italy*. Minneapolis: Augsburg, 1971.

————. *Women of the Reformation in France and England*. Minneapolis: Augsburg, 1973.

————. *Women of the Reformation from Spain to Scandinavia*. Minneapolis: Augsburg, 1977.

BRIDENTHAL, Renate, ed. *Becoming Visible: Women in European History*. Boston: Houghton Mifflin, 1998.

CAMERON, Euwen. "The 'Godly Community' in the Theory and Practice of the European Reformation," in W. J. Sheils and D. Wood, eds. *Voluntary Religion*. Oxford: Oxford University Press, 1986, 131–53.

CRAWFORD, Patricia. *Women in Religion in England 1500–1720*. New York: Routledge, 1993.

DOUGLASS, Jane D. *Women, Freedom, and Calvin*. Philadelphia: Fortress, 1985.

HARRINGTON, Joel F. *Reordering Marriage and Society in Reformation Germany*. Cambridge: Cambridge University Press, 1995.

HSIA, Ronnie P. *Social Discipline in the Reformation: Central Europe 1550–1750*. London: Routledge, 1989.

INGRAM, Martin. *Church Courts, Sex and Marriage in England, 1570–1640*. Cambridge: Cambridge University Press, 1987.

KARANT-NUNN, Susan. "The Economic Position of Pastors in Ernestine Thuringia, 1521–1555," *Archive for Reformation History* 63 (1972): 94–113.

———. "Luther's Pastors: The Reformation in the Ernestine Countryside." *Transactions of the American Philosophical Society*, 69/8. Philadelphia: American Philosophical Society, 1979.

KÖHLER, Walther. *Zürcher Ehegericht und Genfer Konsistorium.* 2 vols. Leipzig: M. Heinsius Nachfolger, 1932–42.

MARSHALL, Sherry, ed. *Women in Reformation and Counter-Reformation Europe: Public and Private Worlds.* Bloomington: Indiana University Press, 1989.

MATHESON, Peter, ed. *Argula von Grumbach: A Woman's Voice in the Reformation.* Edinburgh: T. & T. Clark, 1995.

OZMENT, Steven E. *When Fathers Ruled: Family Life in Reformation Europe.* Cambridge, MA: Harvard University Press, 1983.

ROPER, Lyndal. *The Holy Household: Religion, Morals, and Order in Reformation Augsburg.* Oxford: Oxford University Press, 1989.

SAFLEY, Thomas. *Let No Man Put Asunder: The Control of Marriage in the German Southwest.* Kirksville, MO: Sixteenth Century Journal Publishers, 1984.

TURNER, James Grantham, ed. *Sexuality and Gender in Early Modern Europe: Institutions, Texts, Images.* Cambridge: Cambridge University Press, 1993.

WIESNER, Merry E. "Studies of Women, the Family, and Gender," in William Maltby, ed., *Reformation Europe: A Guide to Research, vol. 2.* St. Louis, MO: Center for Reformation Research, 1992, 159–87.

———. *Women and Gender in Early Modern Europe.* Cambridge, MA: Harvard University Press, 1993.

2. Reformation and Society

BARRY, Jonathan. *Witchcraft in Early Modern Europe: Studies in Culture and Belief.* Cambridge: Cambridge University Press, 1996.

BERINGER, Wolfgang. *Witchcraft Persecutions in Bavaria. Popular Magic, Religious Zealotry and Reason of State in Early Modern Europe.* Cambridge: Cambridge University Press, 1998.

COHN, Norman. *The Pursuit of the Millennium: Revolutionary Messianism in Medieval and Reformation Europe.* London: Pimlico, 1993.

EDWARDS, John. *The Jews in Christian Europe 1400–1700.* London: Routledge, 1988.

EISENSTADT, Shmuel N., ed. *The Protestant Ethic and Modernization: A Comparative View.* New York: Basic Books, 1968.

FICHTNER, Paula. *Protestantism and Primogeniture in Early Modern Germany.* New Haven, CT: Yale University Press, 1989.

FRIEDE, Juan and KEEN, Benjamin, eds. *Bartolomé de Las Casas in History: Towards an Understanding of the Man and His Work.* Dekalb, IL: Northern Illinois University Press, 1971.

FRIEDMAN, Jerry. "Jewish Conversion, the Spanish Pure Blood Laws and Reformation: A Revisionist View of Racial and Religious Antisemitism," *16th Century Journal* 18 (1987): 3–30.

GARNETT, George, ed. and trans. *Vindiciae, contra Tyrannos.* Cambridge: Cambridge University Press, 1994.

GLEASON, Elisabeth G., ed. and trans. *Reform Thought in 16th Century Italy.* Chico, CA: Scholars Press, 1981.

GREEN, R. W., ed. *Protestantism and Capitalism: The Weber Thesis and its Critics.* Lexington, MA: Heath, 1959.

GRELL, Ole Peter, and SCRIBNER, R.W., eds. *Tolerance and Intolerance in the European Reformation*. Cambridge: Cambridge University Press, 1996.

HALLMAN, Barbara. *Italian Cardinals, Reform, and the Church as Property*. Berkeley: University of California Press, 1985.

HANAWALT, E. Albu, and LINDBERG, C., eds. *Through the Eye of a Needle: Judeo-Christian Roots of Social Welfare*. Kirksville, MO: 16th Century Journal Publishers, 1994.

HANKE, Lewis. *All Mankind is One: A Study of the Disputation between Bartolomé de Las Casas and Juan Ginés de Sepúlveda in 1550 on the Intellectual and Religious Capacity of the American Indians*. Dekalb: Northern Illinois University Press, 1974.

HARRISON, Peter. *The Bible, Protestantism, and the Rise of Natural Science*. Cambridge: Cambridge University Press, 1998.

HENDRIX, Scott. "Toleration of the Jews in the German Reformation: Urbanus Rhegius and Braunschweig 1535–1540," *Archive for Reformation History* 81 (1990): 189–215.

HERZIG, Arno and SCHOEPS, Julius H., eds. *Reuchlin und die Juden*. Sigmaringen: Jan Thorbecke, 1993.

JÜTTE, Robert. *Poverty and Deviance in Early Modern Europe*. Cambridge: Cambridge University Press, 1994.

KAMEN, Henry. *Inquisition and Society in Spain in the 16th and 17th Centuries*. Bloomington: Indiana University Press, 1985.

KITTELSON, James M. "Successes and Failures in the German Reformation: The Report from Strasbourg," *Archive for Reformation History* 73 (1982): 153–74.

KOSLOFSKY, Craig. *The Reformation of the Dead: Death and Ritual in Early Modern Germany, 1475–1700*. London: Macmillan, 1998.

LEVACK, Brian. *The Witch-Hunt in Early Modern Europe*. London: Longman, 1994.

LINDBERG, Carter. *Beyond Charity: Reformation Initiatives for the Poor*. Minneapolis: Fortress-Augsburg, 1993.

————. "Tainted Greatness: Luther's Attitudes toward Judaism and Their Historical Reception," in Nancy Harrowitz, ed. *Tainted Greatness: Antisemitism and Cultural Heroes*. Philadelphia: Temple University Press, 1994.

MELLINKOFF, Ruth. *Signs of Otherness in Northern European Art*. 2 vols. Berkeley: University of California Press, 1995.

MICHALSKI, Sergiusz. *The Reformation and the Visual Arts: The Protestant Image Question in Western and Eastern Europe*. New York: Routledge, 1993.

MOLLAT, Michel. *The Poor in the Middle Ages: An Essay in Social History*. Trans. Arthur Goldhammer. New Haven, CT: Yale University Press, 1986.

MONTER, E. William. "The Consistory of Geneva, 1559–1569," *Bibliothèque d'Humanisme et Renaissance* 38 (1976): 467–84.

MUIR, Edward. *Ritual in Early Modern Europe*. Cambridge: Cambridge University Press, 1997.

OBERMAN, Heiko A. *The Roots of Anti-Semitism in the Age of the Renaissance and Reformation*. Philadelphia: Fortress, 1984.

PARKER, Charles H. *The Reformation of Community: Social Welfare and Calvinist Charity in Holland, 1572–1620*. Cambridge: Cambridge University Press, 1998.

QUINN, David B. *Explorers and Colonies. America, 1500–1625*. London: Hambledon, 1990.

SCHILLING, Heinz. *Die Stadt in der frühen Neuzeit*. Munich: Oldenbourg, 1993.

STRAUSS, Gerald. *Luther's House of Learning: Indoctrination of the Young in the German Reformation.* Baltimore, MD: Johns Hopkins, 1978.

THOMPSON, John L. *John Calvin and the Daughters of Sarah: Women in Regular and Exceptional Roles in the Exegesis of Calvin, His Predecessors, and His Contemporaries.* Geneva: Droz, 1992.

WANDEL, Lee P. *Always among Us: Images of the Poor in Zwingli's Zurich.* Cambridge: Cambridge University Press, 1990.

————. *Voracious Idols and Violent Hands: Iconoclasm in Reformation Zurich, Strasbourg, and Basel.* Cambridge: Cambridge University Press, 1995.

About the Author

HANS J. HILLERBRAND (Ph.D., University of Erlangen, Germany) is Professor of Religion and of History at Duke University. He is a specialist on the history of the Protestant Reformation. He has served as the president of the American Society for Reformation Research and of the American Society of Church History and as a member of the Council of the American Academy of Religion. He has taught at the City University of New York and Southern Methodist University and has been visiting professor at several German universities. His publications include the general editorship of the four-volume *Oxford Encyclopedia of the Reformation*, published in 1996, and a large number of articles in professional journals dealing with general issues of the Reformation and its radical fringe.